WILLIAM GODWIN
AS NOVELIST

J. Tysdahl

WILLIAM GODWIN AS NOVELIST

This is the first full-length study of the novels of William Godwin (1756–1836). Godwin was an anarchist and philosopher, the author of *Political Justice*, husband of Mary Wollstonecraft and father-in-law of Shelley, and is becoming recognized as one of the key figures of the English Romantic period. Previous studies have failed to treat his fiction in relation to his works of political philosophy.

Mr Tysdahl rectifies this, bringing together both sides of Godwin's oeuvre. He shows that the novels throw valuable light on the philosophical writings and that they stand as an achievement in their own right.

B. J. Tysdahl is Reader in English at the University of Oslo.

William Godwin
as Novelist

William Godwin as Novelist

by

B. J. Tysdahl

ATHLONE
London

First published by The Athlone Press Ltd
90–91 Great Russell Street, London WC1B 3PY
and by Humanities Press Inc. in the USA

© Athlone Press 1981

British Library Cataloguing in Publication Data

Tysdahl, B. J.
   William Godwin as novelist.
   I. Title
   828′.609   PR 4732.G6
   ISBN 0-485-11223-X (Cased)
   ISBN 0-485-12040-2 (Paperback)

Production services by Book Production Consultants,
7 Brooklands Avenue, Cambridge

Printed in Great Britain by
Biddles Limited, Martyr Road, Guildford, Surrey

Contents

Acknowledgements

First, I want to record my gratitude to friends and colleagues who have given me advice and encouragement. Stephen Prickett, Maren-Sofie Røstvig and Kristian Smidt have commented on a great many important parts of my argument; and I have also been given useful suggestions by Keith Brown, Peter Bilton, H. Neville Davies, Barbara Hardy, Robert Gordon, Erik Kielland-Lund, Olav Lausund and Diderik Roll-Hansen.

My indebtedness to those who have expressed their views on Godwin in print is recorded in the following pages; but more than footnotes are needed to express my gratitude to Burton R. Pollin, David McCracken and Gary Kelly, whose research in Godwin's reading has given later critics indispensable tools. Recently, Don Locke's biography has substantially increased our knowledge of Godwin's life and Godwin's London.

Lord Abinger has kindly given me persmission to consult microfilms of his collection of Godwin manuscripts.

I am indebted to the Norwegian Research Council for Science and the Humanities for a fellowship that gave me a year's leave of absence, for travel grants, and a grant towards publication. In Oslo the staff of the University Library and of the English Department have always done their best to provide books that have not always been easily available. Mrs Kari Riis and Mrs Else Westre have saved me time and trouble by their reliable typing. As always, it is a great pleasure to record one's gratitude to that unique institution, the British Museum, now the British Library Reference Division.

I also want to thank my wife and children who have wished my work well, even though it has sometimes left them with more household chores than they would otherwise have had.

Godwin's first novel *Damon and Delia*, thought to have been completely lost, has recently come to light; and I have added a postscript on this exciting new find.

University of Oslo   Bjørn Tysdahl

I

Introduction

> Our language can be seen as an ancient city: a maze of little streets and squares, of old and new houses, and of houses with additions from various periods; and this is surrounded by a multitude of new boroughs with straight regular streets and uniform houses.
>
> Wittgenstein, *Philosophical Investigations*

William Godwin's position as a novelist is a curious one. He wrote all his important novels after he had become famous as a political philosopher; he wrote them at a time when the French Revolution had given tremendous momentum to those ideas about politics, morality and religion which had preoccupied the second half of the eighteenth century – a time when writers like Burke and Paine formulated political maxims that are still remembered in the language of party politics. The political warfare was bitter, and there was little sympathetic understanding of the views of other parties. When a writer fears that a great many of his potential readers may be disposed to dismiss his most important concerns without giving them a fair hearing, he naturally thinks hard about techniques of persuasion. And Godwin did: some of his novels are striking experiments in narrative form.

Godwin may not himself have realised how complicated his position as a novelist was, but he saw clearly enough that earlier novelists had tended to take the *status quo* in public life too much for granted. He could of course not avoid using these writers as models; no novelist can start from scratch. But his predecessors made use of themes and techniques which could have subverted Godwin's radicalism only too easily: Sentimental novels tended to idealise submission to authority; Gothic stories saw horror everywhere, except where real danger lurked, namely in the power structures of England. Even radical friends like Holcroft and Bage wrote novels which

1

gave only half-hearted support to new ideas: they allowed virtue to be rewarded by a country house and a happy marriage, but by doing so undermined their criticism of those moral and economic conditions which they held responsible for large-scale injustice and unhappiness. Godwin's honest struggle with this tradition is courageous, touching, at times ludicrous, always vigorous.

In a sense Godwin's personal situation parallels the historical. In his private life, too, there had been an *ancien régime* – Calvinism – and a revolution when he left the pulpit and became an atheist. The old Adam lives on in Christians, and in Godwin's case the old Calvinist was not easily suppressed. The result is a tension which is richly reflected in the novels.

If, as I believe, Godwin's fiction is richer in surprises and more multifarious than most critics have recognised, then he is probably best served by a book which does not restrict the presentation of his novels to a scrutiny narrowly organised around one particular theme. As a framework, however, to my examination, from book to book, of his thematic concerns and narrative forms, I propose to consider his relationship to his most important literary models. Godwin was a writer who needed to set in front of himself a concrete example which he then proceeded to imitate, react against, and finally distance himself from. Knowledge of his most important sources is essential if we are to create a critical idiom in which his fiction can be profitably discussed. For all his radicalism Godwin provides a very good illustration of T. S. Eliot's observation:

> No poet, no artist of any art, has his complete meaning alone. His significance, his appreciation is the appreciation of his relation to the dead poets and artists. You cannot value him alone; you must set him, for contrast and comparison, among the dead. I mean this as a principle of aesthetic, not merely historical, criticism.[1]

The most important pressures at work in Godwin's fiction – they are not always immediately conspicuous – emerge most clearly when he is considered in a confrontation with major types of late eighteenth-century novels.

On the other hand, his achievement cannot be profitably assessed by any close comparison with Scott or Jane Austen. Godwin chose to write as an outsider, as a man who lacked the social and literary tact which could have turned him into another kind of novelist; and it is exactly this limitation which gives him his own special signature. The uncertain foothold in a comfortable, conservative world; the fall from this dubious kind of grace; the terror and incidental dignity of isolation; the vulnerability, self-pity and will to survive; the new insight into the society of the rich which is acquired from below – these are themes which he can treat with authority. And, not surprisingly perhaps, the political philosopher is at his best as a novelist when he describes a confused world in which men shudder when they see the emptiness of their own minds, and in which their attempts at moral and intellectual orientation are futile. The language in which these fearful insights are expressed is never sparkling; the stories can be slow and oppressive; the rational philosopher sometimes lectures the reader. But if "faults" of this kind had been corrected, if Godwin had tried harder to be a more traditional novelist, a sense of urgency and authenticity would have been lost. We should also have lost some of the most interesting technical experiments of the Romantic period. If Godwin had felt at home in more traditional kinds of narrative form, he could not possibly have written *Caleb Williams*, which remains one of the most profoundly ambigious novels in the English language, nor could he have conceived a book like *Mandeville*, in which the protagonist-narrator is a madman. Similarly, *St. Leon* and *Fleetwood* owe their vitality to the fact that Godwin finds that he must explode the literary convention on which he builds.

This subversiveness does not make Godwin's career as a novelist shapeless or incoherent. Though his fiction contains such rich variety in ideas and forms that he may seem chaotic in places, unity is found in a characteristic sensibility marked by a tension between calm philosophy and painful exploration of areas of life that refuse to be governed by philosophy. When Godwin thought in terms of narrative he could never for long pose as the author of *Political Justice*. This situation is illustrated most graphically in *Caleb Williams*, but it informs the later novels, too. In sub-chapters called "The other Godwin", "The novel inside the novel" and "The teller and the tale" I have outlined the development of this basic feature in Godwin's art.

But isn't Godwin's style altogether too wooden? Is he, in fact, readable at all? Some of his contemporaries, certainly, argued that he was not. Tory critics of the more enterprising kind found that they could ridicule his politics by debunking his language. *St God-*

win: A Tale of the Sixteenth, Seventeenth and Eighteenth Century, written by
"Count Reginald De St Leon", is a good example.[2] Witty, and
informed by the particular mercilessness of the 1790s, this parody
pounces on longwindedness and stolidity of style in what is ultimately an attempt to expose Godwin's political mistakes. Later, too,
criticism of Godwin's views has often centred as much on style as on
content. And there is certainly something Jacobin – Jane Austen
might have called it an absence of elegance – in his language; he
consciously avoids a style which too definitely presupposes a political and literary tradition of the kind that Burke extols in the *Reflections*. However, this does not mean that Godwin is a hitherto unrecognised nonconformist saint in matters of style. It would be absurd
to suggest that all his adverse critics are perverted by a London or
Home Counties upper-class parochialism; for Godwin's language is
at times open to criticism also on premises that he would himself
share (and that readers of many different persuasions would share).
Indeed, readers in sympathy with some of his most important
themes give strikingly different accounts of his style. Hazlitt praised
"the gorgeous and flowing eloquence" of *Caleb Williams* and *St Leon*;[3]
Walter Allen, who does admire Godwin, talks of his "latinate,
abstract, chilly style".[4] Marilyn Butler finds that in *Caleb Williams*,
"for some reason, the manner he thought appropriate to narrative
was heavy, slack, and verbose".[5] In Godwin's later novels, says
George Sherburn, "everything is humorlessly 'on stilts'".[6] But Gary
Kelly sees a marked improvement on the earlier fiction in *Fleetwood*:
"the style of *Fleetwood* . . . is for the most part a Romantic style, more
evocative, more naturally metaphoric, more subtle, and above all
more refined than anything he had written before."[7] Only one critic,
James T. Boulton, offers a closely reasoned defence of Godwin's
style. Boulton's admirable analysis highlights the ways in which
Godwin's philosophical ideals are reflected in the style of both
treatises and novels.[8]

After this survey of critical views it may sound as an anticlimax to
suggest that Godwin's style is quietly efficient. For most of the time
(when he is neither definitely reflective nor heavily emotional) his
manner is, as a matter of fact, simply workmanlike and unobtrusive.
Let us take an example from *Caleb Williams*:

> I now got to the wall, and had nearly gained half the ascent, when
> I heard a voice at the garden door, crying, Hulloa! who is there?

who opened the door? The man received no answer, and the night was too dark for him to distinguish objects at any distance. He therefore returned, as I judged, into the house for a light. Meantime the dog, understanding the key in which these interrogations were uttered, began barking again more violently than ever. I had now no possibility of retreat, and I was not without hopes that I might yet accomplish my object, and clear the wall. Meanwhile a second man came out, while the other was getting his lanthorn, and, by that time I had got to the top of the wall, was able to perceive me. He immediately set up a shout, and threw a large stone which grazed me in its flight. Alarmed at my situation, I was obliged to descend on the other side without taking the necessary precautions, and in my fall nearly dislocated my ancle.

There was a door in the wall, of which I was not previously apprised; and, this being opened, the two men with the lanthorn were on the other side in an instant. They had then nothing to do but to run along the lane to the place from which I had descended. I endeavoured to rise after my fall, but the pain was so intense that I was scarcely able to stand, and, after having limped a few paces, I twisted my foot under me, and fell down again. I had now no remedy, and quietly suffered myself to be retaken.

CHAPTER XIV

I was conducted to the keeper's room for that night, and the two men sat up with me. I was accosted with many interrogatories, to which I gave little answer, but complained of the hurt in my leg. To this I could obtain no reply except, Curse you, my lad! if that be all, we will give you some ointment for that; we will anoint it with a little cold iron. They were indeed excessively sulky with me, for having broken their night's rest and given them all this trouble. In the morning they were as good as their word, fixing a pair of fetters upon both my legs, regardless of the ancle which was now swelled to a considerable size, and then fastening me with a padlock to a staple in the floor of my dungeon. I expostulated with warmth upon this treatment, told them that I was a man upon whom the law had as yet passed no censure, and who therefore in the eye of the law was innocent. But they bid me keep such fudge for people who knew no better; that they knew what they did, and would answer it to any court in England.[9]

Generally, the description is straightforward and immediate. The new chapter begins at the right time; and the touch of jauntiness is not out of tune. Caleb can say about his gaolers that "they were as good as their word, fixing a pair of fetters upon my legs", because he is really quite relaxed about this escape. This is a moment of considerable excitement, but it does not have, and is not meant to have, the intensity of more portentous occasions in the novel. Above all, Godwin presents himself as a conscientious narrator. He is willing to lose in speed what he can gain in fairness. Accordingly, we learn that there is a reason for the sulkiness of the gaolers – they have had their night's sleep broken. The style thus embodies values Godwin wants to defend. As James T. Boulton puts it, "the qualities it exhibits are precisely those of honesty and openness, confidence and disinterestedness . . . The writer is determined not to sidestep difficulties".[10] This stylistic norm does not make for terseness; judged against it, the sparkling and witty represent dangerous simplifications rather than short-cuts to truth. Godwin never thinks of style as something that can sugar the narrative; his novels must rely for interest on other things than the sweetness or brilliance of their language.

But there is more to Godwin's style than this willingness to be open and conscientious in description and argument. For in the texture of nearly all his novels we find a conflict between the language of the rational philosopher and the idiom of the story-teller. When Godwin wrote his great philosophical work in the early 1790s, he thought that a new world was about to dawn, a world in which life would become less muddled, and thinking – and therefore language – more straightforward. But the novelist found that in fiction the new ideas about man and society had to fight against other kinds of insight. Godwin wanted to write about "things as they are", and when these "things" were given life in character and action they could not easily be encompassed by the political theory and the rational style which he obviously hoped to employ to bring order and coherence and clarity to fiction. In the novels we often hear another voice than that of the confident spokesman of late eighteenth-century radicalism and rationalism. The greatest virtue of Godwin's style is its capacity to capture more than the philosopher's view of life. *Caleb Williams* offers a number of striking examples of a style which may seem clumsy or overloaded until one realises that it reflects a powerful ambiguity.[11]

In his novels Godwin turns out to be more of a *Zauberlehrling* than a philosopher. He releases spirits that are difficult to lay, spirits whose subversive power is greater than he thought. Unexpectedly, Godwin is the kind of artist who is caught by his medium and forced into complexities and irrationalities that he had not foreseen. Multifarious as his novels are, they are all rich in this kind of surprise. Godwin's situation may be a fairly common one in Romantic literature; what gives him a special profile is his staying-power. He refuses to leave as fragments works which threaten to become overwhelmingly complex. The corresponding demands on his style are great, but more often than has been recognised Godwin does achieve a language which well reflects the tensions and anxieties that give a special flavour to his novels.

This flavour is very much one of narrative, not of logical thinking; but Godwin's fiction nevertheless throws an interesting sidelight on his philosophy.[12] The radicalism in the novels emerges as something quite different from the lessons of the assured, logical lecturer whose voice is heard in *Political Justice*. This philosopher seems in comfortable and almost leisurely command of the artillery directed against the establishment. He presents his position as so secure that he does not need to make sudden attacks on the enemy. If not at once, he will win by the slow momentum of his ideas without any violent battles having to be fought. In sharp contrast, the world of the novels is generally seen from the point of view of a frightened and bewildered narrator, a character who suffers badly from feelings of insecurity and who can find little or no comfort and guidance from among his fellow men. The novels are at once more and less radical than *Political Justice*. They are less radical in that they do not preach, point by point, what has gone wrong in English politics and what the duties of social man are. They are more radical in that they are emotionally violent. These tortured characters who cry out in pain are inhabitants of societies that are truly terrible; and their cries are urgent. One particular criticism which can be levelled against the political philosopher is not at all relevant to the novels. It is possible to argue that what *Political Justice* does is to utter radical noises which in practice do nothing but uphold the *status quo*. Does not Godwin's ideal of patient discussion always lead to endless philosophising, lead well-meaning reformers into a wilderness of abstractions, while real power, economic and political, is allowed to remain where it is? One need not be a Marxist to see a large measure of plausibility in such an argument. But this line of thinking does not affect the novels. The picture they present of life can serve the causes of many kinds of reformers and revolutionaries, not only those who believe in the particular route to perfection outlined in *Political Justice*.

In the novels the radicalism is found in the despair and pain which informs the narrative rather than in any black-and-white portraits of the rich and the poor. George Sherburn does not catch the whole truth when he says that "Godwin is traditionally a radical or even a revolutionary. His protagonists are all aristocrats, and they are all, for differing reasons, a bad lot."[13] It is true that after *Caleb Williams* they are all landowners, and they are a sorry lot; but they are not traditional representatives of the ruling class. Falkland does cling frantically to the authority of his social position, and he can thus be seen as a warning against a political system which enables him to become a tyrant. But all Godwin's later protagonists are people who fall, or have fallen, from the security and authority and comfort that their circumstances might have enabled them to enjoy. Emotionally, they are much like Hans Andersen's little match-selling girl: they sit in the cold and dream of the society of those who are warm and comfortable.

On the question of Necessity, too, the philosopher and the novelist are distinct personalities. According to Hazlitt, Wordsworth once told a law student to "throw away his books of chemistry and read Godwin on Necessity".[14] Wordsworth soon changed his mind about Godwin, but his momentary enthusiasm is understandable. The chapter called "Of Free Will and Necessity" in *Political Justice* is well-written and shrewd. Godwin realises that his argument has been made difficult by Hume's *Treatise*, but he patiently and firmly tries to resuscitate the idea that we can only make sense of the human mind by postulating a concept of causation as strict as that of the natural sciences. "Free choice" is an impossibility. But Godwin's fiction pursues less straightforward paths. Gary Kelly insists that "circumstances form character" in Godwin;[15] and this they often tend to do, but never to such an extent that the novels look like early specimens of Victorian naturalism. Indeed, the protagonists are caught precisely in situations in which they feel the pressure both of circumstances outside their control *and* of moral sentiments based on a belief, albeit vague, in something that can be called free will. Often, they feel impotent and unable to act on the promptings of their conscience, but then their situation is felt to be miserable for this very reason. Godwin relies on a humane experience of what life feels like more than on his philosophy when he outlines some of his most memorable scenes, such as the last trial scene in *Caleb Williams*, St. Leon's meeting with the stranger, and Deloraine's feelings about his second marriage. All these depend for interest on a dilemma which the characters experience as a moment of moral choice. We might expect Godwin to present such situations ironically, embedding them in contexts which would remind us that the characters are radically mistaken when they think of themselves as free to choose. But this is not what he does. Such pivotal scenes are enriched by various perspectives created by the rest of the story, but never in such a way that all possibilities of freedom and responsibility are ruled out.

Similarly, Godwin's techniques of characterisation are less obviously philosophical than we might expect. It is misleading to present Godwin as a writer who is always an essayist in disguise:

> When a secondary talent, like Godwin's, portrays aristocrats, servants, or philosophically minded robbers, he seldom thinks of them as men, but rather as persons holding interesting opinions, and the opinions are not smoothly and casually presented: they are explicit. Godwin enriches our conception of how men's minds work, but he does it as a somewhat pedestrian psychologist might do it – by reducing states of mind to fragmenting propositions, whereas what the reader wants is a dramatic fusion of all these elements.[16]

This is true of the robber captain in *Caleb Williams* and of a number of other minor characters. At first, it may also seem a correct comment on Godwin's protagonists. They all hold forth on their "interesting opinions", and Godwin frequently allows one explicit attitude – sometimes an *idée fixe* – to dominate a character. But these plain opinions and explicit attitudes are often used as a protective shell, inside which we find a frightened, intriguing little self. The "fragmenting propositions", which at first do seem to indicate clumsily reduced states of the mind, are really like speeches on a stage. They are answered by other voices, all of them inside the protagonist, that express contrary views, or that murmur or babble in ways which are not easily understood. It is the sum total of such voices which makes up Godwin's most convincing and complex characters.

I ought, perhaps, to make it quite plain here that I shall not be concerned, except indirectly, with Godwin as Mary Wollstonecraft's husband or Shelley's father-in-law. The most important events of Godwin's life are sketched in at the beginning of the following chapters, but I have not attempted to use biography as the master key to the novels. The public man or the philosopher (on whom biographies tend to concentrate) is no reliable guide to the fiction.[17] Instead, I have taken the formal problems of the novelist as a starting-point. This approach enables us to see Godwin's work in a new perspective; and, in its turn, this new insight into the fiction influences our picture of the man. It is of course no completely new face that emerges, but the changes are marked: the novels add to the portrait not a sharper or more rigid profile, but greater complexity and humanity.

II

Early Writings

From pulpit to Grub Street

William Godwin was born in 1756, the son of a dissenting minister in the Cambridgeshire town of Wisbech. When he was eleven William was sent to Norwich to become the private pupil of a colleague of his father's. His tutor was a strict Calvinist; the middle-aged Godwin remembered his creed as "drawn from the writings of Sandeman, a celebrated north country apostle, who, after Calvin had damned ninety-nine in a hundred of mankind, has contrived a scheme for damning ninety-nine in a hundred of the followers of Calvin". As Godwin's first biographer, Charles Kegan Paul, reminds us, Godwin must have thought differently of his tutor when he was younger.[1] He became a Sandemanian himself and suffered for his belief when he was refused admittance to Homerton Academy in 1773 because of his faith. He became a student at another nonconformist college, Hoxton in Kent, later in the same year; and for four of his five years in this lively and learned academic institution[2] he stuck to the creed he had been taught at Norwich.

Godwin's facetious description of Sandeman is not wide of the mark. Robert Sandeman (1718–71), who gave his name to the brand of nonconformity to which the young Godwin subscribed, held that nearly all so-called Christians are heretics, "Jews", in that they base their salvation on works. Sandeman saw these lost souls not only as a pernicious religious majority, but as indistinguishable from the secular establishment. His religious zeal therefore implied a thoroughly suspicious attitude to the Scottish and English governments of his day.[3] However, apart from an exclusivism that out-Calvins Calvin, Sandeman's theology is not unlike Luther's.[4] Thus, though Godwin embraces what was in some ways an extreme belief, it should be remembered that in most questions of faith he was not at odds with other and better known types of Protestantism in the eighteenth century.

11

In his last year at Hoxton Godwin engaged in a discussion with a fellow student about the Being of God:

> I took the negative side, in this instance, as always, with great sincerity, hoping that my friend might enable me to remove the difficulties I apprehended. I did not fully see my ground as to this radical question, but I had little doubt that grant the being of a God, both the truth of Christianity, and the doctrines of Calvinism, followed by infallible inference.[5]

But in spite of these apprehensions Godwin became a minister, first at Ware, later at Stowmarket. He left the latter in 1782 after a disagreement with his congregation "on a question of Church discipline", and, persuaded by friends "to try my pen as an author", Godwin spent some months in London. Though he did write a fairly successful *Life of Chatham*, he may have found Parnassus more difficult to climb than he had hoped, and he returned to preaching. But in the summer of 1783 he took leave of the congregation at Beaconsfield where, for some months, he had been a candidate for the ministry. This departure from the pulpit was final.[6] To earn a living Godwin turned to writing again. In the course of the next two years he saw through the press no less than nine separate publications – the *Life of Chatham*, a collection of sermons with the title *Sketches of History*, two political pamphlets, an advertisement for a school (which he never set up for the good reason that no parents showed any interest), a satire on famous contemporary authors, and three novels: *Damon and Delia*, *Italian Letters*, and *Imogen*.[7] This intense literary activity suggests that Godwin did not look upon his break with the ministry simply as an interlude. His new interest in writing is earnest and sustained: he tries his hand at almost all possible ways of making a living with his pen in the 1780s.

The change of profession accompanied radical changes in Godwin's beliefs. He himself explains that his "faith in Christianity had been shaken" as early as when he was preaching at Stowmarket in the winter of 1781–2. He had then been reading "French philosophers",[8] and he would have liked books such as Holbach's *Système de la nature* and Helvetius's *De l'esprit* for their criticism of religious authority, though not, as Godwin's own writings make clear, for their declared hedonism. In the *Account of the Seminary*, which appeared in 1783, Calvinism is conspicuous by its absence. Godwin outlines his ideas about education without a single line about religious instruction. Moreover, the picture of the child which he gives here has a definitely Pelagian colouring: "nothing is so easily proved, as that the human mind is pure and spotless, as it came from the hands of God, . . .". Childhood and youth would have been a period of complete innocence had it not been for the interference of society: "The vices of youth spring not from nature, who is equally the kind and blameless mother of all her children; they derive from the defects of education."[9] This is an idea of education and of the child which would have shocked Sandeman and his forerunner John Glas, who are in no doubt whatsoever about the awful existence of original sin. Godwin describes his changing views in the following way: "between my twenty-third and my twenty-fifth year [between 1779 and 1781] my religious creed insensibly degenerated on the heads of the Trinity, eternal torments and some others". He has this to say about his further development: "I found myself troubled in my mind on the score of the infidel principles I had recently imbibed, but reading at Beaconsfield the Institutes of Dr Priestley, Socinianism appeared to relieve so many of the difficulties I had hitherto sustained from the Calvinistic theology, that my mind rested in that theory, to which I remained a sincere adherent till the year 1788."[10] Godwin wrote this twenty years after the event; and he probably simplifies a development which was far from being straightforward. For in 1784, the year after the *Account of the Seminary*, he still considered it possible to publish *Sketches of History*, which is a selection of six sermons he preached as a minister. Except for a detail or two, these sermons are orthodox in a general Protestant way. But the direction in which Godwin was moving is clear enough: when he began writing fiction in 1783, he was no longer a Calvinist. He was not yet what he himself would call an atheist; but his half-way house, Priestley's Socinianism, is religion very much watered down. To Sandemanians and Glassites Godwin was now a lost soul: to them God's elect are the few who meet in a pure congregation. There was no room in their conception of holiness for London men of letters.[11] And Godwin was so well versed in Calvinism that he could be in no doubt whatsoever himself about the distance he had travelled.

These are the main facts, as we know them, about Godwin's loss of faith. About the reasons for this development they say very little.

We do not know whether his reading of sceptics like Holbach and Helvetius influenced him decisively or whether he just read them in an attempt to find intellectual allies at a time when he had really ceased to be a Calvinist. Misgivings about doctrines were obviously important, but there may have been other reasons too for the direction Godwin's development took. One is his temperament, neatly summed up by Kegan Paul (who plays down Godwin's radicalism, but is frank about his traits of character):

> All the jealousies, misunderstandings, wounded feelings and the like, which some men experience in their love affairs, Godwin suffered in his relations with his friends. Fancied slights were exaggerated; quarrels, expostulations, reconciliations followed quickly on each other, as though they were true *amantium irae*.[12]

This temperament must have been particularly severely tried, and tried others severely, when Godwin was a young pastor coming to small, closely-knit congregations whose elders may well have thought it their duty to put new-comers in their proper place. Even more important, probably, was Godwin's particular impatience with those who sounded authoritarian. He had grown up under a stern and unpleasant father; and as he came of age intellectually, he could scarcely avoid reacting against what this unlovable parent stood for. This reaction marked him for life: in all his important works he is critical of authority – political, religious and domestic.

When the youthful ex-minister turned to writing in the autumn of 1783, he naturally had to take stock of the kinds of literature he was acquainted with. The picture which we can now piece together of young William's library is not very detailed, but we know that he read the whole of the Old and the New Testament as a boy, and that the first modern book he read was *The Pilgrim's Progress*. Another work which impressed him deeply was an *Account of the Pious Deaths of Many Godly Children*.[13] Later, as a teenager, he read Richardson.[14] These few facts strengthen the inference we can draw from a general knowledge of a relatively poor nonconformist home: the staple literary fare was made up of the Bible and of religious stories in the Bunyan tradition. In addition, there was perhaps a sprinkling of acceptable novels like Richardson's. It was only after the five years at Hoxton College that Godwin began to read more widely in fiction, poetry and drama. He was then under the influence of the Rev. Joseph Fawcett, one of four friends whom Godwin called his "four principal oral instructors",[15] and a man known for his literary interests. At the time when he began writing fiction himself Godwin had caught up on a great deal of what he had missed earlier. In an admirable survey of the literary sources of *Italian Letters* Burton R. Pollin has shown that Godwin took hints from a great variety of books.[16] Moreover, Godwin's own literary hoax of 1783, *The Herald of Literature*, in which he reviews and quotes at length from works that had not appeared, reveals that he had acquired a certain sense of style: with considerable gusto Godwin provides good-humoured parodies of William Robertson and Gibbon, Hayley and Beattie, Burke and Paine, Fanny Burney, Sheridan, and the followers of Sterne.

Godwin's development implies a radical change in his attitude to literature. There was a world of difference between the way in which he absorbed pious stories as a boy and the way in which he was entertained by the fashionable literature of the 1780s and 90s. *The Pilgrim's Progress* had been true and important in a way which *Evelina* and *Cecilia* were not. For to the believer a book like Bunyan's is, in an important sense, real twice over: it is equally true as history and as literature in whose symbols and images there is religious and moral meaning transcending the limitations of the concrete setting. Though Christian's life story is presented as a dream, it is not really thought of as fiction. It is real life; and at the same time it has a richness of connotation and a network of images through which its message is articulated in a manner closely analogous to that of fiction. Compared with this kind of literature a late eighteenth-century novel may well seem trivial: for all its insistence on good behaviour and its sprinkling of pious sentiments, its story fails the test of truth – it does not give us facts, but more or less fanciful incidents thought up by inhabitants of more or less respectable Grub Streets.

When Godwin's religious attitudes changed, the ideas he had been taught about life and literature were by no means shaken off. He could not undo twenty-six years of his life. We find a number of the attitudes of his early years reappearing in what he wrote after 1783, most notably in the novels he wrote just after he had left the pulpit. In particular he retains the impression that human security and happiness are always precarious, and that virtue is always threatened by terrible evil.

But his very first novel is an exception to the rule. *Damon and Delia. A Tale*, a book which was thought to have been lost for ever but recently found, is a *jeu d'esprit*. (A detailed presentation of this "new" novel is given in a Postscript.) A slight story about the vicissitudes of a young Southampton couple is related in a bantering style rich in echoes of *Tom Jones*. Godwin makes fun of sentimental seriousness, of sectarian religion, and of quite a number of late eighteenth-century politicians. In a minor character Godwin combines a self-portrait with a wish for the future: Mr Godfrey is a minister and teacher turned writer whose masterpiece is not recognised by publishers or the public, but who finally finds a generous and discriminating patron in Damon himself. This portrait is not without irony, for as narrator of *Damon and Delia* Godwin emphatically presents his work not as a great artistic achievement but, more realistically, as a good-humoured and unpolished skit. His own masterpiece had not yet been written.

Even while he wrote – and obviously enjoyed writing – this first novel, Godwin must have realised that as a teller of tales he was not really at home in the kingdom of wit; and in his other two early novels he does not imitate the frank awareness in Fielding and Sterne that fiction is fiction. His most important concerns could only be expressed in a style that had a more direct seriousness and urgency, and he proceeded to choose as models literary forms that were as close as possible to religious stories, to the "double truth" of his boyhood reading. Since he could not now use Bunyan's patently Christian form without reservations, he modelled *Italian Letters* and *Imogen* on two of the most morally serious stories he had read, Richardson's *Clarissa* and Milton's *Comus*. In 1783 there were no theological reasons why Godwin should prefer Milton and Richardson to Smollett, Sterne and Fielding. In many ways the newly fledged freethinker must have felt more immediate fellowship with the latter group of writers. Milton's and Richardson's moral and religious assumptions made his use of their work problematical, for even the writing of simple moral tales involved Godwin in questions of faith and artistic form to which there were no simple, traditional answers. But his sense of urgency won.

Later, in the course of a long and chequered career as a writer, Godwin tried to emulate a number of writers – not all of them as serious as Milton or Richardson. But whatever models he made use of (for moral, artistic, or pecuniary reasons), he tried to make sure that the requirements of the chosen form did not involve him in inconsistencies. At the same time his stories always tend to acquire a life of their own. The resulting clash between the wish for intellectual integrity and the equally powerful requirements of a story which refuses to be the handmaid of theoretical thinking is one of the most characteristic traits in Godwin's fiction, and it is well illustrated in his two serious novels from this period. *Italian Letters* and *Imogen* cannot claim much attention in their own right today, though they are considerably better than most run-of-the-mill fiction of the 1780s.[17] They are primarily of interest because they teach us something about the author of *Caleb Williams*, *St Leon* and *Mandeville*.

Italian Letters

Italian Letters, or, The History of the Count de St. Julian, is a sad story.[18] The Count de St Julian is cheated of his inheritance and is then unsuccessful in his attempt to save his best friend from a life of debauchery. Happiness does come within reach in the form of Mathilda, who is rich, virtuous, and beautiful; but while St Julian is sent on an expedition to Spain for his friend, this treacherous libertine lures Mathilda into marrying him. In spite of his philosophic evenness of temper St Julian seeks redress in a duel and kills his former friend. After a year he offers Mathilda his hand; but, always a paragon of decorousness, she refuses his offer.

As we have seen, Godwin's background prompted him to choose a serious model, in this case Richardson, for his novel;[19] and he presents the reader with moral object-lessons on seduction, duelling, over-indulgence by parents, rashness, and a handful of other weaknesses and vices. The epistolary mode is convenient: moral advice tends to sound less sanctimonious in a letter written by one of the characters than when it comes straight from the author. Moreover – and this was important to Godwin – a novel that consists of letters sounds less like fiction than a novel in the tradition of *Tom Jones*. The epistolary mode makes for verisimilitude; and Godwin follows Richardson in letting some of the letters reveal characters in the process of sorting out an emotional problem. Godwin is not yet capable of a description of mixed feelings like Caleb's for Falkland, but in Letter XV, for instance, he gives us St Julian's disappointment and hope in paragraphs that are appropriately incoherent. St Julian begins by sounding more stilted than usual:

> I have waited, charming Mathilda, with the most longing impatience in hopes of receiving a letter from your own hand . . . If you knew, fair excellence, how much pain and uneasiness your silence has given me, you could not surely have been so cruel. The most rigid decorum could not have been offended by one scanty billet that might just have informed me, I still retained a tender place in your recollection. (p.50)

He then goes on to describe her lovely person and outstanding virtues and, indirectly but forcefully, his own fear of losing her: "And is it possible that this all-accomplished woman can stoop from the dignity of her rank and the greatness of her pretensions, to a person so obscure, so slenderly qualified as I am?" In spite of the suspicions which he has more than hinted at, he begins the next paragraph in this manner:

> But no, my Mathilda, I am a stranger to these fears, my breast is unvisited by the demon of suspicion. I employ no precaution. I do not seek to restrain my passion. I lay my heart naked before you. I shall ever maintain the most grateful sense of the benevolent friendship of your venerable father, of your unexampled and ravishing condescension. But love, my amiable Mathilda, knows no distinction of rank. We cannot love without building our ardour upon a sense of a kind of equality. (p.51)

With considerably immediacy Godwin here gives us a picture of a poor, somewhat muddled lover. Though desperately uncertain, St Julian is unwilling to confess his fears. But at the same time he gives in to the need to argue his case: we must be honest to each other, and we must realise that if we love each other truly, we also enjoy "a kind of equality". His argument helps him to overcome his suspicions, the very writing of the letter eases his strain, and the language becomes warmer and more direct: "fair excellence" becomes "my amiable Mathilda". But it does not make sense to say that the letter improves in style. The stilted beginning is entirely in character for the poor lover who fears that his rich fiancée is drifting away from him and who must find a new kind of language in which to approach her.

A précis of the story of *Italian Letters* may sound as if Godwin sets himself up as a kind of simplified Richardson, producing a string of lifelike incidents that serve as moral warnings. And up to a point this is what he actually does. But *Italian Letters* resembles a number of Godwin's later novels in that there is in it a considerable tension between the popular form which Godwin emulates and basic concerns in the book. In spite of its moral insistence *Italian Letters* presents a world in which there is really little room for moral responsibility. Though no longer a Calvinist, Godwin retains a rudimentary idea of predestination. St Julian is portrayed as a character who is not responsible for his own fate. In his first letter he confesses that he is "born with a heart too susceptible for [his] peace" (p.5). He has the good fortune to meet Mathilda and her kind father, but he is still in doubt: "Is it possible I should not have been born to uninterrupted misfortune?" (p. 34). Even when he has been accepted by both he continues complaining: "Alas . . . the greatest sublunary happiness is not untinged with misfortune" (p. 44). Finally he reaps what his fears have painted for him, his own lasting unhappiness. Still, the story is readable. For St Julian is not pusillanimous in spite of his many misgivings. He is brave, and he can be insistent, resourceful and disinterested. Nor can he be said to be out of touch with reality. Though he is naïve at times (on one occasion he is so gullible as to be unbelievable), the really sad thing is that his many presentiments of disaster are not chimeras. His response to his surroundings is shown to be realistic in the sense that the whole world of *Italian Letters* is one of impending disasters against which decent young people fight in vain.

A net of ironies connected with this theme enriches a style which is often rather melodramatic.[20] In the first letter St Julian says to his friend: "With my Rinaldo I was early, and have been long united; and I trust, that no force, but that of death, will be able to dissolve the ties that bind us" (p. 5). In retrospect, this is an intriguing observation: for when death comes to one of them, it is by the hand of the other; and the death of Rinaldo does not dissolve ties, but binds both St Julian and Mathilda in a situation which they cannot escape from. In a similar way other passages gain in vitality on a second reading: in rural security St Julian begins his correspondence by warning his friend against the dangers of a town, but it is in the country that he is soon after cheated of his patrimony by a younger brother. Some of St Julian's thoughts at this early stage raise questions that transcend the more straightforward kinds of dramatic irony. An example is found in the very first paragraph when St Julian says reassuringly about his friend, who has just inherited his father's estate and title, that "it is not the voice of flattery, that can render him callous to the most virtuous and respectable feelings that can inform the human breast" (p. 3). It is probably true – but far from certain – that it is not flattery that causes the moral corruption of Rinaldo; but he *is* "rendered callous"; and the sentence, which on a first reading invited us to take Rinaldo's moral fibre for granted, now directs our thoughts to what other causes of corruption we may find in Rinaldo's life: is it sexual passion which transforms a friendly young man into a ferocious beast? Or is the irony at work still more subtle since the novel later suggests that in Naples sexual passion and flattery are indivisible?

In this dangerous world of *Italian Letters* young persons must fend for themselves without the guidance of fathers or father-figures.[21] Mathilda's father was an exemplary old gentleman, but he dies before the time when Mathilda's life becomes really entangled. The other three fathers in the story all illustrate unfortunate relationships. Rinaldo's father was over-indulgent, the results are seen in the unrestrained life of the son. Rinaldo himself becomes an example of what St Julian had warned against: "And can a man of the smallest sensibility think with calmness of bringing children into the world to be the heirs of shame?" (p. 26). St Julian has had a stern father: "The outcast of my father almost as soon as I had a being, I was never sensible to the solace of paternal kindness, I could never open my heart, and pour forth all my thoughts into the bosom of him to whom I owed my existence" (p. 34).

Nor are the young people of the novel helped by God. The numerous moral ideals of *Italian Letters* are expressed in a conspicuously humanistic language. There are a few perfunctory mentions of God as creator and of heaven as a moral standard, and revenge is once said to be "equally the disgrace of reason and Christianity" (p. 119); but Godwin does not let his characters find strength and guidance in religion. God is non-existent in their inner lives; and there is no symbolic patterning of events, as in *Caleb Williams*, which can be read as a Christian interpretation of the world.

The setting of the novel should, I think, be seen as related to Godwin's humanistic standpoint. The Italy and Sicily to which we are taken do not differ radically from the traditional view in English fiction of the South of Europe; and Godwin probably liked a southern setting for the obvious reasons: the landscape is – or is meant to be – breathtaking in its beauty and majesty; and in these more lawless parts of the world people are capable of fascinating enormities which, as Catherine Morland realised, could not easily be perpetrated in the more civilised counties of Southern England. But another consideration must have been at least equally important. In such a setting the author could come as close as possible to describing a real world in which religion did not interfere. He therefore takes us to an Italy in which Christianity is no longer a living presence. On the few occasions when we hear of the Roman Catholic Church it is presented as an institution out of touch with reality; it is never seen as a place of worship. Once this has been realised, we can account for the somewhat surprising fact that *Italian Letters* does not exploit the Gothic possibilities of its location: Godwin could not use – or play with – Walpole's castle-cum-ghost recipe, for this would automatically have involved him in metaphysical speculations of the very kind that he wanted to avoid in this novel. He was to have his full share of such difficulties when he was tempted to write a Gothic novel in the late nineties.

In his next story, *Imogen*, on which he spent four months as compared with the three weeks given to the writing of *Italian Letters*,[22] he courageously makes use of a properly allegorical setting. The choice of a fairly ordinary European setting for the former attempt was probably wise. By placing his story in a real country like Italy Godwin could avoid an open discussion of the essential nature of man and society of the kind which a fully worked-out allegory necessitates. He was not prepared, in the autumn of 1783, to write in the style of *Rasselas* about a metaphorical Abissinia.

One reason for this caution is probably found in the very natural fact that Godwin had not sorted out all his ideas in the new position in which he found himself. It is interesting to note that in *Italian Letters* his view of authority is still traditional. Though, as we have seen, the parents cannot really help their children, Godwin does not query their right to control their offspring, or indeed any of the traditionally sacred family ties. Even when he finds himself unjustly disinherited, St Julian submits to what he thinks is his father's will; and Mathilda is praised for her absolute obedience to her father. Godwin is not yet consciously aware of the conflict which his own narrative in fact embodies between the traditional concept of submission, as we find it in sentimental fiction,[23] and a sense of justice which is incompatible with this kind of obsequiousness.

Imogen

The epistolary mode with its built-in verisimilitude was only one way in which a story could be made "real". In his next novel, *Imogen: A Pastoral Romance from the Ancient British*, [24] Godwin explores another literary form which has considerable pretentions to the serious, the pastoral allegory. At first glance it may seem strange that Godwin should turn from the psychological realism of letters to the abstractness of a stylised Arcadia; it is easy to think of these two forms as totally different in all respects. But this is not the case: both can be seen as attempts to overcome or bypass the fictional in literary art. An allegory can attempt this by presenting a story which is so obviously stylised that nobody can miss the vital point: here the story is nothing but a straightforward illustration of the book of life.[25] When thought of in this way, an allegory is very far from being fiction. The allegorist has not invented a set of incidents. His art is descriptive; he has just drawn some simple illustrations of important events and forces in life.

It is interesting to note that five of the six sermons which Godwin published are firmly based on an event from the Old or the New Testament – an event which Godwin first relates, then comments on so as to bring out the general truths that it embodies. The collection of sermons was given the rather curious title *Sketches of History* obviously because Godwin wanted to stress the importance of real events, of history, as the basis for his reflections.[26] By the time he was writing *Imogen* he was no longer sure that the Bible was history, but in the romance he retains the structure of the sermons in that an explicit commentary is tied to particular events.

Godwin's choice of *Comus* as a model for his story is understandable in the light of this development. Milton's masque has a simple and serious story which serves as a basis for a rich and persuasive moral commentary on life. But Godwin could only use Milton with great modifications, for the classical and local deities in *Comus* are manifestations of Christian concepts which Godwin did not now share. To make it clear from the beginning that we are not invited to read *Imogen* as a thinly veiled Christian story, Godwin begins his narrative not *in medias res* but with an introductory chapter in which three bards praise the deity in songs that, for all their highflown language, really damn religion with faint praise. It is only the last song, a hymn to creation, which can be read as a tribute to religion: it does reflect a pale belief in a creator. The first bard sings a fantastic story of a wanton shepherd pursuing a chaste maid whom the gods help by allowing her to change her form whenever she is about to be overtaken. Tongue in cheek, Godwin out-Ovids Ovid in these metamorphoses; and the message of the song is completely undermined by the main story in which the heroine is *not* helped by gods in her sore need. The second bard relates how a lovely and loving couple are separated when the young man is chosen as a sacrifice to the gods in a time of drought. The song gives us, in effect, a highly ambiguous description of a particularly unpleasant religious sacrifice.

The choice of pre-historic Wales as a setting serves the same purpose.[27] Godwin's "Preface" leaves no doubt that his knowledge of classical pastoral literature was extensive enough to enable him to use a Greek Arcady as a background to his story. When, instead, he takes his readers to a Welsh rural paradise, he avoids the Christian overtones which Greek myth had acquired in the tradition which Milton makes use of. As in *Comus* the gods and heroes of *Imogen* represent a blend of tradition and invention, but Godwin has concocted a special mixture which does not easily lend itself to a syncretistic interpretation.[28]

The main story in which we meet another young couple, may seem to counteract the humanism which Godwin carefully introduces in the setting and the first chapter: Imogen is abducted by a villain in a storm created by a goblin who can be seen striding along between the clouds.[29] We can thus be in no doubt that supernatural powers are abroad. But when Edwin goes to an old Druid for help, we realise that the supernatural has a special, limited role only in this set of events. The Druid gives the young man sympathy, encouragement, and moral and practical advice. Edwin also receives a root which "is a sovereign antidote against all blasts, enchantments, witchcrafts, and magic" (p. 48). The gift of the root is linked with Edwin's acceptance of the moral lesson he has been given. He first convinces the old man of his courage, rectitude and sagacity, then he receives the charm. The amulet does not give Edwin supernatural energy. It is, as the Druid said, an "antidote", a defence against the supernatural powers of the villain. The attack on evil which is

necessary to set things right must come from Edwin's moral resources. This pattern, which is first brought out in the gift of the
root, becomes increasingly clear in the course of the story. Edwin
and Imogen are victorious because of their moral strength:

> Goblins, and spirits of darkness, are permitted a certain scope in
> this terrestrial scene; but their power is bounded; beyond a certain
> line they cannot wander. In vain do they threaten innocence and
> truth. Innocence is a wall of brass upon which they can make no
> impression. Virtue is an adamant that is sacred and secure from
> all their efforts. (p. 45)

Imogen's tempter has a thrilling variety of supernatural agents at
his disposal whereas she has recourse to no such help in her trials.
There is an interesting contrast to *Comus* here. The Lady and Imogen both have a soul of sterling virtue, but the sense of the *holiness* of
chastity, "the sublime notion and high mystery", has been exchanged in Godwin for sexual love: in the first phases of her trials
Imogen's moral sense is reinforced by her warm feelings for Edwin.

Thus, Godwin's world is not Christian except in a highly
rudimentary way; on the side of good there is only a pale Deism.
Evil, on the other hand, is described as working in supernatural
ways.[30] The villain's magic is not reducible to moral and psychological symbolism in the way in which we can account for Edwin's
root. Godwin, who always wanted his thinking to be tidy, could not
have been blind to the half-way position which the book occupies
between the rationalistic and the mysterious; and in his next novel,
Caleb Williams, he carefully gives an account of evil in terms of social
roles and ideals. In *Imogen* his starting-point precludes this kind of
social realism: we are in a valley where equality, justice and benevolence reign. But Godwin needed a potent evil force in his work.
Obviously, evil must be present to set the story going and to bring
out the theme which is announced with Johnsonian emphasis on the
first page: "False and treacherous is that happiness, which has been
preceded by no trial, and is connected with no desert" (p. 25). But
there is also another reason – one that suggests an interesting kind of
honesty in Godwin – for the presence of the evil goblin in the sky.
Even at this time, when he was rapidly becoming an atheist, he
realised that when he turned to narrative his sense of evil was so
powerful that he could express its overwhelming and bewildering
presence only in manifestations of a supernatural kind.

Evil is met in *Imogen* by moral strength and, on the part of the lovely heroine, with anti-aristocratic principles which point directly towards *Political Justice*. In the valley of the shepherds "all lived in happy equality" (p. 25); and when Imogen is detained by the servants of the villain, she reacts with great vigour against the servile attitude which they reveal:

> "Your master! and your lord!" replied Imogen, with a tone of displeasure, "I understand not these words. The Gods have made all their rational creatures equal. If they have made one strong and another weak, it is for the purpose of mutual benevolence and assistance, and not for that of despotism and oppression. Of all the shepherds of the valley, there is not one that claims dominion and command over another . . . ". (p. 59)

There is no doubt about the inference to be made: the happy valley where the shepherds live represents what England should have been; the next valley, in which the lustful Roderic reigns, is a picture of what it has been reduced to.

Even by modest standards, *Imogen* is no success. It does illustrate both the philosophical bent in Godwin's fiction and the tension between philosophy and narrative which marks his later novels; but Godwin is not in command of the tact with which Milton or Johnson could treat an allegorical setting. Edwin and Imogen begin life in a peaceful valley and later find themselves in the rough-and-tumble of the world. The parallel to *Rasselas* is thus conspicuous, but Godwin involves himself in difficulties of his own when he describes his valley both as perfect (in fact so good that the all-important test of moral fibre cannot take place there), and as normal: this valley is the home of all except the very few who have gone their evil ways across the mountains into other territories. The moral geography of *Imogen* thus becomes forced. Young people must be taken out of the world, so to speak, to undergo the difficulties which will steel them so that they can be happy and good ever after. Had he read *Imogen*, Johnson would certainly have been sarcastic about their reward: they go back to a world of men in which there is really no choice, no challenge, and no tension.

With *Italian Letters* and *Imogen* Godwin began his literary career as a writer of serious stories, and he continued in the same vein. It is perhaps natural that he has been thought of as a life-long prisoner of his own somewhat wooden earnestness. This, however, is a view which must be modified in the light of his literary attempts in the 1780s. Godwin *chose* a serious style. His early writings reveal that he toyed – and not without some success – with other modes. The parodies in *The Herald of Literature* are vigorous, to the point and good fun, and his *Instructions to a Statesman* contains biting political irony. *Damon and Delia* includes elements of literary burlesque and political satire in a light-hearted story. The most subtle example of Godwin writing in this vein is found in the "Preface" to *Imogen*. Here he revels in ironies about the authorship of the romance.[31] He first presents the story as the work of an ancient bard:

> The manners of the primitive times seem to be perfectly under-stood by the author, and are described with the air of a man who was in the utmost degree familiar with them. It is impossible to discover in any part of it the slightest trace of Christianity. And we believe it will not be disputed, that in a country so pious as that of Wales, it would have been next to impossible for the poet, though ever so much upon his guard, to avoid any allusion to the system of revelation. On the contrary, every thing is Pagan, and in perfect conformity with the theology we are taught to believe prevailed at that time. (p. 21)

This incontrovertible proof is more than a good-humoured gibe at the Welsh; it is also, of course, a signpost set up by Godwin to notify his readers that they will not be reading a Christian work. The ironies surrounding the question of authorship are continued. The author of the preface, who is also the translator of the tale into English, realises that readers will notice the striking resemblance of this romance to *Comus*. But he is indefatigable: as the masque was written on the borders of Wales, Milton may well have come across the manuscript of the romance and himself have been the debtor in this literary relationship! Then, the author of the preface abruptly leaves his initial position and boldly states that the writer was one of his own ancestors, a Welsh squire said to have lived at the time of William III. There is no reason given for this attribution, except, of course, what the intelligent reader may infer: all editors and trans-lators are archegoists who want to make as much as possible of their own importance. To reinforce this impression, the preface is sprin-kled with satirical references to Macpherson and to the publishing business of the 1780s.

When the story proper begins, the style changes to the serious. Wisely, Godwin discarded the mode of a witty London man of letters. He could probably have competed with some success for a Grub Street distinction on this basis;[32] but if he had been swallowed up by this kind of eighteenth-century sophistication he would not have become the writer of *Political Justice* or of his best novels. Godwin pursues interests and obsessions in his novels that are often different from the thoughts which he outlines in his political philosophy, but in both kinds of works the style of his argument is that of a nonconformist, a lonely writer engaged in a very earnest endeavour to communicate with other people, a great many of them belonging to a more elegant world whose witty dialect he does not really share and is not willing to share.

III

Caleb Williams: A Question of Genres

> An example of the seventh type of ambiguity, or at any rate of the last type of this series, as it is the most ambiguous that can be conceived, occurs when the two meanings of the word, the two values of the ambiguity, are the two opposite meanings defined by the context, so that the effect is to show a fundamental division in the writer's mind.
>
> William Empson, *Seven Types of Ambiguity*

After *Imogen* Godwin found a precarious living in journalism. For sixty guineas a year he wrote the historical part of the *New Annual Register*; he contributed to the short-lived *Political Herald*, and became acquainted with leading Whig politicians without, however, securing any lucrative appointments.[1] He supplemented his slender income by tutoring a boy who boarded with him, and later he also undertook the education of a poor, orphaned cousin. Notes and letters from these years give us glimpses of a tutor who is no born pedagogue. He is harsh and sometimes unimaginative. But, as Godwin himself argues in a letter to his young cousin after a quarrel, behind the sternness are "motives of kindness": "I am poor, and with considerable labour maintain my little family; yet I am willing to spend money upon your wants and pleasures. My time is of the utmost value to me, yet I bestow a large portion of it upon your improvement."[2]

Godwin's moments of exasperation are understandable. He was a poor hack writer living in chambers that he shared with a pupil and sometimes a friend as well. During the first eleven years in London – from 1782 to 1793, when at last he had a house to himself – he changed his lodgings no fewer than thirteen times.[3] Behind these moves we can glimpse Godwin's practical difficulties: there must have been quarrels with landlords about noisy teenagers and perhaps about the rent; and the writer must quite often have had the sinking feeling that the peace and quiet necessary for intellectual work was nowhere to be found.[4] Still, Godwin read widely, and he continued writing the historical part of the *New Annual Register*, an appointment which enabled him to study English history in a systematic fashion for six years.

In 1790 he was unsuccessful in an application for a position in the Natural History Department of the British Museum but by this time his leanest years were over. He now found himself a member of a group of friends and associates who were enthusiastic about the early stages of the French Revolution and who took part in the lively discussion triggered by Dr Price's Old Jewry sermon and by Burke's *Reflections*. Godwin dined with Stanhope, Sheridan and Fox, and was generally considered a knowledgeable and philosophically minded Whig.[5] Then, in 1791, he persuaded the well-known London publisher George Robinson to support him while he wrote a comprehensive treatise of political philosophy. The *Enquiry Concerning Political Justice and Its Influence on Morals and Happiness*, famous even before it was published, appeared in 1793. It sold well and Godwin's name was firmly established as that of a profound thinker among the radicals. The government disliked the work, of course, but it was not suppressed. Pitt is reported to have opposed action against it because, he said, it was too expensive to be harmful.[6]

It makes sense to think of Godwin as having now arrived where he really belongs. He has sorted out his ideas about life, is a confirmed atheist and a confirmed radical, though no revolutionary. He has acquired a style and a knowledge of Europe which give his writings authority, and he is respected by those whose views he cares about. There is indeed a sense of homecoming about *Political Justice*: now, at last, a firm standpoint is found from which the workings of society can be seen for what they are. With an air of calm and security, almost of leisure, Godwin conducts his readers through his work.

Still, when Godwin began the writing of a novel in 1793, he was not at rest with himself and his surroundings. He was, he said later, in a "high state of excitement" (p. 338). This is really no wonder. For all its calm assurance, *Political Justice* is a breathtaking break with the past. In it Godwin denounces all kinds of institutions and all kinds of authority – social, moral and religious – except a stark principle of justice. Any author might turn giddy at having completed such root and branch work; and in Godwin's case the restlessness arising from the fact that he had tried to abandon so much in his cultural heritage and in his own earlier life was heightened by changes in the political climate.

The government decided to curb what they thought of as revolutionary activities in England. In the very months when Godwin was writing *Caleb Williams*, Joseph Gerrald, a well-known radical, was charged with sedition. Godwin visited him in prison and corresponded with him.[7] Though more severe action, for instance the trial of twelve London radicals on a charge of high treason, was taken only after Godwin had virtually finished the novel, he knew all through 1793 and '94 that radicals were in danger of being prosecuted. Godwin probably found a little comfort in the fact that he was not a member of a Corresponding Society and that he had consistently preached non-violent evolution as the road to a better society. But he also knew that, if necessary, he would stand by his radical friends even if he thus risked his personal freedom. In 1794 he actually rushed back to London from the country to write his courageous *Cursory Strictures* in defence of his friends in the dock. They were acquitted; but the political climate was nevertheless hardening. Five years of intense, far-reaching and profound political debate were coming to an end.[8]

This background helps us to understand why Godwin chose what at first sight seems to be the most unlikely of themes from the pen of the philosopher:

> I bent myself to the conception of a series of adventures of flight and pursuit; the fugitive in perpetual apprehension of being overwhelmed with the worst calamities, and the pursuer, by his ingenuity and resources, keeping his victim in a state of the most fearful alarm. (p. 337)

It is not really an unlikely theme. It does, in fact, suit Godwin's political purposes, and it also captures more elusive presences from the past that he still struggled with.

As a rule it is easy to discover what model or models Godwin makes use of as a starting-point for his novels. *Italian Letters* is heavily indebted to Richardson, while *Imogen* is Godwin's version of the *Comus* story. Later in his career Godwin tries his hand at the Gothic in *St Leon* and at the Sentimental in *Fleetwood*. *Caleb Williams*, on the other hand, seems radically different from all likely models. One reason why it does look like a sport in the history of English literature is found in historical circumstances: an open discussion of the political issues raised by the French revolution found its way into the English novel only two or three years before *Caleb Williams*; Godwin attempted to write in a nascent form of fiction. Moreover, as admirable surveys by J. M. S. Tompkins and Gary Kelly demonstrate,[9] Jacobin novelists were experimenting with various narrative modes; and no tradition on which Godwin could easily build had been established.

Another difficulty is of a more radical kind. It is hard to give a satisfactory account of models when the work in front of you will not stand still. For *Caleb Williams* is a particularly elusive book; nearly all the extant criticism of the novel illustrates the bafflement that readers have experienced. "We are", said the *Analytical Review* in 1795, "somewhat at a loss how to introduce our readers to an acquaintance with this singular narrative."[10] Later critics have proceeded to explain their bafflement either by reference to a flaw in the novel (which most of them are willing to condone because of the book's virtues), or by suggesting that they have only been faced with an initial difficulty which can be overcome: a careful reader will eventually learn what the novel is about and will find it a unified narrative. Leslie Stephen's analysis from the turn of the century represents an intelligent version of the former approach;[11] the last twenty years have seen interesting attempts by P. N. Furbank, Eric Rothstein, Rudolf Storch, Mitzi Myers and others to present *Caleb Williams* as one and whole.[12]

It is my impression that Godwin's novel has no complete thematic unity in any traditional sense. *Caleb Williams* can, in fact, be seen as two or three different novels which behave in much the same way as the rabbit and the duck which psychologists produce in studies of perception. The picture can be seen as either a rabbit or a duck; and, as E. H. Gombrich reminds us in *Art and Illusion*, though "it is easy to discover both readings", it may be more difficult "to describe what happens when we switch from one interpretation to the other".[13] When confronted with analogous difficulties in *Caleb Williams*, a reader should not, I think, succumb too easily to one of the critic's sweetest temptations – the wish to present an interpretation of a work of art which makes it look very complex and absolutely coherent. In this case such a generally profitable attempt may be unrewarding, for it is only when the curiously unstable relationship between different readings is kept in mind that the novel's particular liveliness can be accounted for.

It is important to realise that *Caleb Williams* is an example of Empson's most radical kind of ambiguity, the one which brings out "a fundamental division in the writer's mind". It is this that the duck-and-rabbit analogy can illustrate: a reader's view of *Caleb Williams* may shift in a much more thoroughgoing way than do our impressions of most other stories. A number of critics have commented on the intriguing moral nature of the main characters. Caleb can be seen as a young hero or a misguided youth, Falkland as basically noble or essentially depraved. But the moral ambivalence in these portraits is in fact encompassed by a much more radical ambiguity, one in which two entire *Weltanschauungen* vie in catching our attention. A modern student of irony like Wayne Booth would have to call *Caleb Williams* an instance of Unstable Irony, as opposed to Stable Irony which enables a reader to reconstruct one definite meaning once the literal statement has been seen through or rejected.[14]

Angus Wilson was, I think, the first critic of *Caleb Williams* to make the point that the novel wavers between two different accounts of life: he finds the novelist "a courageous opponent of the cruelties and injustices that scarred the surface of eighteenth-century order and decency, but also . . . a man peculiarly sensitive to the spiritual terrors and despairs that lay beneath its intellectual composure and certainty".[15] A Freudian critic, Rudolf F. Storch, takes as his point of departure an experience of the book as "social protest" and "Calvinist obsession".[16] In his shrewd analysis Storch successfully shows that the story can be read as "a study of neurosis"; in the following an attempt will be made to demonstrate that it can also – and with at least equal profit – be read as the story of a character caught between beliefs or philosophies that may be true and all-important, and not only rationalisations of feelings of guilt and protest.

We can never know for certain the extent to which Godwin himself may have been consciously aware in 1794 of the simultaneous presence of Calvinism and atheistic political theory in the novel. In retrospect, in the preface of 1832, he approaches an interpretation of the novel which indirectly highlights this very tension. But it is pointless to look for such an acknowledgement in the 1790s; then, Godwin could release such pressures only in the language of fiction. But tensions of this kind were not uncommon in writers sensitive to the intellectual climate of the nineties; important links can be established between Godwin and the first generation of Romantic poets.

This chapter is organised as a study in Empsonian ambiguity, and I believe that this approach to the novel can expose more of the exciting stuff that the story is made of than other readings. But I have tried not to disregard those aspects of *Caleb Williams* that are less directly relevant to my own overall impression of the book. One of the following sub-chapters is devoted to a reading of the novel as a study in Caleb's (and Falkland's) psychological and moral development. Though my argument will present reasons why such a reading, if final and absolute, destroys great parts of the novel, all students of *Caleb Williams* must be thankful to those critics who, in the course of the last fifteen years, have emphasised the importance of Caleb's growth from a raw, unthinking lad to an experienced and thoughtful man.

"The spirit and character of the government"

Things As They Are; Or, The Adventures of Caleb Williams appeared in May 1794, fifteen months after *Political Justice*. A short preface, which was withdrawn from the first edition at the request of the booksellers, had this to say about the novel:

> The following narrative is intended to answer a purpose more general and important than immediately appears upon the face of it. The question now afloat in the world respecting *Things As They Are*, is the most interesting that can be presented to the human mind. While one party pleads for reformation and change, the other extols in the warmest terms the existing constitution of society. It seemed as if something would be gained for the decision of this question, if that constitution were faithfully developed in its practical effects. What is now presented to the public is no refined and abstract speculation . . . of things passing in the moral world . . . It is now known to philosophers that the spirit and character of the government intrudes itself into every rank of society. But

this is a truth highly worthy to be communicated to persons whom books of philosophy and science are never likely to reach. Accordingly it was proposed in the invention of the following work, to comprehend, as far as the progressive nature of a single story would allow, a general review of the modes of domestic and unrecorded despotism, by which man becomes the destroyer of man. (p.1)

Here it is the political philosopher who comments on the novel. At this crucial time in the history of England one party actually defends a society characterised by destructive despotism, another wants things changed. But Godwin, who makes no bones about where he belongs, does not preach another French Revolution. The constitution can be "developed in its practical effects" when people in general know more about the workings of the social machinery. Hand in hand, philosophical treatises and novels can disseminate this kind of information.

There can be no doubt that critics who see *Caleb Williams* against the background of late eighteenth-century politics and who find in the book an exemplification of ideas from *Political Justice*, bring out something essential to any understanding of the book.[17] Although much more than a political tract, *Caleb Williams* insistently and fairly consistently presents a picture of the kind of society which Godwin attacks in his political philosophy – a society governed not by justice but by crude power and by false ideals of chivalry inherent in the social tradition.[18]

Caleb's life story highlights this concern. A poor, bright lad becomes the secretary of the local squire; eager to learn more about the world, Caleb studies his employer and his strange history, and concludes that this seemingly noble figure is a murderer. Once, when there is a fire in the house, Caleb is on the point of opening a secret chest in Falkland's room, but he is intercepted by the arrival of his master. When Falkland realises what Caleb thinks, he actually confesses the murder and threatens Caleb with awful punishment should he attempt to leave his service. After some months Caleb can no longer stand life under this kind of surveillance and leaves one night for London. He is found on the way, and in his innocence agrees to go back and defend himself against charges now made against him. When his belongings are produced before the magistrate, he realises to his horror that valuables have been planted in one of his boxes. For all his protests Caleb is sent to prison. In a second attempt to escape he is successful; and he finds refuge for some time with a band of robbers headed by a latter-day Robin Hood. But Caleb sees clearly enough that robbery, even though only from the rich, is a debasing profession; and he leaves as soon as he can, disguised as a beggar. After various adventures on the road, he goes into hiding in London. Here Falkland's dedicated spy, Gines, gets hold of him; but at a new hearing Falkland does not prefer any charges against Caleb who, rather bewildered, is taken by force to meet his old master who now tries to press Caleb to sign a declaration that he, Falkland, is innocent. Caleb refuses, and in the course of the next years he is constantly pestered by the ever-vigilant Gines who follows him and sees to it that he is calumniated and deprived of the means to earn a living and to settle down with a family of his own. In desperation Caleb finally returns to his own county and requests a second hearing of Falkland's case. They meet, and, in the first version Godwin wrote of the ending, Caleb fails to convince the meeting, is taken to prison, suffers bouts of madness and dies, perhaps poisoned by Falkland's servant.[19] Godwin then had second thoughts about the last pages and wrote the published version of the ending in which Caleb is overwhelmed by kind feelings for the man he accuses of murder, and in which Falkland melts, confesses his crimes, and dies some few days later. Caleb is free, but despised as cruel and vindictive by those who know him and, what is worse, tortured by guilt because he has brought this essentially noble master to an ignominious end. Both endings can be seen as clinching the political argument, though, as we shall see below, on somewhat different grounds.

The social criticism embedded in the story is coherent. What is said about prisons, courts of justice, assemblies of squires and bands of robbers is all linked with a simple and basic fact: power rests with landowners who only too easily find that might is right. This point is firmly established in the first chapters about Falkland when Mr Clare, an old poet who is a model of persuasive wisdom and integrity, is still alive. He, of all human beings, ought to be able to counteract evil tendencies in the neighbourhood. Energetically, he warns Falkland about future dangers. But when Falkland's moment of crisis comes, Mr Clare's good advice is lost in a flood of wounded pride and rage which an aristocratic upbringing has made virtually inevitable. Even Mr Tyrrel, Falkland's polar opposite in most ways, stops to consider the poet's good principles, but he quickly decides to pursue his own gratification. He causes the death of his sweet, little cousin who has fallen in love with Falkland; and his obstinacy, pride, and love of power send both Hawkinses on the road to destruction. In the later chapters of the novel Caleb again and again experiences from below the power of wealth. Outraged, as he is not believed when he accuses his master of the murder, he cries out on one occasion: "Six thousand a year shall protect a man from accusation; and the validity of an impeachment shall be superseded, because the author of it is a servant!" (p. 277).

In other words, Godwin is in no doubt what is "base" and what is "superstructure" in Caleb's world. In the novel one of the most important ideas of *Political Justice* is clothed in flesh and blood: "the period that must put an end to the system of *coercion* and *punishment*, is intimately connected with the circumstance of property being placed upon an equitable basis" (Vol. ii, p. 421).[20] Godwin's treatise does not develop this insight along the lines that Marx later pursued. In a most un-Marxist way Godwin believes that the individual can learn, though slowly, to live according to a principle of justice which will ensure the greatest possible happiness for all. But, like the founders of Communism, Godwin sees the institutions and the morality of a society as formed largely by its economic structure. Economic power, reflected in the political establishment, is much more insidious than we often consider it. Indeed, "the spirit and character of the government" insinuates itself into all regions of the minds of men. Godwin devotes crucial chapters in the first volume of *Political Justice* to an examination of how "political institutions have a more powerful and extensive influence, than it has generally been the practice to ascribe to them" (Vol. i, pp. 24–5).

That Godwin wants to bring out something more fundamental than the shortcomings of any one social institution is seen in the grotesque workings of the legal machinery in *Caleb Williams*.[21] Because of Falkland's position, no proper investigations are being carried out when he is suspected of having murdered Tyrrel; he is brought before an informal meeting of squires, not a proper court; and he is then acquitted after a summary hearing – largely because of his own tortured eloquence. Next time we are taken to a courtroom it is the murderer, Falkland, who is in charge of the proceedings against a likeable young man accused of manslaughter. The victim was a lower-class Tyrrel, a boorish villain who seemed to find pleasure in pestering the innocent. The situation is rich in parallels to Falkland's case and for Caleb it serves as a mousetrap scene. The verdict seems fair enough: Falkland discharges the young man who has won our sympathy; but by doing so he adds new ironies to the ways in which courts work. The legal system is presented as equally erratic on the occasions when Caleb himself appears in the dock or on the accuser's bench. Caleb is first detained on false evidence produced by Falkland. Later, though the falseness is not exposed, the accusation is withdrawn. When Caleb finally *feels* guilty during the hearing of Falkland's case which he has requested, he is victorious and Falkland's guilt is revealed. Minor characters like the noble prisoner Brightwel, the robber captain Raymond, and Falkland's servant Gines, reinforce the impression that no real justice can be expected from the English legal system. But the novel does not mechanically show us that judges are corrupt or that so and so many laws ought to be repealed. Judges can, in fact, be upright like Mr Forester or sensitive and at least potentially benevolent like Mr Falkland. What *Caleb Williams* reveals is a legal system which is itself a kind of hostage in a society so hopelessly alien to justice and happiness that the decisions of its institutions cannot be expected to coincide with any generally shared concept of justice.

This is illustrated most graphically in the prison scenes. Some of the prisoners seem to be guilty of what they have been charged with, some not; some are charged with deeds that only the letter of the rich man's law finds offensive; and some are killed by the hardships of the life they have to endure long before their cases are heard at the Assizes. Imprisonment tends to dull energy and humanity; prisoners and gaolers alike must be callous in order to survive. The prison scenes of *Caleb Williams* are didactic; here and there Godwin almost forgets that he is no longer writing a political essay. But Caleb's memory of imprisonment is most often full of intense life, and it is not difficult to accept his own excuse:

If it should be said, these are general remarks; let it be remembered that they are the dear bought result of experience. It is from the fulness of a bursting heart that reproach thus flows from my pen. These are not the declamations of a man desirous to be eloquent. I have felt the iron of slavery grating upon my soul. (p. 182)

Caleb Williams does not illustrate the theoretical treatise in a mechanical way. For one thing, Godwin wisely leaves out in the story his ideas about the future of mankind. The novel is concerned not with the development towards a better society, but with "things as they are". Though written later, the story can be read as a preparatory document describing those evils which prompted the writer of *Political Justice* to spend time and energy on a theoretical treatise. Because the novel is concerned with the present, it is not open to the criticism which has been levelled against Godwin's optimism about the future. Not that the novel and *Political Justice* disagree in their assessment of man as he is now. That man is capable of impartial thinking and just conduct (and therefore of future improvement) is never, in Godwin's philosophy, a truth which can be exemplified everywhere. Falkland and Caleb fail because they belong to a society not permeated by truth and sincerity and justice. Neither character can be used as an argument against *Political Justice*, which may be a naïve work in certain respects, but not so simple-minded as not to recognise the presence of blind passion and flagrant dishonesty in Godwin's own England. Godwin believed that truth is great and will eventually prevail; but this idea, central to *Political Justice*, is a possibility only, not a fact, in the novel. Caleb is optimistic at first: "Why have we the power of speech, but to communicate our thoughts? I will never believe that a man conscious of innocence, cannot make other men perceive that he has that thought" (p. 171).

The situation, Caleb's first appearance in court, is patently ironic, for Caleb is not believed. Moreover, the whole question of innocence is not as simple as Caleb here takes it to be. But in spite of Caleb's disappointment here and later, there are encounters in the book in which Caleb is believed, not because of circumstantial evidence, but because the hearer is sensitive to a trustworthy note in Caleb's voice and argument. The best example is probably the good Mrs Marney, who helps Caleb in London. Caleb himself fails in the end when he does not believe in truth only, but puts his trust in a social institution: "I now see that mistake in all its enormity. I am sure that, if I had opened my heart to Mr Falkland, if I had told to him privately the tale that I have now been telling, he could not have resisted my reasonable demand" (p. 323). *Caleb Williams* describes man as a surprisingly resilient being who can think logically and justly even when in chains. But it also argues with *Political Justice* that in insidious ways society corrupts our vision and our ability to consider things impartially. It is this corruption which Caleb finds inside himself in the last pages of the book. The ending highlights an emotional difference between the two works: whereas *Political Justice* keeps up a calm belief in the final victory of reason some time in the future, the novel ends in defeat.

Godwin's rewriting of the ending is another indication of the extent to which he has become sensitive to the demands of the fictional world he had created. Originally, the political message is straightforward enough: a poor, honest man can expect no justice from a society in which the rich are only too well prepared to victimise those that threaten their peace. The published version of the ending is no retractation of what the story as a whole says about society. Here, too, Caleb is a loser. Now he realises that he has not only been buffeted by an evil world; his own mind has been invaded by its destructive modes of thinking so that he now wants to destroy Falkland by the very means that Falkland had applied towards him. Both endings hinge on spectacular scenes that smack of stage melodrama, but the final version also forcefully reminds us that Godwin does not need to present a society in which people become either black or white. In fact, the final ending does not only give us more interesting portraits of the main characters, it is also politically more effective: it enlists a more subtle pity, and not only righteous anger and indignation, on the side of reform; and it is less defeatist than the first ending, in which Caleb alone is the loser and Falkland is victorious. This first rounding-off invites an emotional response which does not support the radical cause: the anger readers may feel is imprisoned and impotent, for this ending suggests that revolt, even by courageous and upright young men, will fail and the tyrannical rich will survive.

In another way, too, the final ending testifies to the extent to which Godwin has become a novelist. Caleb is forced to realise how elusive the ideal of calm reasoning advocated in Godwin's philosophy can be. He was first convinced that his course of action was a "piece of equity and justice, such as an impartial spectator would desire" (p. 319), but confronted with Falkland he finds that these "fine-spun reasonings" evaporate. How then can man be certain that what looks like justice is really so? *Political Justice* argues that we shall know what is true when we see things at close quarters, but in its last pages *Caleb Williams* suggests that this is no panacea. For the speech that wins the meeting and Falkland himself over to Caleb's side is not at all a model of truth. Caleb has seen through one set of false assumptions, but this new version of his own history is at best only a curious mixture of newly acquired insight, misunderstandings and uncertainties. Against the evidence in his own narrative Caleb now believes that he would have been successful in accusing Falkland of murder had he only done so while still in his service (p. 321). He grossly exaggerates Falkland's kindness at a time when Falkland allows Gines to continue his bloodhound search (p. 322); and in summing up his last action, "I have been a murderer, a cool, deliberate, unfeeling murderer" (p.323), Caleb is blind to the flaming intensity of the mixed feelings he entertains for Falkland at this stage. Again, the effect of such complexities is not to undermine the social criticism in the novel, but they force the reader back to the story to reassess the relationship between the teller and the tale.

The common sense and the literary tact with which Godwin treats his political themes in *Caleb Williams* can be fully appreciated only when he is seen struggling with the models available to him. One cannot simply say that he chose the language of fiction for his attempt to reach a wider audience, for his problem was precisely that there was no one literary language ready-made for this particular purpose. The subject-matter was to be "things as they are" and, as Godwin conceived of these things in 1793, they could not be brought out by the allegorical mode of *Comus*, nor by the kind of domestic scenes in which Richardson excels. This does not mean that Godwin had forgotten – or tried to forget – earlier novels. Richardson could still teach him a lesson about ways in which the human mind can be dissected and conflicting motives and wishes laid bare. A number of incidents in the first volume of *Caleb Williams* are reminiscent of *Clarissa* and *Sir Charles Grandison*,[22] and in the first version of the last pages there are heavy borrowings from *Clarissa*.[23]

By 1793 Godwin's knowledge of English literature had become considerable; his diary shows us that his reading was of a size and range which many modern students of literature probably must admit that they have equalled only for very short spells.[24] But though he could draw on wide reading by the nineties, and though he does make frequent use of Richardson, Shakespeare (who is sometimes brought into the novel in ways which give little credit to Godwin's taste) and a number of other great writers, he knew that he was writing in a new world. A great revolution had occurred in the heart of Europe, and new questions were "afloat in the world respecting THINGS AS THEY ARE", questions "the most interesting that can be presented to the human mind". In this situation Godwin must have turned with a particularly keen interest to the few examples provided by the radical novelists of his own day, those who had been trying out bottles for the wine of the new era.

One of these, Thomas Holcroft, was Godwin's very good friend; Godwin called him one of his most important "oral instructors",[25] and Holcroft may well have contributed to the ideas expressed in *Political Justice*.[26] Holcroft's novel *Anna St Ives* had appeared in 1792, when Godwin was still at work on *Political Justice*. When he wanted to write a novel himself, there must, I think, have been three important lessons to be had from Holcroft's attempt. Two of them were encouraging: first, Holcroft tries to be realistic; he had chosen a form, an epistolary narrative like Richardson's that makes for psychological realism. Secondly, he manages to weave an open discussion of political questions into the whole of the story. In *Anna St Ives* the main points made by Burke in his *Reflections* are taken up and encountered one by one. And in spite of its epistolary lectures on property, aristocracy, equality, reason and promises, *Anna St Ives* remains a novel, and for long stretches at a time even an enjoyable novel.

A third lesson was probably equally conspicuous to Godwin: Holcroft's approach is at once high-handed and half-hearted. It is overbearing in that we must accept an *a priori* conception of Frank Henley as the ideal young man of the new age. Political teaching flows copiously from Frank's pen, and gradually also from the pen of Anna, whom he educates and wins by his blameless conduct. Frank's excellence – in a world which has been made frivolous and dangerous by the rich – is brought out by all his admirable words and deeds. For radical readers there must have been great emotional uplift (one in which twentieth-century liberal readers can easily share) in some of the scenes in which Frank displays his clear thinking, high morality and undaunted courage. But an epistolary novel of the 1790s needs greater verisimilitude for the author to be able to reach those who are not already converted. Had Holcroft been another Fielding, he might have written a comic allegory in the mode of *Tom Jones*, a book that laughed its way into the hearts and minds of conservative readers. But in this novel Holcroft, who wrote clever comedies for the stage, is serious in the sense that he tries to be plain and factual in his description of men and manners. (The only attempt in the grotesque is the portrait of Frank's father.) As a consequence, there is something incongruous about the perfect Frank and his ideals. The incongruousness does not seriously detract from the entertainment value of the novel, but the political teaching suffers because of it. I imagine that when *Anna St Ives* came out, the message appealed to those who were already convinced, while conservative readers, though irritated by what they would look upon as tedious asides on dangerous subjects, enjoyed the sentimental sweep of the story and the happy ending.[27] This ending might have given Burke a wry pleasure had he read the novel. For the moral victories of Frank and Anna are crowned by wealth and a country estate. They will, in effect, be excellent illustrations of Burke's ideal:

> When the useful parts of an old establishment are kept, and what is superadded is to be fitted to what is retained, a vigorous mind, steady persevering attention, various powers of comparison and combination, and the resources of an understanding fruitful in expedients are to be exercised: they are to be exercised in continued conflict with the combined force of opposite vices; with the obstinacy that rejects all improvement, and the levity that is fatigued and disgusted with every thing of which it is in possession.[28]

Holcroft probably did not notice that his symbols of victory eventually landed him in the wrong camp.[29] But Godwin's concept of how "things as they are" can be described in fiction is more radical; and his friend's novel must have served as a warning: the wrongs of English social life cannot be properly brought out by letting clean-living and right-thinking young people settle down to a happy married life in comfortable circumstances. In Godwin rich and poor alike are imprisoned – symbolically and sometimes literally – by the social system of which they are a part. A traditional rounding-off of Holcroft's kind will hide the basic truth that an Englishman is doomed to live in a social tradition which has become destructive of happiness:

> Government was intended to suppress injustice, but it offers new occasions and temptations for the commission of it.
> By concentrating the force of the community, it gives occasion

42

to wild projects of calamity, to oppression, despotism, war, and conquest.

By perpetuating and aggravating the inequality of property, it fosters many injurious passions, and excites men to the practice of robbery and fraud. (Vol i, p. xxiv)

Godwin is true both to his theory and to his more immediate feeling about life when – in both endings of the story – he lets Caleb's life end in misery.

Robert Bage, a northerner, did not belong to Godwin's circle of friends and acquaintances in 1793, but Godwin certainly read Bage's *Man as He Is* which appeared in the same year as *Anna St Ives*, 1792. The original title given to *Caleb Williams*, "Things as They Are", seems to be a conscious echo of Bage's title. *Man as He Is* is a much more genial novel than *Anna St Ives*. Bage has a keen eye for the ludicrous and incongruous in life; and his protagonist is a "man as he is", a passionate and generous young man, but no paragon of all virtues like Frank Henley. As Bage's bantering narrative takes the young Sir George from county to county in England, and later to the Continent, we are given pleas – put into the mouths of various respectable characters – for natural rights and for full civil rights to dissenters (vol. i, pp. 44, 94)[30] and attacks on the buying of votes and on promises (pp. 118 ff., 240–1). In the third volume the admirable la Fayette is brought in to suggest how freedom and equality can be introduced: "Purge – purge well, – if that will not do, – bleed a little" (p. 115).

In *Man as He Is* the narrator poses as a sophisticated man of letters who knows what his audience, predominantly female, will like and who promises to give them what they relish. Which he does. The novel takes us to the centres of fashion and to idyllic rural retreats; we follow the various fortunes of young innocents, London rakes, courtesans, crusty rich relatives, and a mother who is an unpleasant nitwit. In the middle of all this there is an engaging young man who blunders on – among rakes and radicals – towards greater moral insight. Behind it all is the narrator's detached, ironic attitude to his fiction.

The writer of *Things As They Are* could take a number of hints from Bage (and behind Bage stand Fielding and Smollett). Like Sir George, Caleb is fatherless and has to fend for himself; and Bage's occasional psychological penetration, as evinced in the portrait of

Birimport,[31] may have encouraged Godwin to attempt descriptions of characters in which there are fine shades of guilt, shame and honesty. But the echo of Bage in the title implies that Godwin goes further: his novel is not primarily concerned with the nature of man; it is about "things", which here must mean man *and* his surroundings. And in spite of his interest in the representative features of English life, Godwin moves his story one step further away from the picaresque. Both novelists take their heroes to a great many different scenes in which the workings of society are criticised; but we pass a watershed between Bage and Godwin. In *Caleb Williams* it is very definitely the interest we take in two individualised and complex characters engaged in a complicated and internecine struggle that carries us forward, not the excitement engendered by a series of happenings on the road.[32]

Two female novelists of some note were associated with the radical cause in the early 1790s, Elizabeth Inchbald and Charlotte Smith. Mrs Inchbald's *A Simple Story*, which appeared in 1791, was well known to Godwin – he had assisted the authoress in the last stages of the writing.[33] Mrs Inchbald gives us a memorable sketch of a woman torn between irresponsible levity and profound love, but the story was probably not one which Godwin felt that he could make use of. It is firmly set in the old order of things, which it does not openly criticise, except, perhaps, for a last-page insistence on the supreme importance of education. There is more social criticism in one of Elizabeth Inchbald's plays, *Such Things Are* from 1787, which may have given Godwin another hint towards a title for his novel. The play has prison scenes in which we witness the suffering of the innocent because of political rivalry, but the main target of criticism is not of Godwin's kind: the central character is an unpleasant young man who plays on the vanity of the rich in a callous attempt to gain wealth.

Charlotte Smith's epistolary *Desmond* (1792) is openly political. Mrs Smith had been to France and was very knowledgeable about the Revolution, and her novel is livelier and richer in incidents than most Jacobin fiction. She was in no doubt as to where her sympathies lay: "I have given to my imaginary characters the arguments I have heard on both sides; and if those in favour of one party have evidently the advantage, it is not owing to my partial representation, but to the predominant power of truth and reason". Moreover, she realised that the form of her novel would be more readily criticised because of this: "For that asperity of remark, which will arise on the part of those whose political tenets I may offend, I am prepared; those who object to the matter, will probably arraign the manner".[34] This awareness of the special difficulties a radical novelist had to face obviously appealed to Godwin. However, Charlotte Smith does not really attempt to solve the problems of presentation which this situation involved her in. She resorts too often to a black-and-white characterisation which can amuse only those whose sympathies are radical anyway. Nor is her case improved by the many letters in which the good characters reflect at length on such worthy topics as prisons, poverty and Paine. From Godwin's point of view the most promising feature in *Desmond* must have been the young hero who writes most of the letters, for he is no ideal human being (as a middle-aged friend repeatedly reminds him) but a young man foolishly in love and naïvely enthusiastic about the Revolution. In this context it is a pity that his mentor, Mr Bethel, is so consistently wise and enlightened in his opinions. Since he becomes the final and perfect authority in political questions, the part assigned to the reader is too passive. We are not asked to begin thinking on our own as the novel would have invited us to do had we been left with the naïve and likeable Desmond as our guide through France and French politics.

In all his novels Godwin is at times overcome by his wish to preach; but his own philosophy can, as a matter of fact, offer the novelist better guidance: *Political Justice* argues that life must be experienced at close quarters before it can be properly understood and that generalisations therefore tend to be dangerous short-cuts to truth. Mankind is not easily saved by generalised good advice, not even when it comes from the lips of the best of men. Therefore, Charlotte Smith's and Holcroft's epistolary form – a handful of letter-writers, one of whom is the good norm against which everything can be judged – was not one that Godwin could easily use. There is an eloquent paragon of virtue in *Caleb Williams*, Mr Clare, but he dies before the story reaches its first climax. He becomes one of a number of benevolent father-figures in the novel who all die or are caught in situations in which they cannot help those in need. There is no room for Mr Bethel, or for Frank Henley, in the world of Godwin's novel.

Bage's mode of narrative is different from Holcroft's and Charlotte Smith's, but equally foreign to Godwin's most important concerns. The light, bantering style of Bage's non-committal narrator might have been within Godwin's range, but to tell a story from such a point of view is to insinuate that life can be considered at a distance and its vicissitudes be mastered and compartmentalised by means of detached and good-humoured satire. Godwin wanted to bring out a troubled intensity that required another approach:

> I began my narrative, as is the more usual way, in the third person. But I speedily became dissatisfied. I then assumed the first person, making the hero of my tale his own historian; and in this mode I have persisted. . . . It was infinitely the best adapted, at least, to my vein of delineation . . . (p. 339)

Thus Godwin in his preface of 1832. He did in fact choose what to us sounds like a modern solution: he placed the story in the mouth of a sensitive and intelligent, but immature and bewildered main character. Eric Rothstein's brilliant analysis of Caleb as the teller of the story reveals how uncertain Caleb is when he begins his narrative. He must rely heavily on material borrowed from other authors; later, as he gains personal experience of life, he can refer to characters and incidents in a language that smacks less of romance and more of real eighteenth-century life. But he never reaches any full and reliable understanding of his own complicated situation. The reader is all the time forced to evaluate what Caleb says in each chapter against the rest of the book.[35]

Caleb's position as narrator and protagonist is well chosen for a novel with a political aim. His story implicates us in a way which Anna's and Desmond's do not; but the same Caleb also provides a political reading of *Caleb Williams* with certain discomforts. There are a number of irritants in the picture which emerge when we consider the novel as an illustration of Godwin's political theories. For one thing, Caleb is not consistent in the way in which he accounts for his misfortunes. Most often Caleb implies that his life is determined by external circumstances: in the spirit of *Political Justice* he blames things as they are in the England of his day for his misery. But on other occasions he describes himself as being persecuted by the "malignant destiny" (p. 16) that governs Falkland, as being in the hands of "death dealing mischief" (p. 37), or impelled by a "fatal impulse that seemed destined to hurry me to my destruction" (p. 121). In the last pages of the novel Caleb puts forward still another interpretation of himself; he now feels that he is a free agent and therefore responsible for his actions.[36] At this stage it is his feeling of guilt which is the heaviest burden he has to bear. That Caleb nourishes such remorse is no proof of a disagreement between the novel and *Political Justice*: the political theory does not, of course, deny the existence of feelings of guilt. And Caleb is not, and is not meant to be, a philosopher writing a thesis; in his various moments of calm and rage he may well be allowed to ascribe his downfall to a variety of causes. Few of us are consistent when we search for reasons for our short-comings. Still, the force of Caleb's remorse, coming, as it does, as the last note, is considerable. Though it may be contained within the boundaries of a political reading, it also points beyond such an interpretation.

It is not only Caleb's feelings in the last pages which blur the firm outlines of a work intended to "comprehend . . . a general review of the modes of domestic and unrecorded despotism" (p. 1). It has recently been shown with what mixed feelings even radicals in the 1790s would look upon Caleb's dual role of servant and "spy".[37] It has also been suggested that "the tinder of the plot", Caleb's curiosity and Falkland's love of fame, does not seem "to be socially determined or even socially encouraged".[38] Most readers will, I think, easily notice the way in which Falkland's obsession with his reputation is presented as a result of the history of his own class; but Caleb's curiosity is certainly not closely related to the main concerns of *Political Justice*. And, as Leslie Stephen noticed, Falkland is really no clear example at all of the kind of rule Godwin argues against.[39] For in most respects Falkland is a benevolent, wise, and just landowner. It is only in the particular series of actions resulting from the quarrel with Tyrrel that he is at fault.

Suddenly, then, as we look at the novel, it may change like the rabbit-and-duck picture – and our impressions come to rest in a different pattern for a time.

"The power of the omnipresent God"

It is in the perspective created by nearly two hundred years of literary history that the second reading I want to outline emerges with greatest clarity. Walter Allen, who sees Godwin as the fore-runner of a novelist like Graham Greene, gives an emphatic account of such a new reading:

Godwin overthrew God, and having done so, went on to finish the job by overthrowing, on paper at any rate, the very basis of all government, secular and ecclesiastical. But thorough-going intellectual though he was, emancipated from the 'mind-forg'd manacles' as he might conceive himself to be, he was still tied to God emotionally by the profoundest sentiments of fear and remorse for his action, tied to Him perhaps even by love.

... Falkland himself tells him [Caleb]: "You might as well think of escaping from the power of the omnipresent God, as from mine! " This the progress of the novel proves to be true. And when Williams does kill Falkland he realizes he has killed the being whom he most dearly loves.

My conclusion, then, is that *Caleb Williams* is not, as it has been conventionally assumed, an allegory of the political state of England in the seventeen-nineties, but rather a symbolic statement of the author's relation to God.[40]

Those of us who have had the curious experience of seeing the novel which illustrates a political treatise disappear before our eyes, its place taken by a dreadful version of the 139th Psalm, may well ask ourselves whether we are in the same danger as those who find Blake's "dark Satanic Mills" primarily a symbol of the Industrial Revolution. Are we seeing, inside the covers of *Caleb Williams*, a work which Godwin and his contemporaries could not perceive? In one sense, the answer to this last question must of course be "yes". We shall never be in the situation in which Godwin's first readers found themselves, and we must – sometimes probably with considerable benefits – read literature in the light of a number of twentieth-century assumptions. But few, if any, modern readers would feel happy about an interpretation which could not possibly be shared by the first readers of an old work. We ought, therefore, to ask ourselves whether contemporary evidence can be found to support Walter Allen's reading.

We have seen that in his first preface Godwin stressed the novel's political implication; but in the 1832 preface to *Fleetwood* (which deals with the writing of *Caleb Williams*) the following is presented as more important:

I formed a conception of a book of fictitious adventure, that should in some way be distinguished by a very powerful interest.

Pursuing this idea, I invented first the third volume, then the second, and last of all the first. I bent myself to the conception of a series of adventures of flight and pursuit; the fugitive in perpetual apprehension of being overwhelmed with the worst calamities, and the pursuer, by his ingenuity and resources, keeping his victim in a state of the most fearful alarm. (p. 336–7)

This summary from forty years later may possibly tell us more about Godwin's development after *Caleb Williams* than about the novel itself,[41] but it does mention several of the sources which Godwin used and it indicates what kinds of stories of flight and pursuit Godwin was interested in in 1793.

Godwin made use of the fair-maid-in-distress stories of *Pamela* and in particular of *Clarissa* for the chapters devoted to Emily in the first volume, but the flight and pursuit theme of the rest of the novel is not of Richardson's kind. It is thus only natural that Richardson is not mentioned when Godwin describes how "it was ever my method to get about me any productions of former authors that seemed to bear on my subject" (p. 339). Of the five works which he proceeds to mention, two are stories of criminals, the "Newgate Calendar" and the "Lives of the Pirates"; the other three are stories of pursuit of another kind. The first is the anonymous *History of Mademoiselle St Phale*, which, in Godwin's words, describes "a French Protestant in the times of the fiercest persecution of the Huguenots, who fled through France in the utmost terror . . . by scarcely any chance finding a moment's interval of security" (p. 340). Thus *Caleb Williams* is linked with the idea of *religious* persecution. From a Roman Catholic point of view, the Mademoiselle is pursued by the righteous wrath of God; from the point of view of the author of the story her flight illustrates the way in which a good Christian must flee the nets of the Devil. This pattern is reflected in *Caleb Williams* in more than one way, in that either Falkland or Caleb can be thought of as the pursuer. In all cases (since Caleb and Falkland, respectively, can be either God or the Devil, there are four possible interpretations of the flight pattern) this model has a metaphysical colouring.

However, the account Godwin gives of the *History of Mademoiselle de St Phale* in 1832 is curiously distorted. It is not quite correct to say that the young lady fled "in the utmost terror, in the midst of eternal alarms and hair-breadth escapes, having her quarters perpetually beaten up" (p. 340). For one thing, the flight begins only half-way

49

through the book. In the first part Mademoiselle has the sublime joy of seeing her good brother outwit a Jesuit and of being strengthened by her father's exemplary death-bed. There are machinations; and she is abducted, and later forced to flee the country. But even at this time speedy interventions by her brother save her from the threatening imprisonment in a convent, and there are long spells in the blissful company of the reformed. Moreover, we know from the first page that the whole story is written down as the young lady tells it to good friends, all safe and sound. We eventually realise that they are on board a ship which will take them to safety (and to certain very eligible young men) in Northern Germany. Godwin's account of this edifying story is thus lop-sided, but this lop-sidedness is significant: it brings out very clearly what Godwin thought of as relevant to his own concerns – a flight "in the utmost terror".[42]

The next source Godwin mentions, *God's Revenge against Murder*, is one in which he found that "the beam of the eye of Omniscience was represented as perpetually pursuing the guilty, and laying open his most hidden retreats to the light of day" (p. 340). Indeed, in *God's Revenge against Murder and Adultery; Remarkably displayed in a Variety of Tragical Histories, containing Examples, Historical and Moral* (as the full title of the 1770 London edition goes), all lust and greed and wrath are punished; but God's pursuit and punishment are found almost exclusively in a brief, perfunctory last paragraph. The pages of this "penny dreadful" are largely filled with crimes and preparations for crimes, committed – and described – with considerable gusto. Again, we see Godwin's account bringing out what was important to *him*: stories in which man flees from "the eye of Omniscience".

The same pattern is reinforced in the more straightforward reference which Godwin makes to Bluebeard in the 1832 preface: "Falkland was my Bluebeard, who had perpetrated atrocious crimes . . . . Caleb Williams was the wife, who in spite of warning, persisted in his attempt to discover the forbidden secret" (p. 340). Godwin immediately goes on to describe Caleb's curiosity and its results in terms of the supernatural (with an echo of *Macbeth*): Caleb, "when he had succeeded, struggled as fruitlessly to escape the consequences, as the wife of Bluebeard in washing the key of the ensanguined chamber, who, as often as she cleared the stain of blood from one side, found it showing itself with frightful distinctness on the other" (pp. 340–1).

But aren't these references most easily accounted for as part of

Godwin's strategy in the 1832 preface – he wants *Caleb Williams* to look less like a political pamphlet and more like a novel with an outright popular appeal in story and mood? A curious entry in Godwin's diaries from the early nineties suggests that this is not the only answer. That we find Godwin reading Burke, in a certain sense the arch-enemy in *Political Justice*, at this time is no wonder; but it is puzzling to find that Godwin studied not only the *Reflections* but also Burke's early *A Philosophical Enquiry into . . . the Sublime and Beautiful*.[43] Godwin's interest in Burke's personality and in the *Reflections* is understandable, and it has been well and fully analysed by James T. Boulton[44] and David McCracken. But why this steady interest in an aesthetic treatise, which, judged against the ideas of *Political Justice*, is dangerously one-sided? In Godwin's own terminology it is a textbook for a "man of taste and refinement", but not for the truly virtuous man:

> The sublime and pathetic are barren, unless it be the sublime of virtue, and the pathos of true sympathy. The pleasures of the mere man of taste and refinement, "play round the head, but come not to the heart." There is no true joy, but in the spectacle and contemplation of happiness. There is no delightful melancholy, but in pitying distress. (*Political Justice*, vol. i, p. 447)

The *Enquiry* is therefore a book which Godwin could easily dismiss, if he so wanted: from the point of view expressed in the passage just quoted, it is a trivial work about the trivial problems of over-refined pleasure-seekers. Still, Godwin persistently returns to this treatise. The reason is scarcely found in Burke's discussion of the beautiful: Godwin was never a diligent worshipper of beauty. It must have been the other main part – the one devoted to the sublime – which fascinated Godwin. Burke holds that one particular feeling, that of terror, is the strongest of which the human mind is capable; and terror is linked with sublimity: "Whatever is fitted in any sort to excite the ideas of pain, and danger, that is to say, whatever is in any sort terrible . . . is a source of the *sublime*: that is, it is productive of the strongest emotion which the mind is capable of feeling." Burke lists a great many sources of the terrible sublime, such as obscurity, privation, vastness, power, and suddenness. The one which is described at greatest length is, as we might expect, power; and this is also the most interesting item in our context. For here Burke describes the power of kings and then turns to theology: since all power must ultimately be traced back to God, He is the final source of terror. Nothing, says Burke, "can wholly remove the terror that naturally arises from a force which nothing can withstand".[45] To Godwin, atheist and radical, this must have been engrossing reading. Here was a study in what we would call psychology and aesthetics which praised terror as the strongest emotion and which found this sublime passion caused by the power of kings and by the majesty of God. These were not only academic problems. Godwin knew that he might be in danger of being persecuted for his political views, and he could be in no doubt that according to the disciples of Sandeman he had reason to fear the wrath of God. Terror, even metaphysical terror, was thus something which Godwin, for all the calm reasoning of *Political Justice*, wanted to know more about in the early 1790s.

These sources make it clear that to read *Caleb Williams* as a study in sublime, metaphysical terror need not be to indulge in a twentieth-century anachronism. But how substantial and how persistent can such a reading be?

The development of the story lends itself quite naturally to this kind of investigation. It is, as a matter of fact, possible to give a summary of the novel which is strikingly different from the one given in the preceding sub-chapter. Caleb is first described as living in a world of innocence:

> I was born of humble parents . . . and they had no portion to give me, but an education free from the usual sources of depravity, and the inheritance, long lost by their unfortunate progeny! of an honest fame. I was taught the rudiments of no science, except reading, writing and arithmetic. But I had an inquisitive mind, and neglected no means of information from conversation or books. My improvement was greater than my condition in life afforded room to expect. (pp. 3–4)

There is a Master, an owner of the garden, in this Eden:

> I had never had occasion to address a person of this elevated rank, and I felt no small uneasiness and awe on the present occasion. I found Mr Falkland a man of small stature, with an extreme

52

delicacy of form and appearance. . . . every muscle and petty line of his countenance seemed to an inconceivable degree pregnant with meaning. His manner was kind, attentive, and humane. His eye was full of animation, but there was a grave and sad solemnity in his air, which, for want of experience I imagined was the inheritance of the great, . . . His look bespoke the unquietness of his mind, and frequently wandered with an expression of discon-solateness and anxiety. (p. 5)

This is a picture of a worried deity, but in this world Mr Falkland is an omnipotent character. Caleb is characterised by a thirst for wisdom which becomes dangerous. He is not merely inquisitive; he has an obsessive curiosity:

The spring of action which, perhaps more than any other, charac-terised the whole train of my life, was curiosity. . . . I could not rest till I had acquainted myself with the solutions that had been invented for the phenomena of the universe. In fine, this produced in me an invincible attachment to books of narrative and ro-mance. I panted for the unravelling of an adventure, with an anxiety, perhaps almost equal to that of the man whose future happiness or misery depended on its issue. I read, I devoured compositions of this sort. (p. 4)

Caleb's curiosity is not only obsessive, it is also strangely biassed in that it leads his thoughts away from facts towards "narrative and romance". As James Walton remarks about this passage, "the 'natural philosopher' is vanquished by the fictionist, and actual causes by 'invented' ones".[46] There is a spectacular lack of logic in this search for knowledge. Caleb does not realise that between his initial question and his search for an answer the ground shifts in a curious way. But this little glimpse of his mind at work prepares the reader for the confrontation between "phenomena" and "narrative" which in fact informs the rest of the novel.

When Caleb's story is resumed in the next volume, we expect the irresistible apple to make its appearance, which it does in the form of a mysterious trunk in Mr Falkland's apartment. It is appropriate that flames should seem to surround Caleb as he is about to open the chest:

In a window-seat of the room lay a number of chissels and other carpenter's tools. I know not what infatuation instantaneously seized me. The idea was too powerful to be resisted. I forgot the business upon which I came, the employment of the servants and the urgency of general danger. I should have done the same if the flames that seemed to extend as they proceeded, and already surmounted the house, had reached this very apartment. (p. 132)

In terms of the Old Testament parallel this is a moment of fatal sin. The flames rise round the sinner, and he forgets his original good intention and the "general danger". Caleb's curiosity, which was briefly outlined in the first pages of the novel, now shows itself for what it is; it is an obsession which is callous and unrelenting. Even though Caleb can at times see what Falkland suffers – "What he endured in the intercourse between us appeared to be gratuitous evil" (p. 123) – he cannot stop prying into Falkland's affairs. There is an irresponsible egocentricity in this search for the "truth".

Caleb in his turn is not allowed to forget the power of his Master who suddenly appears in the room where Caleb tries to open the chest. Falkland is a jealous authority, and one from whom he cannot escape:

At this moment you are enclosed with the snares of my vengeance, unseen by you, and, at the instant that you flatter yourself you are already beyond their reach, they will close upon you. You might as well think of escaping from the power of the omnipresent God, as from mine! (p. 144)

The rest of Caleb's story is an illustration of a dark version of the Psalm which Falkland had alluded to:

Whither shall I go from thy spirit? or whither shall I flee from thy presence?

If I ascend up into heaven, thou art there: if I make my bed in hell, behold thou art there.

If I take the wings of the morning, and dwell in the uttermost parts of the sea;

Even there shall thy hand lead me, and thy right hand shall hold me.

If I say, Surely the darkness shall cover me; even the night shall be light about me.

Yea, the darkness hideth not from thee; but the night shineth as the day: . . . (Psalm 139:7–12)

Wherever Caleb flees, he is found by Falkland's servant. Caleb can hide from this malicious angel neither by the sea (he is stopped twice as he is about to leave England) nor in the darkness of London where he never ventures out of doors in daylight. Caleb himself sums up this part of his life: "It was like what has been described of the eye of omniscience pursuing the guilty sinner, and darting a ray that awakens him to new sensibility, at the very moment that, otherwise, exhausted nature would lull him into a temporary oblivion of the reproaches of his conscience" (p. 305).

The biblical analogy can be turned upside down without losing its religious force. Since Falkland for long periods seems to be an evil despot, Caleb can sometimes look upon himself as a courageous scout who, like his namesake in Numbers, explores enemy country. When he realises that Falkland is a murderer, his mental state is expressed in the language of religious ecstasy:

My blood boiled within me. I was conscious to a kind of rapture for which I could not account. I was solemn, yet full of rapid emotion, burning with indignation and energy. In the very tempest and hurricane of the passions, I seemed to enjoy the most soul-ravishing calm. (pp. 129–30)

Falkland, of course, overhears Caleb's soliloquy. Towards the end of the novel it is the flames of Hell which illuminate the portrait of Falkland:

His visage was haggard, emaciated and fleshless. His complexion was a dun and tarnished red, the colour uniform through every region of the face, and suggested the idea of its being burnt and parched by the eternal fire that burned within him. . . . His whole figure was thin to a degree that suggested the idea rather of a skeleton than a person actually alive. (pp. 280–1)

But in these last chapters, too, the novel explores the ambiguity in Falkland as Caleb sees him. At this stage Caleb himself begins to think of this weak and emaciated squire as noble and benevolent, "endowed with qualities that partook of divine" (p. 321); and he regards himself as a Judas who has sold his master, not for money but to please his own mistaken sense of justice.[47]

The metaphysical interpretation of *Caleb Williams* thus embodies a profound ambiguity (which from my point of view is an ambiguity inside the more comprehensive one constituted by the simultaneous presence in the book of a rational and a religious universe): Falkland sometimes looks like a benevolent God, sometimes like a devil. Conversely, Caleb is either a transgressor who is rightly punished for having entered forbidden tracts of land or the scout of the chosen people. The novel even explores the possibility that Falkland is like the God of the Book of Job. Falkland says to Caleb: "I meditated to do you good. For that reason I was willing to prove you" (p. 281), and Caleb himself seems to believe this in the end. But common to these conflicting attitudes and guesses in the novel is the sense of holiness, of something irreducible and unfathomable, of *mana*, that they contain. In this frame of reference man is not the political being that *Political Justice* presents, but a creature that must be defined in relation to awful, supernatural powers working both outside and inside him.

As we have seen, Godwin brings his political themes into *Caleb Williams* with a well-developed sense of the requirements of the novelist's art and craft. It does not quite make sense to praise him for incorporating his religious theme with a similar consciousness of what the novel demands. For Godwin was obviously not fully conscious of the extent to which he was writing a desperate and tortuous version of Calvinism between the covers of *Caleb Williams*. Still, the novel can deserve praise for the way in which this theme is brought out, too. Some of the quotations given above approach a biblical style, but this kind of language is used sparingly and only for moments of great intensity. Generally, the evenness and even flatness of his ordinary style is effective in its own way: it gives to the Old Testament analogy an insinuating force which it could scarcely have had if more consistently phrased in an imitation of the easily recognisable style of the Authorised Version. It is one of the virtues of *Caleb Williams* that biblical images can work without being too conspicuous. In the chest scene, for instance, the action is so rapid, the style so straightforward, and Caleb's psychological state so vividly portrayed that the analogy with the Bible does not seem superimposed. It can rather be thought of as a submerged element that one notices only slowly and gradually.

Caleb Williams does not present us with a bald and definite religious allegory in which the squire is either God or a tortured minion of the devil, and in which Caleb must be categorised either as sinner or as Old Testament saint. Whereas the political content is positive enough, there is something tentative about the novel's exploration of religious territory. It is through action, mood, symbol, and allegory that an awareness of the holy is conveyed, not through direct commentary. The language often shies away from the religious as when Caleb considers what had become of Falkland: "The idea of his misery thrilled through my frame. How weak in comparison of it is the imaginary hell, which the great enemy of mankind is represented as carrying every where about with him!" (p. 284). Indeed, though the biblical analogy is a major structural element in the story, a metaphysical reading of the novel embodies important "irritants", as did the political interpretation. In this story, where man grows up in a happy garden, where he sins out of curiosity, is expelled from happiness and hunted by a jealous Master, God is not great enough. Falkland is an absolute ruler of his domain, but he is also a man of "small stature, with an extreme delicacy of form and appearance" and with a look that testifies to "the unquietness of his mind" (p. 5). As we continue looking at this fascinating landowner, we may discover that his "divine" nature is soluble in the social environment in which we find him. There are historical and social reasons why he may look like God or the Devil to an inexperienced, poor young man. In similar ways, Caleb – transgressor or explorer – can exasperate the critic who finds, or wants to find, a metaphysical novel only. Caleb's curiosity is easily seen as a modern version of the fatal apple, but what Caleb finally looks upon as his worst shortcoming is his use of indirect means to bring Falkland to justice; he should have trusted in face-to-face honesty. This is an idea which belongs to the world of *Political Justice*. Similarly, the old man whom Caleb meets when he is arrested on his way to Ireland reminds us of an angel or a divine father-figure: there is something "extremely venerable and interesting in his appearance", and "his hair . . . was as white as the drifted snow" (p. 246). But as we continue looking at this good old man and the incident in which he appears, he changes; and we are left with a picture of a kind but timid grandfather sadly misled by his unthinking regard for the landed gentry. An extended example is provided by Falkland's agent, Gines. He seems invested with supernatural powers of perseverance in his search for Caleb and becomes an angel of revenge in the story. At the same time it makes sense to see him as a particularly well motivated servant of the cruel and unfair legal system which Godwin attacks in the novel. Many other characters and incidents in *Caleb Williams* embody the same kind of "trigger" effect.

"The private and internal operations of the mind"

The two readings outlined above and the duck-and-rabbit effect which they create seem to me to have a force and a comprehensiveness absent from most other approaches to the novel. Needless to say, the two readings constitute no formula capable of explaining every detail; but when seen together, in their curious reciprocal relationship, they have a special virtue; they can account both for the power and for the incongruity that a reader experiences in *Caleb Williams*. This approach also makes this strange novel less of an oddity than it may seem at first sight. The simultaneous presence of religious and secular explanations of life links the novel in interesting ways with the poetry of the Romantic period.

At this stage a number of critics may raise objections. Surely, in actual fact, whether he knew it himself or not, Godwin wrote a psychological novel, a story in which the study of character becomes the unifying centre. As long ago as 1906 Johannes Meyer suggests that "bei der Ausarbeitung ist dann aber das Nebensächliche zur Hauptsache geworden", and to Dr Meyer the new "Hauptsache" is the psychological content of the novel.[48] Godwin himself can be quoted in support of this argument:

> the thing in which my imagination revelled the most freely, was the analysis of the private and internal operations of the mind, employing my metaphysical dissecting knife in tracing and laying bare the involutions of motive, and recording the gradually accumulating impulses, which led the personages . . . to adopt the particular way of proceeding in which they afterwards embarked. (p. 339)

Meyer's account of the psychology of Caleb and Falkland has been followed by other studies. P. N. Furbank's interesting "Godwin's

Novels" sees the books as "a highly dramatized symbolic picture of Godwin himself in the act of writing *Political Justice*. . . . Caleb Williams is clearly Godwin himself, Falkland the ancien régime, and the opening of the trunk is the writing of *Political Justice*".[49] Furbank's argument implies a kind of flicker (though less radical than the one I have outlined above): the novel is ostensibly an illustration of ideas contained in *Political Justice*, but really, and more interestingly, about the act of writing a dangerous political document.

The novel is not unamenable to a Freudian interpretation. Rudolf Storch argues that Falkland, Tyrrel and Caleb must be seen as aspects of one mind, a neurotic personality which is in fact that of Godwin himself.[50] The divided feelings of Caleb for Falkland and Falkland for Caleb express the ego's split attitudes to the super-ego and the libido. Given Freudian premises, there is no flicker in the novel: on the contrary, there is a natural and logical connection between what the story says about God and guilt on the one hand, and landowners and social repression on the other.[51] Though I find it impossible to share premises which translate the questions the novel asks about ultimate power and ultimate authority into an exclusively psychological language, there can be no doubt that a Freudian approach illuminates with particuar sharpness the terrible and painful stalemate in the second half of the novel.

In any case, *Caleb Williams* is impressive as a psychologically realistic account of two main characters. The novel succeeds because as we read we can be convinced that Caleb is alive and important in the same way as we are (and not only because Caleb is a striking portrait in a piece of literature whose inner relationships we may find instructive and entertaining). Caleb begins his adult life as an inquisitive and profoundly egocentric young man. His egocentricity is revealed in his dealings with Falkland and, indeed, with all other members of the household. As we see his curiosity at work on the history of his master, we realise how ruthless and inconsiderate our young hero is. He is right, too, of course. It *is* a good thing to detect murderers. True, Falkland killed Tyrrel a long time ago, and there is an eloquent plea in the novel for all Eugene Arams (p. 228); but though Godwin suggests that old crimes should be condoned when the criminal has lived a spotless life for years afterwards, there is no defence in the book for lies and subterfuges of the kind that Falkland has been forced to use. Fully and convincingly Godwin bring out both Caleb's mixture of blindness and insight, and the complex moral demands bearing on his activities as a sleuth. Caleb's situation is made the more acute in that he is not completely unimaginative; he can, though only intermittently, imagine what Falkland's life must be like.

In the course of his adventures Caleb learns more about other people both through suffering and during the brief periods in which he can observe goodness in others;[52] and when he meets Mr Collins on the road towards the end of the novel we realise, in a poignant scene, that Caleb is now a wiser man. The basic situation is not unlike Caleb's early pursuit of Falkland's hidden secret. Now, too, Caleb feels the force of the indubitable demands of a general principle of truth and justice. Again, the man confronting him is one whom Caleb can help as a friend or a son. Collins's position is much less desperate than Falkland's, but Caleb's moral eyesight is keener now – he can realise more easily what another human being's difficulties are like. His inner conflict in this interview is made the more intense by the fact that Collins is the only good guide and comforter that Caleb knows of. He even calls the old man, rather melodramatically, his father: "My father! exclaimed I, embracing one of his knees with fervour and delight, I am your son! once your little Caleb, whom you a thousand times loaded with your kindness!" (p.309). When Caleb considers his choice of action in the course of this interview, his strong emotions are supported by his whole history. We follow his train of thoughts with all the excitement that belief in a real human being engenders. Caleb has matured, but exactly how much we do not know. We therefore read the passage as we meet crises in ordinary life: we can form plausible hypotheses about the outcome, but it is not entirely predictable:

What could I say to such a man as this? Amiable, incomparable man! Never was my mind more painfully divided than at that moment. The more he excited my admiration, the more imperiously did my heart command me, whatever were the price it should cost, to extort his friendship. I was persuaded that severe duty required of him, that he should reject all personal considerations, that he should proceed resolutely to the investigation of the truth, and that, if he found the result terminating in my favour, he should resign all his advantages, and, deserted as I was by the world, make a common cause, and endeavour to compensate the general injustice. But was it for me to force this conduct upon him, if, now in his declining years, his own fortitude shrunk from it? Alas, neither he nor I foresaw the dreadful catastrophe that was so closely impending! Otherwise I am well assured, that no tenderness for his remaining tranquillity would have withheld him from a compliance with my wishes! On the other hand, could I pretend to know what evils might result to him from his declaring himself my advocate? Might not his integrity be brow-beaten and defeated as mine had been? Did the imbecility of his grey hairs afford no advantage to my terrible adversary in the contest? Might not Mr Falkland reduce him to a condition as wretched and low as mine? After all, was it not vice in me to desire to involve another man in my sufferings? If I regarded them as intolerable, this was still an additional reason why I should bear them alone.

Influenced by these considerations, I assented to his views. (p. 311)

As Caleb leaves Collins after this meeting, the narrative catches up with the present time in the story; the portrait of Caleb is as complete as it can be before the final great scene in the "Postscript".

There is thus no doubt that *Caleb Williams* has considerable interest as a study in Caleb's psychological and moral development. Moreover, one of the most important reasons why Godwin succeeds as a Jacobin novelist is precisely the fullness and complexity of his portraits of Falkland and Caleb:

Godwin, all too aware of how Holcroft had erred in trying to construct a novel as an argument in *Anna St Ives*, threw all his energy into creating striking characters. . . . His emphasis was on character, but it was not the Theophrastan 'Character' which was used by Bage, Holcroft, and Mrs Inchbald in their Jacobin satires. In an undated MS essay on tragedy and fiction Godwin wrote, "The real essence of every story of human affairs is character. Without this it is all rottenness and dust. It is by character that I understand a story, and come to feel its reality."[53]

Caleb Williams is firmly built on the idea that it is by character that we come to feel the reality of a story. Caleb is only a listener for virtually the whole of the first volume, but perhaps for this very reason his presence is established with great realistic force. We experience how naturally his suspicions grow and in the end become so virulent that they govern him completely. There is great dexterity in the way in which a volume devoted almost entirely to Falkland's history establishes Caleb as a character in whom we believe. Falkland in his turn becomes properly alive when he becomes Caleb's antagonist in the second volume; through Caleb's eyes we see a mysterious landowner, but one who is terribly real to Caleb.

The growth and modulation of powerful passions in Falkland and Caleb give great intensity to the story. Still, it is deceptively easy to overemphasise the interest of the novel as a study of character. It may be salutary to remember that the first volume does not give us a very exciting picture of Falkland. For long stretches his early history is related by Caleb in such a way that we must simply take his word for it; and it is a history which at times consists of rather wooden blocks of information. Later, Falkland is sometimes too mysterious for us to be able to piece together a coherent picture of him. We are, as a matter of fact, left in remarkably great doubt about Falkland's whole attitude to Caleb. This doubt has its obvious virtues in that it adds to the ambiguity of the metaphysical reading; but when the book is considered as a study of character, this doubt becomes an awkward blank spot. Some of the crucial incidents of the story leave us with too many open questions about Falkland's motives. Why, for instance, does he confess the murder to Caleb? He says himself that otherwise he might murder Caleb as well. But Falkland has been willing to "murder" the two Hawkinses, and he all the time stresses his own resourcefulness, which indeed is considerable. Can it be possible that Falkland's cruel words and seemingly cruel intention are balanced, even at this stage, by a wish to keep Caleb as a friend, the only confidential friend he could have? The idea is hinted at, but it remains sadly undeveloped. Similarly, why does Falkland allow Caleb to wander throughout Great Britain while he keeps an eye on him and deprives him of social acceptance and a safe income wherever he goes? Since Falkland's prime concern is with his own reputation, we would have expected him either to get rid of Caleb by engineering his death or deportation, or to let him leave as a free man in the hope, which would be realistic enough, that Caleb would keep his mouth shut. Absurdly, Falkland pursues the one course of action most likely to goad Caleb to the very revelation that Falkland fears. We can, of course, ask whether this is a sign that Falkland's deepest self really wants to be caught, but this is to indulge in guesswork that takes us outside what the story says. *Caleb Williams* does not give us sufficient information to consider this particular kind of psychological ambivalence in Falkland in anything but the baldest outlines. Neither Caleb nor the reader does, as a matter of fact, know much about Falkland's mind.

The portrait of Caleb is much fuller and finer, but sometimes, and notably in the first chapters of the third volume, his development depends rather mechanically on external factors.[54] His reactions are plausible, but do not really add much to our understanding of his inner life. And since Caleb exists only in relation to Falkland, the sketchiness and the uncertain strokes in the portrait of his master leave the reader in a position in which it becomes impossible to evaluate important aspects of Caleb's character with any great precision. This is also the point where Godwin's uncertain ear for dialogue becomes most embarrassing. Conversations in *Caleb Williams* tend to have a tense excitement about them, but they are often too melodramatic or bookish or theoretical to serve the purpose of psychological description. Godwin does not attempt finely tempered dialogues like those of Jane Austen or George Eliot. Judged against the loving psychological detail in which memorable scenes in *Mansfield Park* or *Middlemarch* are painted, *Caleb Williams* must appear crude and melodramatic.

However, it would be absurd to judge Godwin's novels against this kind of model only. A reading of *Caleb Williams* invites us to consider a different set of questions about the characters. Both Caleb and Falkland are frequently described in a psychological shorthand which turns our thoughts to their function in patterns suggested by the story as a whole rather than to fine shades in their inner lives. Godwin's extensive use of parallels and contrasts in the portrait-gallery, carefully analysed by Rothstein,[55] does not depend on the characters being fully drawn as do the corresponding patterns in George Eliot. By analogy, Gines, Brightwel, Collins, and Raymond – none of them fully developed characters – can illuminate Caleb's situation; and in the same way Forester, Tyrrel and Raymond teach the reader a number of important things about Falkland. This approach to *Caleb Williams* has the great and obvious advantage that it does not presuppose an unbroken psychological verisimilitude in all the characters, and it helps us to see how Godwin can give us an exciting picture of Caleb's moral development in spite of the sketchiness in his portrayal of individual figures. The various parallels and analogies between the characters reach a powerful and natural climax in the final version of the ending when Caleb finds that he and Falkland have in effect changed roles: Caleb has now, out of an exaggerated and mistaken idea of personal honour, destroyed his old master, whereas Falkland now realises, in word and deed, the truth that concern for others and simple honesty are greater and better values than personal reputation.

This latter reading is not at odds with the "flicker" I have described earlier. A novel that works by analogy and parallels of this kind must base its meaning quite definitely not on the story alone but also on some outside system of ideas. Fielding openly tells us in the preface to *Joseph Andrews* that the morality of the story consists in its being an illustration of something outside the book – the well-known and only too well-beloved vice of Affectation. *Caleb Williams* does not only work by Fielding's methods; but in so far as it does, it turns the reader's thoughts to the question of what system of values is being illustrated.

Caleb Williams thrives as a novel when it is seen in the context of the war of ideas and beliefs in the 1780s and 90s; and the price one has to pay for reading it as a self-contained account of Caleb's psychological and moral development is considerable. If, for instance, what the novel says about political power in the 1790s is regarded as background only, a fine urgency gets lost: *Caleb Williams* was thought of by Godwin and his early readers as a dangerous book, much more explosive than a story whose main point was the development of an ethical awareness in an individual. The anonymous reviewer in *The British Critic* put it this way: "When a work is so directly pointed at every band which connects society, and at every principle which renders it amiable, its very merits become noxious as they tend to cause its being known in a wider circle."[56]

The rabbit and the duck – and the 1790s

Gestalt psychologists who have studied perception remind us that one of the basic ways in which we organise our sense impressions is by a figure-ground contrast. From the myriad of impressions on the retina we tend to single out something as a "figure" and the surroundings are experienced as receding and making up a background. It is possible to make simple drawings such as the vase-and-two-faces, in which the figure-ground relationship is unstable. That the "seeing" of a literary work may imply a similar relationship between figure and ground is neatly illustrated by the German critic referred to earlier: Johannes Meyer argues that what for Godwin was a background feature, "das Nebensächliche", became "Hauptsache". Meyer thus suggests that it is natural to read *Caleb Williams* as a work in which there is a figure and a ground, and that, in the course of the writing, Godwin changed ground to figure and figure to ground.[57]

My earlier discussion highlights some of the reasons why such changes can occur quite frequently in the course of one's reading of *Caleb Williams*; but it is not reasonable to assume that all readers see the book in this way with equal facility; and a number of readers would probably find it easy to resist switches from one "picture" to the other. Critical analyses illustrate the variety of responses prompted by the novel; and another analogy from the psychology of perception suggests one of the more straightforward reasons for this variety. Different kinds of tests show that our expectations, our "mental set", will necessarily influence our perception. If you flash nonsense words briefly on a screen telling some observers that they see names of animals whereas other observers are told that the words have been taken from some other area of life, say travel, those who have been instructed to expect names of animals actually find such names in the nonsense words, which by the other group are constructed as names of hotels, cars and ships. This simple experiment pinpoints what common sense and awareness of literary history suggest, too: we tend to see what our training has conditioned us to expect.

In the particular context of this study I have tried to show that a greater awareness of the literary models that interested Godwin makes us see more clearly that there may be a basic instability in Godwin's novel.[58] But isn't it, might it be argued, a gross exaggeration to talk of two different pictures? Surely, a squire can be a symbol of God and a servant can represent mankind in such a way that what we see in the novel is not so much an alternation between two different pictures as *one* painting so shaded that it becomes capable of somewhat different interpretations. It would be an empty quarrel about words to pursue to the bitter end an argument whether *Caleb Williams* must be looked upon as one or two pictures. The illustrations from psychology textbooks treat a perceptual situation which is simpler and more clear-cut than a reader's response to a 300 page long story. Still, these illustrations may serve to impress upon us the fact that a resort to an easy formula in which landowner and God merge can provide no valid account of the particular jolts which the novel gives its readers. The better attempts (see above) to read the book as Caleb's psychological history and to find cement for the whole book in this development make valuable points; but when an attempt is made to make the development of Caleb the *only* main concern of the novel *Caleb Williams* seems to me to become a sadly amputated book. For Caleb develops – morally and otherwise – in a world about the nature of which we remain radically uncertain.

This uncertainty informs the style of the novel. A critic[59] has chosen the description of Tyrrel in Volume I, Chapter 3, as an example of Godwin's clumsiness: to bring out the bodily strength of Falkland's antagonist, Godwin compares him to three different strong men of antiquity – Hercules, Antaeus and Milo, "whose prowess consisted in felling an ox with his fist, and devouring him at a meal" (p. 17). Indeed, one of these is enough; taken together, the three confuse the picture of this boorish landowner: he is strikingly unlike the heroic Hercules in most respects; and how seriously are we meant to take the reference to Antaeus, son of the earth, and in Christian interpretations of the myth, a son of the Devil? But Godwin's case is worse than this. In this passage Tyrrel is presented in what is a virtual plethora of allusions. His first name is Barnabas, "which is, being interpreted, The son of consolation" (Acts 4:36), or, in another rendering of the Greek of which Godwin was certainly aware, "the son of exhortation". His family name reminds us of Sir James Tyrrell, murderer of princes in the Tower of London.[60] He is even more firmly related to English history when he is called a typical English squire (p. 16). Finally, and abruptly, he is described in terms of natural life: he has "the fangs" of a "wild beast" (p.19). A sardonic smile enlivens two of these references. This "son of exhortation" has had a nitwit of a mother absolutely incapable of giving him an education; and the nasty Tyrrel, named after a murderer, is summed up as the "true model of the English squire" (p. 16). But altogether the passage seems sadly overloaded with allusions that point in too many different directions.

It seems overloaded. But what we witness in a passage like this is not simply a deplorable inability to write neat, clear English. These many references illustrate a consistent search in *Caleb Williams* for a frame of reference inside which Caleb can express his strange story. Therefore we find a great many passages in which allusions may seem to spread in all directions; and, since Caleb never solves these problems, we must not expect him to achieve a more homogeneous and straightforward style towards the end of the story. This description of Falkland is taken from the last pages of the novel:

> What – dark, mysterious, unfeeling, unrelenting tyrant! – is it come to this? – When Nero and Caligula swayed the Roman sceptre, it was a fearful thing to offend these bloody rulers. The empire had already spread itself from climate to climate, and from sea to sea. If their unhappy victim fled to the rising of the sun, where the luminary of day seems to us first to ascend from the waves of the ocean, the power of the tyrant was still behind him. If he withdrew to the west, to Hesperian darkness, and the shores of barbarian Thule, still he was not safe from his gore-drenched foe. – Falkland! art thou the offspring in whom the lineaments of those tyrants are faithfully preserved? Was the world with all its climates made in vain for thy helpless, unoffending victim? (p. 314)

On the one hand, this passage is built on references to political history (there may even be a submerged allusion to Montesquieu's theories about the political importance of climates here); on the other, it draws strength from the language of the Old Testament. Here, as elsewhere, Caleb becomes aware of the extent to which his language is biblical and recoils: the sun only "seems" to arise from the sea. But he is never able to remain quietly in a style which reflects only the world of *Political Justice*.

Largely, of course, the stylistic ideal behind Caleb's narrative is the one suggested by Locke's empiricism. By the time Godwin was writing *Political Justice* he used Locke with certain reservations,[61] but Godwin is always quite insistent that it is only by observing the external world that the basis of true knowledge can be laid. In "Of the Mechanism of the Human Mind" Godwin dismisses Hartley's theory of vibrations as unnecessary, but otherwise this chapter of *Political Justice* rests firmly on Locke's *Essay* and the first part of Hartley's *Observations*. In Godwin's case this philosophy encourages one particular approach to narrative: the best style is one which patiently and factually describes observations in such a way that the reader's mind can be filled with ideas that in the course of the reading merge into more complex clusters of thoughts, what Hartley called "complex ideas".

Sterne might have served Godwin as a warning that a novelist cannot use Locke's theory of the mind in any simple way. *Tristram Shandy* highlights the curious ways in which the mind is filled to overflowing with ideas and the curious plight of the novelist who tries to describe the minds of human beings. In Sterne the organising faculty of the mind – and of the novelist – is shown as incapable of keeping pace with the ideas which the brain amasses at such tremendous speed. We shall never know all the opinions of Tristram Shandy (there is not time enough), nor see all those that we are acquainted with in any tidy pattern (we have glimpses of too many). As a philosopher Godwin does not share Sterne's sly pessimism. He optimistically believes that, placed where he can observe life at close quarters, man is able to combine his sense-impressions in such ways that he can form well-balanced and correct conclusions about life.

As a novelist Godwin is in two minds about the road to knowledge. Caleb tells his story *à la* Locke. He presents himself as a *tabula rasa* which is filled in the course of the story. His mind is furnished in the manner outlined in *Political Justice*: "The actions and dispositions of mankind are the offspring of circumstances and events, and not of any original determination that they bring into the world" (vol.i, p. 26). Moreover, in this optimistic version of Locke man's memory will enable him to survey the sum total of his experiences so that he is no longer at the mercy of each individual impulse received from his surroundings: "the great stream of our voluntary actions essentially depends, not upon the direct and immediate impulses of sense, but upon the decisions of the understanding" (p. 26). Unfortunately, this understanding, "the opinion of men", is, "for the most part, under the absolute control of political institution" (p. 26); but this does not undermine the Lockean basis of this kind of understanding. Caleb faithfully tries to tell his story in such a way that the individual bits of evidence on which he bases his conclusions are evident. But he, too, has to face Tristram's difficulties. A life story contains such an immense mass of individual impressions that the biographer cannot simply give us these cumulatively; he must resort to symbols, analogies, allusions to make his story reasonably short and orderly. And this, as we have seen, is where Caleb is made to waver, and where radically different ways of understanding life emerge.

There are even moments in the novel when Caleb seems to leave a style based on empiricism completely behind. When he is in great pain, he accounts for his misery by reference to another kind of insight. In the texture of *Caleb Williams* this is signalled by a special style marked by short sentences, apostrophes, questions, and repetitions of easily recognisable syntactic structures. We find examples of this style in the first paragraph of the novel, in the last pages of Volume III, Chapter XV, and in the Postscript, in other words in the parts of the book in which Caleb gives the reader the last and final impression of his story. Caleb says that these passages are written in a "solemn" mood (p. 316). The opening of Chapter XV explains the reason for this solemnity; Caleb feels that he exists in a world of prophecy: "It is as I foreboded. The presage with which I was visited was prophetic" (p. 312). It is possible to dismiss this as nonsense on Caleb's part; he is half-mad, and at this stage his "insight" must be taken with more than one pinch of salt. But such an attempt at dismissal does not really iron out the discrepancies. Caleb's feeling of doom is described with considerable force, and its crucial place in the narrative gives it great authority. The very last page modifies, as we might expect, the impression of fate as all-powerful. Here Falkland's (and Caleb's) misery is said to be the result also of historical forces, "the poison of chivalry" (p. 326). Thus, the "flicker" which we can find in incidents and characters is kept up in the style to the very end.

The importance which is here assigned to the duck-and-rabbit effect may seem to indicate that *Caleb Williams* is a very special rarity. In a way it is. Though a great many novels create responses that hover between the political and the metaphysical, few offer the kind of radical shifts which we find in *Caleb Williams*. Perhaps there is reason to be grateful that most other novels which deal in profound ambiguity do so in less radical ways. For the ambiguity of the duck-and-rabbit picture is only possible because of the drawing's sketchiness, and the related effect in Godwin's novel is possible only because of a corresponding sketchiness in his portrayal of character. If he had attempted a more finely shaded account of a more restricted set of relationships between man and his surroundings, he would probably have found that this necessitated more gradual changes from one view of the world to another. But *Caleb Williams* must not be thought of as that absurd or impossible phenomenon –

a novel which exists only in relation to itself and not in a kind of dialogue with the literature of its age. The novel is Godwin's attempt to deal with problems which, in different ways, occupied Wordsworth, Coleridge and others in the 1790s.

The closest parallel to *Caleb Williams* is found in another novel of this period. In *The Monk*, written in 1794 and published two years later, M. G. Lewis presents the miraculous in different lights from chapter to chapter. The first page tells us that "in a city where superstition reigns with such despotic sway as in Madrid, to seek for true devotion would be a fruitless attempt".[62] The novel then proceeds to show us, through the eyes of a man of the world, the entertaining variety of motives which are at work when people crowd into a church to listen to a celebrated preacher. The novel begins with a distrust of the supernatural so definite that it smacks of atheism; but Lewis later introduces a ghost into the action, allows a figure we must understand to be the Wandering Jew to help the hero, and finally gives us the privilege of witnessing the Devil himself give the villain his due. Moreover, one of the main characters, Mathilda, is poised dangerously between two roles: we are not quite certain whether she begins as a smart young woman with a great appetite for that handsome young man, the Abbot Ambrosio, or whether she is all the time an evil spirit, commanded by the Devil to lure Ambrosio to destruction.

The Monk is no imitation of *Caleb Williams*. Lewis did not care for the social and political problems which Godwin could never forget; and beside the sustained intensity of *Caleb Williams* Lewis's novel seems, what in fact it was, a hastily written book by a nineteen-year old. However, *The Monk* is no trivial work. Lewis shows considerable psychological shrewdness, and he has the courage to do what Mrs Radcliffe fights shy of: he relates his feeling that life is terrible (the standard starting-point for the better kind of Gothic fiction) to a discussion of divinity. This discussion does not bring out a consistent ambiguity like that of *Caleb Williams*; but there are suggestions of a similar "flicker" when, in the early parts of the novel, we are not quite sure whether the metaphysical is real or not. Later, when Lewis does suggest that we are visited by supernatural powers, these visitations are presented as overwhelmingly destructive.[63] In the case of both novelists, the narrative acquires a speed and a direction not clearly foreseen. Godwin wrote a tale which is much more than an illustration of political wrongs; Lewis begins by ridiculing superstition only to find that the supernatural forces itself into his story.

As we shall see in the next chapter, Godwin found himself in trouble when he used the Gothic novel, with all its paraphernalia, as a model for *St Leon*. Still, Godwin and Lewis share what one might call a Gothic sensibility. In the novels of each, the sense of terrible evil is no passing thrill as in *The Mysteries of Udolpho*, where in the end everything is idyllic. The lonely, dark dilapidated castle represents no intermediate stage in the development of Godwin's protagonists – it is a fitting symbol of the very flavour of life as presented in *Caleb Williams*, *St Leon* and *Mandeville*.

It is in the context of this central image that we must consider what is perhaps the most surprising feature in *Caleb Williams*, the fact that this story about an active young man is not organised round the who-is-going-to-marry-whom theme. For Richardson, Smollett, Mackenzie, Holcroft and Bage this was staple fare. They were all happy to have the two-fold benefit that this theme provides: there is an interesting element of suspense in it; and both story and moral commentary reach a natural conclusion when people get married or suffer defeat in the marrying game. Godwin had used this framework for earlier stories. The most obvious reason why it is absent from this novel is found in *Political Justice*, in the first edition of which the domestic virtues were given short shrift. Godwin may have felt that because of important principles in his moral philosophy he had to restrain whatever inclinations he might have had to focus on the sweet flutters of love. An unsympathetic critic might add another explanation: Godwin needed no restraint – a man who could write as he did about Archbishop Fénelon and his mother must have been thoroughly unemotional anyway.[64] The argument I have put forward in this chapter suggests another answer. Godwin *was* emotionally involved in what he was writing, indeed so involved in a feeling that the world is awful that he had little emotional energy left in *Caleb Williams* to describe at length other and sweeter climates of the mind. When, for some weeks, Caleb can think of marriage, we read about his hope with a sinking feeling that it will be crushed, which it is. The absence from most of the novel of the marriage theme is a sign of Godwin's honesty as a novelist. The energy of the main characters is expended in desperate struggles in a world the nature of which is sadly uncertain: baffled and thwarted, they can have no appetite for an activity as hopeful as wooing.[65]

Marriage is the most public of private events; and the absence – or near-absence – of the theme in *Caleb Williams* and in some of Godwin's contemporaries is partly due to the high winds in the political climate of the nineties. No calm havens in which domestic bliss could thrive were in sight for radicals caught up in a whirlwind of hope and despair. A dramatic illustration is found in Wordsworth's relationship to Annette Vallon; a more suggestive analogy to Godwin's novel is found in Coleridge's "Christabel" in which the heroine is caught in a situation as destructive as that of Caleb. She has "her own betrothéd knight" (line 23), and her mother

> did say
> That she should hear the castle-bell
> Strike twelve upon my wedding-day.
> (ll. 199–201)

But when the castle bell has struck twelve Christabel finds herself embraced by a lamia. Coleridge may originally have intended the poem to proceed to illustrate the hopeful theme with which he concludes Part I:[66]

> But this she knows, in joy and woes,
> That saints will aid if men will call:
> For the blue sky bends over all!
> (ll. 329–31)

The sky, however, is not blue in "Christabel", it is covered by "the thin gray cloud" (line 16); and the innocent Christabel is overpowered by Geraldine's spell and by her father's new coldness to her to such an extent that *she* begins to hiss and looks at her father with snake-like eyes.

There may be a direct influence in "Christabel" from Godwin's story about a young boy who begins life believing that reason and justice make up a blue sky over us all, who is confronted with unexpected evil but still thinks that he can "dally with wrong that does no harm" (line 668), and who finally sees himself as having exchanged roles with his enemy and as completely destroyed. But the question of indebtedness is less important than the actual analogy. Both writers embed in their stories a sense of evil which is less easily mastered by systems of thought or belief than they had thought; both give highly ambiguous portraits of father-figures; and

"Christabel" and *Caleb Williams*, as well as *The Rime of the Ancient Mariner*, confront the reader with the same problem of interpretation: are we being told what are essentially Christian legends, or are these stories more easily and naturally interpreted in a language which comes from non-metaphysical philosophy?[67] It is not surprising to hear that Godwin and Coleridge got on well together in the late nineties, and that one of the things they discussed was the existence of God.[68] Nor should we wonder that both writers came to a point in the composition when it seemed impossible to proceed. Like other radical, sensitive intellectuals in the nineties, they found themselves in a war of ideas where the fronts were changing in confusing ways. This situation did not make the writing of poetry impossible – a great many of Wordsworth's and Coleridge's best poems can be read as responses to challenging changes in the intellectual climate. But this flux did not provide any firm basis for long narratives. Typically, both Wordsworth and Coleridge failed to complete projected long poems in the nineties; and Godwin nearly discontinued his writing of *Caleb Williams*: "When I had proceeded as far as the early pages of my third volume, I found myself completely at a stand. I rested on my arms from the 2nd January, 1794, to the 1st April following, without getting forward in the smallest degree" (p. 341). Godwin's stock of incidents was not running out; he had already made up his mind that the third volume was to be a story of pursuit. What made him pause must have been the feeling – perhaps vague and largely unconscious – that his story was becoming overwhelmingly complex. It had ceased to be a simple account of how a landowner perverted by high notions of honour pursued an innocent servant.

The similarities between Wordsworth's poems and Godwin's fiction are less striking, but a poem like "Tintern Abbey" gains in interest when it is seen not only as a poem about the psychological development of the poet, but as an account of what might be called an epistemological watershed. Everything in the poem can be explained by reference to Locke and Hartley; indeed, "Tintern Abbey" is a very neat illustration of Propositions 1–14 in the *Observations on Man*.[69] However, the cup made up by Hartley's laws runs over when the poet, overwhelmed, feels,

A presence that disturbs me with the joy
Of elevated thoughts; a sense sublime

Of something far more deeply interfused,
Whose dwelling is the light of setting suns,
And the round ocean and the living air,
And the blue sky, and in the mind of man:
A motion and a spirit that impels
All thinking things, all objects of all thought,
And rolls through all things.

(ll. 94–102)

This experience "disturbs" the poet because he is, in a sense, getting more than he had bargained for. He is experiencing what, in the language of the Intimations Ode, he called "the visionary gleam".

Primarily, however, Wordsworth responded to Godwin's philosophy and not, as did Coleridge who knew Godwin better, to the fascinating human being who hides behind the rather impersonal voice of *Political Justice*. *The Borderers* examines some of Godwin's philosophical ideas; and some of the poems in the *Lyrical Ballads* engage in a dialogue with *Political Justice*. "The Last of the Flock" attacks Godwin's view of property; and in a number of ballads Wordsworth insists that emotions, and in particular the domestic feelings which Godwin had given short shrift in the first edition of his treatise, are important and valuable. But "Simon Lee", though it can be read as extolling gratitude in a pointed exchange with *Political Justice*, at the same time reveals the way in which social circumstances, in this case changes in the ownership of land, reduce an honest man like Simon to poverty. Both to Godwin and Wordsworth it is a sad thought that Simon should have to exercise his gratitude in this particular situation. In "The Female Vagrant" the description of how the power of property and Whitehall politics destroy human happiness looks as if it comes straight from certain chapters in *Political Justice*. But in all these poems it is Godwin the philosopher who is glimpsed, not the novelist. In fact, though Godwin and Wordsworth faced some of the same problems in their imaginative writing, their tales belong to different worlds. Wordsworth could see life as leading "from joy to joy"; in Godwin's novels man never lives in a world where "all which we behold/Is full of blessings".

Clashes between literary traditions must be only too obvious in *Caleb Williams*: nearly all criticism printed in the last thirty years makes them a starting-point, a puzzle, which the critic sees it as his task to solve. In the preceding argument I have tried not to solve the puzzle. Unresolved, the clashes between traditions and beliefs seem to me to be the novel's ultimate source of strength. It is their existence which makes the book such an intriguing account of the mental climate of the 1790s. To describe this novel I have used words which may seem to imply both high praise and radical condemnation – honesty, courage, intensity, uncertainty, vacillation. No contradiction is intended. The uncertainty in Godwin's grasp of life makes for imaginative honesty in this novel. Disparate elements in what is a complex and bewildering experience of life are not silently dropped by the wayside to permit the author to come up with something tidy and whole. Nor are the two or three main attempts at an explanantion of life balanced in any orderly fashion. Life is baffling in *Caleb Williams*, and a main virtue of the novel lies in the fact that Godwin tells us a story which gives imaginative life and intensity to this bafflement and its premises.

In the literature of the 1790s *Caleb Williams* acquires its special profile by the fact that Godwin completed a tale whose themes became so involved and threatened to become so contradictory that nobody would have been surprised had the story been left unfinished. But the novel also points forward, both in its social criticism and in its ambiguities. *Hard Times* resembles it inasmuch as Dickens not only attacks representatives of the rich, but presents Bounderby and Gradgrind as formed by, and expressing, a philosophy which is a danger to man and society. It is a far cry from Burke's and Falkland's theories about chivalry to Gradgrind's utilitarianism, but the strategy of the two novelists is the same.

Walter Allen stressed the way in which *Caleb Williams* points towards certain kinds of twentieth-century religious novel. In one of its aspects it does; but in its ambiguity and in its corresponding search for a language in which to tell its tale it provides a more powerful commentary on later novels of another kind. When, for instance, Hardy's *Tess of the d'Urbervilles* invokes both the historical necessity which sends the *nouveau riche* from the North marauding into Wessex and the unfathomable mysteries of Stonehenge, we are in a fictional world that Godwin might have recognised. Hardy's language reaches out in different directions, as did Godwin's in the last pages of *Caleb Williams*, when Tess is caught towards the end:

The eastward pillars and their architraves stood up blackly

against the light, and the great flame-shaped Sun-stone behind them; and the Stone of Sacrifice midway. Presently the night wind died out, and the quivering little pools in the cup-like hollows of the stones lay still. At the same time something seemed to move on the verge of the dip eastward – a mere dot. It was the head of a man approaching them from the hollow beyond the Sun-stone. . . . The dawn shone full on the front of the man westward, and Clare could discern from this that he was tall, and walked as if trained.

The mere dots turning out to be policemen who walk "as if trained" represent the Wessex of social fact and matter-of-fact concreteness, while the language of the preceding sentences has taken us into another world. Hardy is more poetic and elastic than Godwin, whose search for styles can seem helpless at times. But in this context the helplessness is a virtue in disguise; a supple, fluent, sophisticated language would not have served Godwin at all well. It is interesting that another nineteenth-century novel which offers close resemblances to *Caleb Williams* is *Moby Dick*. Melville's story is quite different in setting and range; but there are similarities in story and characters, and in particular in the fact that Ishmael desperately casts about for a language, a set of analogies that can make sense of his existence. In both Godwin and Melville a certain uncouthness of style is appropriate. They cannot use a literary heritage which imposes traditional order and neatness on its stories.

IV

St Leon:
Recalcitrant Gothicism

Caleb Williams is a kind of literary curiosity – a monstrous hybrid between different species – which gains its interests by a fortunate confusion. But if any one should be prompted to push his study into other works, I fear that he is destined to disappointment.

Leslie Stephen, "William Godwin's Novels"

Godwin's life was intense in the first half of the 1790s. His work on *Political Justice* and *Caleb Williams* filled the years from 1791 to 1794: the writing of the philosophical treatise "exalted my spirits", said Godwin; and he hoped that the novel would afford "no inadequate image of the fervour of my spirit".[1] In May 1794, the month in which the latter was published, Godwin's acquaintance Horne Tooke was imprisoned. Other arrests followed; and in October twelve English radicals, among whom was Godwin's very good friend Holcroft, were facing charges of high treason. Godwin returned from the country where he had been peacefully discussing the principles of political justice with Dr Parr, attended the trial and wrote his *Cursory Strictures* in defence of his friends. Horne Tooke later said that Godwin's plea had saved his life.[2]

After these years of extraordinary political excitement and of very hard creative work, Godwin lowered the pace. He spent the next two years revising *Political Justice* and writing occasional essays. It was not an easy time for a writer with a radical reputation. Though the October 1794 trials ended with acquittals, Godwin's friend Joseph Gerrald, who had been found guilty of sedition, was transported to Australia where he died in 1795.[3] Whig Members of Parliament retreated to their country homes, and Tory attitudes to Jacobins were becoming more and more aggressive. The later stages of the

French Revolution provided them with powerful ammunition, as did the war with France. Godwin kept a relatively low profile for another reason, too. Tory attacks and personal danger apart, he realised himself that the French Revolution had gone wrong. The reorientation he needed was emotional; the ideal of change outlined in *Political Justice* was not at all invalidated by the Terror. But for all his consistent philosophical insistence on a peaceful, non-violent exchange of ideas as the only road to a better world, he had been enthusiastic about the early stages of the Revolution, and had entertained high hopes for Europe. As a novelist he now had to find his bearings in a new Europe in which a revolution had failed. It is tempting to think of a new role as lying very near at hand: he could present himself in fiction as the calm philosopher *au-dessus de la mêlée*, as the kind of writer he had tried to be in *Political Justice*. That Godwin considered writing a biography of Bolingbroke, who assumed such a role after his return from France, is a sign that he found this attitude attractive.[4] But such serenity did not really present any solution to his problems as a novelist; for Godwin's fiction is successful only when the reader finds himself immersed in struggle, faction, defeat, in the smoke and din of confused battles. Godwin was wise enough not to attempt to write fiction over which the calm light of disinterested philosophy shines.

Nor, for all his determination not to be engulfed by domesticity, did Godwin's relationship with Mary Wollstonecraft provide him with more immediate energy for writing. Instead, it gave him a happy year. On Mary's death in September 1797 the forty-year old philosopher had to rearrange his life in such a way that he could both write and be a father to Fanny and Mary. The two claims were not easily reconciled. In 1799 Coleridge was sadly impressed by a dinner with Godwin: little David Hartley can be "somewhat too rough & noisy", but "the cadaverous Silence of Godwin's Children is to me quite catacomb-ish: & thinking of Mary Wolstencroft I was oppressed by it the day Davy & I dined there".[5]

The main literary outcome of the first two years following *Caleb Williams* is found in *The Enquirer*, a collection of essays on "Education, Manners and Literature". Most of these essays read like footnotes to *Political Justice* – generally humane and sensible, but insignificant and superficial compared with the earlier treatise. There is a long essay on style which, to the disappointment of readers interested in Godwin's own language, is only a facile defence of late eighteenth-century English. But Godwin's mind had not lain completely fallow. An interesting essay "Of Beggars" points forward to his attacks on Malthus, and an examination "Of Personal Reputation" discusses a theme that had been central in *Caleb Williams* and that was to be reconsidered in *St Leon*.

Then, in early 1798, Godwin wrote one of his best books – the impressive *Memoirs of the Author of A Vindication of the Rights of Woman*. Mary Wollstonecraft's life is told briefly, and in an episodic manner which eminently suits Godwin's purpose: "Every benefactor of mankind is more or less influenced by a liberal passion for fame; and survivors only pay a debt due to these benefactors, when they assert and establish on their part, the honour they loved."[6] Later biographers of Mary Wollstonecraft have presented their readers with pictures of this outstanding woman which are quite different from Godwin's; but the *Memoirs* survives, easily, because of the openness of Godwin's design. He presents his approach as one of affection *and* honesty, and he is aware throughout that this union is not always easily established. The most remarkable section of the book deals with Mary's affair with Gilbert Imlay. If Godwin felt jealous, he leans over backwards not to show it. Mary is described as exquisitely happy when she is in love with Imlay:

> Her sorrows, the depression of her spirits, were forgotten, and she assumed all the simplicity and the vivacity of a youthful mind. . . . She was playful, full of confidence, kindness and sympathy. Her eyes assumed new lustre, and her cheeks new colour and smoothness. Her voice became cheerful; her temper overflowing with universal kindness; and that smile of bewitching tenderness from day to day illuminated her countenance, which all who knew her will so well recollect, and which won, both heart and soul, the affection of almost every one that beheld it. (pp. 112–13)

It is, of course, possible for readers to respond with different degrees of approbation or enthusiasm to this passage. A disciple of Godwin would find in it an admirable instance of that justice which is not limited by personal consideration. Early reviewers tended to find the account of his wife's affair tasteless;[7] twentieth-century readers may speculate on the psychological undercurrents in Godwin's mind that enabled him to luxuriate in the idea of his wife being so happy with another man. More significant in the context of this study is the fact that the situation points towards Godwin's fiction. In the *Memoirs* he casts himself in the role of the little man whose spouse has been "shared" with others. In the novels Godwin's "heroes" are never strong and brilliantly successful in love; for all their pride, they are failures, always haunted by images of their own littleness. It is not fortuitous that the *Memoirs* remind us of Joyce's *Exiles* in which Richard, motivated by a curious mixture of wishes, virtually arranges for his wife to go to bed with a friend of the family. Both Joyce and Godwin are interested in characters whose aggressiveness – sexual or otherwise – is mixed with an awareness of their weakness or insignificance. But Godwin needed time to consider thoroughly some of the more startling repercussions of such insights into marital attitudes. St Leon is a traditional lover, and the account of his marriage is conventional. It was only when Godwin had recovered from the loss of Mary Wollstonecraft and had himself experienced another kind of marriage that he could return to some of the problems that he touched in the writing of his first wife's biography. *Fleetwood* (1805) is a study in a husband's strange mixture of insecurity and agression.

It can come as no surprise to a reader of the biography of Mary that Godwin would be toying with the idea of writing novels at this time. But that he should be thinking of fiction is not as natural as it may seem in retrospect. *Caleb Williams* was written as a companion piece to a philosophical work; Godwin looked upon himself more as a political thinker than as a writer of tales; and in the lists of projects which he made in 1796 and 1798 the first titles are philosophical or historical works. In both lists there is a book "on the Reasons and Tendency of Religions Opinion", in which he hoped to "demonstrate the absurdity and impossibility of every system of Theism that has ever been proposed".[8] This dissertation was never written. Godwin's lukewarm conversion to theism, brought about by Coleridge in 1800,[9] probably prevented it. But the partisan interest in atheism in the late nineties should be noted – it is reflected, in quite a surprising way, in *St Leon*. In 1798 Godwin also wanted to write a treatise on the "First Principles of Morals" because he now thought that the power of feelings had been underrated in *Political Justice* and because he had realised that the domestic affections need not at all be the enemy of the public good. It is easy to understand why this dissertation was postponed: Godwin had incorporated his new views in the third edition of *Political Justice*;[10] and he could give imaginative life to them in *St Leon*, which abounds in praise of family love, and in *Fleetwood*, which is throughout a study in sentiment. Three "tales" are mentioned in the 1796 list of projects: The Coward, The Lover, and The Adept.[11] The lover became *Fleetwood*; the coward and the adept combined to make up important themes in *St Leon*.

Godwin's Gothic problem

Godwin read widely, as usual, in the years between *Caleb Williams* and *St Leon*. Gary Kelly sums up the reading recorded in the diaries: "The novels of Richardson, Prévost, Smollett, Fielding and Goldsmith gradually gave way to those of Mary Robinson, Mary Hays, Mary Wollstonecraft, Rousseau, and Goethe, as well as lesser works in the Gothic vein."[12] What is new is thus a more pronounced interest in the Gothic, in novels of sentiment, and – what was only to be expected – in the fiction written by Mary Wollstonecraft and her circle. It was the Gothic that Godwin chose as the mould for his new tale. He had approached this genre in *Caleb Williams*, which explores a question underlying much Gothic fiction: in a world which terrifies us, what is the nature of the terrible? But the use of standard Gothic paraphernalia in *Caleb Williams* is insignificant; the ostensible concern in this work is with political problems which no other Gothic writer would dream of treating in his or her novels. *St. Leon. A Tale of the Sixteenth Century* (1799)[13] is Gothic in a more obvious sense. The setting is historical (the sixteenth century was quite as popular as the Middle Ages with Gothic novelists) and Continental; and the story hinges on supernatural incidents. One reason for Godwin's choice is not far to seek. In the five years that had passed since his previous novel, Ann Radcliffe's name had become famous with the publication of *The Mysteries of Udolpho* in 1794 and *The Italian* three years later; and "Monk" Lewis had earned both fame and notoriety by *The Monk*, which appeared first in 1796 and then in three more editions in the course of two years.[14] Necessity had sharpened Godwin's eye for the financial successes of his contemporaries. He had tried his hand at a pastoral romance in the eighties, and he was later to imitate the Waverley novels in *Mandeville* and *Cloudesley*. *St Leon* is his deliberate attempt to win a prize in the Gothic race which promised such substantial rewards.[15]

Godwin did not openly hail Walpole, Radcliffe and Lewis as his sources of inspiration; but his "Preface" is meant to leave prospective readers in no doubt as to the kind of book they may now acquire. The story is based on a mysterious old tale, *Hermippus Redivivus*, "said to be written by the late Dr John Campbel", which features an enigmatic stranger in Venice, who, we must infer, possesses the *elixir vitae*. Godwin feels that this kind of story needs an apology:

> The hearts and the curiosity of readers have been assailed in so many ways, that we, writers who bring up the rear of our illustrious predecessors, must be contented to arrive at novelty in whatever mode we are able. The foundation of the following tale is such as, it is not to be supposed, ever existed. But, if I have mixed human feelings and passions with incredible situations, and thus rendered them impressive and interesting, I shall entertain some hope to be pardoned the boldness and irregularity of my design. (p.ix)

There *is* a certain amount of novelty in *St Leon*, but Godwin is misleading when he suggests that the plan outlined in these quotations had much originality in it. The same recipe can be found in the preface to the second edition of *The Castle of Otranto*: it is Walpole's programme[16] which Godwin, like Clara Reeves, Lewis and Coleridge in "The Rime of the Ancient Mariner", wants to use and tries to refine.[17]

When he chose this Gothic recipe, Godwin had to face difficulties that would probably have overwhelmed somebody who had no need to live by his pen. The "Preface" shows him as uneasy about the warmth with which he now describes "the affections . . . of private life" (p. ix); he defends this new emphasis by arguing that though he has changed his mind about some of the practical conclusions to be drawn from his philosophy, there is no need for him to "make any change respecting the principle of justice, or anything else fundamental to the system" (p. x). It is, however, in other areas that we find Godwin struggling with really difficult problems created by his choice of genre. The Gothic novel was, in fact, a danger to something quite fundamental to the intellectual system of the calm, rational radical.

First, though suspicions of immorality always hovered over late eighteenth-century fiction, the Gothic novel is generally conservative in political and moral matters: a fundamentally good and just aristocratic society is upset by a villain, whose machinations are exposed towards the end so that we can witness a happy return to the *status quo* of the first chapter. Individuals may have gained in the course of the events in moral fortitude and insight; but this development in the characters does not influence society except by turning the clock back to where it was. Even *The Monk*, for all its display of forbidden fruit, is such an implicit defence of an aristocratic and static social order. Of course, Gothic novels can nowadays be read the way Blake read Milton. It is possible to see a subversive element, political and ethical, in their flirtation with the demonic and loathsome. But the connection between this fascination with evil and the kind of political thinking Godwin advocated is slight. The nearest descendant of the Gothic villain-hero who rises in protest against conventionality is Byron's noble Manfred – a creature existing in a precarious social vacuum in which he spends his time alternatively praising and blaming himself for having had an incestuous relationship with his sister. Godwin generally tackles social and psychological problems in another language and another setting than this.[18]

Nor do the common attitudes to religion in Gothic fiction lend themselves easily to Godwin's obvious interests. Lewis, Mrs Radcliffe and later Maturin make much of the attacks on Roman Catholicism which were becoming almost compulsory in Gothic novels, but it is only a sadly amputated Voltaire which is reflected in their works. Maturin consistently invites belief in the supernatural; Lewis's diatribes against superstition are silenced by his own last chapters in which evil spirits are the leading actors; and though Mrs Radcliffe takes pains to explain all her mysterious incidents as having been inside the bounds of nature, there is a comfortable feeling in her novels that it may be possible in religion (and in particular, we may infer, in a moderate denomination like the Church of England) to find room both for awe and for commonsense morality.

Godwin's problem was not limited to the political and metaphysical attitudes that he might only too easily be burdened with. The narrative technique of Gothic fiction was equally unamenable to the writer of *Political Justice*. Most of these novels rely heavily on belief, or a willing suspension of disbelief, for their supernatural machinery, and their plots, to work. But the Godwin of *Political Justice* cannot build his story on ghosts and supernatural incidents, or even playfully introduce them into his tale, without opening himself to charges of inconsistency, not simply because a professed atheist would have to deny them, but also because they represent a danger to the ideal of calm, commonsensical reasoning that his whole philosophy of justice depends upon. Throughout *Political Justice* the emphasis on clearsightedness is strong.[19] For the man of duty there is no holiday to be taken from the slow, continuous and arduous task of seeing things as they are; and there is absolutely no short-cut to truth through metaphysical revelations.[20] In fiction the corresponding attitude must imply an approach which allows characters and incidents to appear in all their uniqueness, as full and clearly differentiated portraits and scenes, not in a metaphysical shorthand in which general traits only are conveyed, and not behind a veil of mystery. But supernatural incidents and beings work in Gothic fiction just as such a shorthand language, as signs representing generalisations of doctrine or sentiment. Godwin realised this danger when he wrote *Caleb Williams*: where there is incidental use of Gothic trappings – in the chapters describing the band of robbers and in the prison scenes – he steers clear of the supernatural; he does not even resort to Mrs Radcliffe's trick of letting something seem supernatural until the suspense is wrung out of it to the last drop. We are left in no doubt whatsoever that the mysterious and terrifying in these parts of *Caleb Williams* is due to natural causes. If *Caleb Williams* mutters a great deal about God and the Devil, as I believe it does, this is expressed by other means than the fantastic furniture of the standard Gothic plot. Godwin's novels have no colonies of this sort outside the bounds of nature. The only exception is *St Leon*.[21]

It may perhaps be argued that in Gothic novels the supernatural is a trick pure and simple, employed to create suspense and to simplify the narrative, and that it should not be looked upon as contributing towards the definition of the world of the novel and the values in this world. This contribution, however, it nearly always makes. The supernatural has a downright moral function in Gothic novels – in dramatic interventions it punishes and rewards, most often according to desert. And, what is even more important in this context, it influences the idea and ideals of human insight implied in the fictional world. When the supernatural influences the action, there is automatically a suggestion that life is capable of climaxes and intensities that cannot be accounted for by common sense and/or natural philosophy, and that life can at times be understood, not by the slow and laborious process of unravelling human motives and physical possibilities, but by reference to quite different sources of knowledge. Even a phantasmagoria like *Vathek*, with its Arabian Nights pantheon in which English and French readers were scarcely invited to believe, implies the existence of direct revelations of a kind which is completely foreign to Locke's *Essay*, Hartley's *Observations* and Godwin's *Political Justice*. In some Gothic tales the supernatural is treated with such raillery that ontological questions are scarcely raised; but Godwin was no Thomas Peacock or Oscar Wilde. There is nothing flippant about his presentation of the supernatural in *St Leon*. Had there been a more sustained ambiguity in the point of view (as there was to be in some of the later novels), Godwin might have avoided a direct clash with his own theories. But Reginald St Leon is obviously a trustworthy narrator of his own story, and this story is at odds with the account of the world given in *Political Justice* where everything is seen as governed by a lawful necessity, not in any case by inexplicable, mysterious agents. Godwin had read Hume and is circumspect when he mentions causation; but even his guarded sentences in *Political Justice* read as a damaging criticism of *St Leon*:

> That mind is a topic of science, may be argued from all those branches of literature and enquiry which have mind for their subject. What species of amusement or instruction would history afford, if there were no ground of inference from moral antecedents to their consequents, if certain temptations and inducements did not, in all ages and climates, introduce a certain series of actions, if we were unable to trace a method and unity of system in men's tempers, propensities and transactions? (vol. i, p. 369)

Up to the point when the stranger arrives with his strange gifts, *St Leon* can serve as an illustration of this view of the mind. Afterwards, it relies for interest and coherence on something which does not provide "amusement or instruction".

Godwin may not have been consciously aware of the extent to which the Gothic novel as a genre would involve him in difficulties that might affect his integrity as a writer. If he was, perhaps he felt that a certain incongruity might be excused since the ostensible message was so obviously of a piece with his political philosophy: from beginning to end *St Leon* can be read as an attack on Burke's idea of chivalry and on an aristocratic England which had become reactionary in the course of the 1790s. The Gothic elements in the novel are made to serve this purpose; and the supernatural (in this case the *elixir vitae* and the philosopher's stone) is presented, quite emphatically, as a symbol of those aspects of society which Godwin wants to criticise.[22]

As a fifteen-year old boy St Leon is taken to the Field of the Cloth of Gold, the illustrious meeting between Francis I of France and Henry VIII. From then on he is helplessly in love with an idea of honour and chivalry which his mother had systematically prepared the ground for: "My mother loved my honour and my fame more than she loved my person" (p. 4). The two other main ingredients in the young protagonist's psyche are his capacity for married love – he is capable of loving his wife, Marguerite, to a great extent for what she is, not for the antiquity and nobility of her maiden name – and his obsessive love of gambling. St Leon's love of his wife is a simple virtue (granted the modifications of Godwin's early views on domestic affections); and gambling is of course an outright vice, the most common road to ruin for young men in dozens of late eighteenth-century stories. It is, in fact, a particularly handy vice for the novelist. It places the interesting young man in a colourful society where his moral stamina is severely tested; it makes for great, though not irreparable, calamities and for delicious showers of tears, most of them falling from the eyes of the loving female who can cry and converse more freely about his losses at table than about his conquests in bed. Godwin is not blind to these virtues of gambling, but he is more interested in linking it with psychological and social insights that are peculiarly his own. St Leon does not really gamble to improve his finances, though he does live in a style which exceeds his means. He seeks exactly the same thing – fame, an "illustrious career" (p. 27) – in war, in keeping a long train of servants, and in gambling. When "the nobility of France exchanged the activities of the field for . . . the sordid and inglorious passion of gambling" they were all the time moved by the same "concentrated spirit" (p.27). St Leon knows that he ought to avoid cards and dice, but he does not see to the roots of his own danger: "I mistook profusion and extravagance for splendour and dignity", he says (p. 27), but the readers realise that this confession is not good enough. His basic weakness is not that he is blind to whatever distinctions there may be between extravagance and splendour, but that he lacks the inner peace and stability that might have enabled him to see that he could live a better and perhaps also a happier life outside the "theatre of honour and fame" (p. 28). This situation – "I did not suffice to myself", says St Leon (p. 42) – is one that Godwin returns to in all his later novels. It brings out a theme which enables him to combine psychological and political insights: his gifted young men are driven to desperation by their lack of inner security; consequently, they exploit others and try to find comfort either in money and titles or in political and religious fanaticism.

Because St Leon's gambling is placed in this context, it foreshadows his later commerce with the stranger. In both parts of the novel Godwin exposes that love of chivalry which Burke had extolled. He had attacked this ideal in *Political Justice*,[23] but he realised that a corresponding attack in fiction required a strategy chosen with considerable care. He could not begin his story by flatly denouncing honour, dignity and splendour. Such an attack could not possibly be convincing; and it might seem naïve: Godwin was not blind to the fact that though fame is always a dangerous temptation, there is also a "species of reputation" which is valuable because it can give "efficacy to our services to others".[24] Therefore, his approach is indirect. We first listen to St Leon's venerable mother addressing her last words to her son:

> When I am gone, you will be compelled more vividly to feel that singleness and self-dependence which are the source of all virtue. . . . Be careful that your career may be both spotless and illustrious. Hold your life as a thing of no account, when it enters into competition with your fame. A true knight thinks no sacrifice and suffering hard, that honour demands. Be humane, gentle, generous, and intrepid. Be prompt to follow wherever your duty calls you. Remember your ancestors, knights of the Holy Cross. Remember you father. Follow your king, who is the mirror of valour: and be ever ready for the service of the distressed. . . . May Heaven shower down a thousand blessings, upon your innocence, and the gallantry of your soul! (p.9)

It is only in the light of what happens later that this noble piece of advice becomes patently ironic. That a true knight should think no suffering and sacrifice hard that honour demands, is exactly the attitude which makes St Leon accept the fatal gifts from the stranger. The *elixir vitae* and the philosopher's stone represent the idea of chivalry as Godwin wants us to see it: in an aristocratic society it is a destructive ideal. St Leon is driven to seek the gift from the stranger by the same motives that prompted his admiration for King Francis and that drove him to the gambling table. When he is reluctant (in his marriage he has glimpsed another hierarchy of values), the stranger addresses him with "a look of ineffable contempt":

> Feeble and effeminate mortal! You are neither a knight nor a Frenchman! In vain might honour, worth, and immortal renown proffer their favours to him who has made himself the basest of all sublunary things – the puppet of a woman . . . (p. 126)

St Leon finally accepts the gift because of the ideas he has imbibed in his childhood and youth. To most readers it will not seem obvious that a love of chivalry and honour should have such dire consequences. This ideal can sound both virtuous and challenging; and Godwin manages to let us feel this in the mother's good advice. It is necessary that we should be made to see the plausibility and attraction of the ideal at this stage. Godwin is not attacking something which is loathsome anyway, as Mrs Radcliffe nearly always does; he tries to do something much more interesting and difficult – to criticise a value which is generally taken for granted.

It is thus as a symbol central to the discussion of values throughout the novel that the supernatural can be forced to work for the political philosopher. St Leon's inability to resist the stranger is the sad result of his mother's pious words. The supernatural powers give him unbounded wealth, the elegance and vigour of youth, and even a chance to do good, but they are acquired at a high price – the disintegration of a happy marriage, the estrangement of his son, the death of one daughter and separation from the other two. Moreover, he is not really able to help other people with his gold; and though he does become famous in Hungary and Austria, his renown eventually becomes a notoriety that he shuns. Translated into the language of *Political Justice*, this goes to show that a society built on the ideal of chivalry is a state in which there is no room for sincerity, justice, and real affection.

It is therefore no doubt true, as W. A. Flanders says in his interesting article on "Godwin and Gothicism" that the novel "uses the supernatural trappings of Gothic fiction for didactic purposes".[25] In itself, this is perhaps no innovation on Godwin's part. A didactic element is found in supernatural manifestations from *The Castle of Otranto* onwards. It is present even in *Vathek*, in which the trappings are exceptionally lush. Godwin's novelty does not lie in the bare fact that he uses the genre for moral and educational purposes; but he is the first to use it as a weapon against the ideals of honour and the political establishment of late eighteenth-century England. This innovation is one of the reasons why *St Leon* makes livelier reading than most Gothic novels.

But isn't the reading presented above absurd? Can Godwin be thought of as damning a gifted man for what is after all a very natural wish for distinction? Kelly and Woodcock (see note 22) save Godwin from such suspicions by seeing St Leon not as an example of a man who must be condemned, as men eventually must be when they build their lives on Burke's moral premises, but as another radical out to improve society. However, this view presents us with two St Leons; the first, as all must agree, is the slave of an aristocratic idea of fame; the second, who must then be thought of as appearing suddenly in the middle of the novel, is the champion of causes analogous to those that English radicals fought for in the 1790s. It seems to me that this reading creates more problems than it solves. Godwin does, after all, create a protagonist who is recognisably the same all through. What may mislead readers is the fact that St Leon is a decent and likeable man. He tries to do what he can for his daughters and later for his son; and the misery he witnesses in Hungary moves him to large-scale benevolence. But Godwin needed a fine character of this kind to make his point: even the kind, old St Leon, steeled in misfortune and rich in experience, is hopelessly the prisoner of honour. In starving Buda-Pest he buys for himself "a spacious and beautiful mansion", a house which "had for centuries been the principal residence of the illustrious family of Ragotski" (p. 372). Later, he finds an ally in Bethlem Gabor whose sense of honour is at least as exalted – and more obviously destructive – than his own. Godwin again illustrates one of the main points in *Political Justice*: there is no private sphere of life in which man can be his own master; "political institutions have a more powerful and extensive influence, than it has generally been the practice to ascribe to them" (vol. i, pp. 24–5). The truth of this observation is brought out in St Leon's shortcomings, but more forcefully in his benevolence. He always finds himself in societies in which individual kindness is crippled in the mind that fosters it and where it can do little to redress wrongs.

The other Godwin

Godwin's choice of the Gothic was hazardous; and not even when the Gothicism is forced to work as a sermon on certain chapters in *Political Justice* can he be completely at home in such a setting. However, the uncomfortable presence of the Gothic creates tensions in which the other Godwin, the writer who is an almost complete antithesis to the philosopher, can be seen.

Caleb Williams hovers between two interpretations of life – one political in the sense in which the word is used in Godwin's philosophical writings, the other metaphysical. A great part of the strength and fascination of the novel is due not to either of these two interpretations, but to the oscillation between them which the reader experiences. There is a corresponding vigour under the surface of *St Leon*. Godwin the convinced atheist (not yet converted to theism by Coleridge) is seen in the stern criticism of theocracies, Roman Catholic and Protestant, and in the advocacy of a way of life sign-posted by a non-religious morality; and the political thinker wants to show his readers how religion may aggravate the dangers inherent in aristocratic ideals. At the same time *St Leon* suggests, in its Gothic elements, that overwhelming and mysterious powers may suddenly confront us, and that our response to such powers may make or mar us for life (and perhaps eternity – St Leon himself may live for ever!). There are ways in which these powers may be explained away by Godwin or by a sceptical reader, for instance by postulating different levels of reality inside the novel. But such attempts involve amputations of the book. It *is* a fact, on a level with all other facts in this story, that St Leon is endowed with supernatural gifts; he does not only believe that he has them.

This oscillation between two views of life is not only seen in the basic outlines of the story: it creates an interesting double irony in individual passages as well. When St Leon has been imprisoned by the Inquisition in Spain, the inquisitor tells him that:

> every thing that was valuable to mankind, not only in the future state, but also in the present, depended upon preserving in full vigour and strength the sacred institutions of the Christian faith;

and that those who were endowed with the powers sufficient for that purpose would be in the highest degree inexcusable in the sight of God if they did not vigilantly and inflexibly maintain the exertion of those powers. It was an egregious mistake of self-willed and opinionated men, to suppose that the maintenance of our holy religion was sufficiently provided for by the clearness of its evidence. (p.314)

This is simple irony from the pen of the political philosopher. The inquisitor is thus placed very firmly at the outset as an enemy of truth and justice. Godwin makes the direction of the irony perfectly clear by letting St Leon, as he narrates his story, refer to Godwin's own day: "'there is nothing new under the sun:' two centuries perhaps after Philip the Second shall be gathered to his ancestors (he died in 1598), men shall learn over again to persecute each other for conscience sake . . ." (p. 338). But the inquisitor has also been given this to say, in the same speech as the one quoted above:

Of all the crimes, he added, to which the depravity of human nature had given birth, the most astonishing and the most horrible was that of diabolical commerce. That human creatures should be so far infatuated, as to enter into league with the declared enemy of souls, and for the possession of a short-lived and precarious power to sign away their spirits to eternal damnation, was so extraordinary as to have been wholly unworthy of credit were it not supported by evidence as strong and irresistible as that of the miracles of Jesus Christ himself. (p. 318)

The irony is more complex here. For one thing, the inquisitor is right about the brevity of the pleasures St Leon has gained by his special gifts; and the word "infatuation" is an apt term for St Leon's attitude to honour. But this arch-enemy of truth, the inquisitor, is also right, in the light of the story, about something else: you *can* acquire supernatural power, and it can be had at the price of your moral integrity. Of course, the novel does not support all that the inquisitor says in this speech; but, though on terms rather different from those of the Roman Catholic priest, *St Leon* does bear out a belief in fiends. In fact, the stranger who comes to St Leon's happy home on the Lake of Constance is one.

This double vision is not so fully brought out in *St Leon* as in *Caleb Williams*. The Gothic novel does not create for us a world which makes sense, in its entirety, in either interpretation. It is a basic virtue in *Caleb Williams* that if it is looked upon as a Jacobin novel all the important elements in the story find their place in a coherent pattern, and so they do, but in another concatenation, when it is seen as a forerunner of religious novels with a Kafkaesque sense of terror and ignorance. *St Leon* is less subtle; the Gothic could not work as a very precise correlative for Godwin's complicated response to life. But the novel is more complex than the political message may at first lead us to think; the use of what was for Godwin an incongruous genre necessitated a confrontation of his humanistic philosophy with a metaphysics which he had left behind in the eighties. Of course, to say that he had left it behind is only partly true. His various manuscript notes in the Abinger Collection reveal how often throughout his life he felt it necessary to confirm to himself his position as an unbeliever.[26] These repeated assertions were needed because his years as a minister of the Gospel were a part of his life that he could not completely exorcise by the seemingly calm reasoning of *Political Justice*. The optimism and reassurance in the tone of this treatise can, in terms of Godwin's biography, be read as an attempt by the philosopher to save himself and mankind from a truly terrible God. But in *St Leon*, as in *Caleb Williams*, the novelist allows his early fears to rise again: when the hero receives gifts from outside the bounds of nature, they are evil; and earlier in the story it has been an "act of God" – a storm – which has driven him into his worst misery.

But the sense of evil that hangs over St Leon must not be understood as giving us a complete theology in disguise. An evil destiny is here presented as it is felt, as a cluster of emotional responses to pain and loss, and not as a detailed system of belief. In an oppressive rhythm of defeats the strong and resourceful St Leon is reduced to misery. He is frightened and destroyed by what he did not, and could not, foresee. In spite of St Leon's tendency to make his own life the subject of philosophical speculation, the more elusive powers at work in his story remain elusive; and their folk-tale suggestiveness stands out as a striking contrast to those areas of life that St Leon successfully masters by his intellect.

The price

The Gothic genre gave Godwin what he had not consciously bargained for, a world in which he could find room for a double vision of
life; and it gave him ample opportunities to exercise one of his main
virtues as a story-teller – the establishment of ironic situations in
which generalisations made by the characters must be reconsidered
in the light of the actual story. Once noticed, such ironies inform the
style with new vigour. The inquisitor's speech is a good example,
another is the dying advice of St Leon's mother. As the quotation
above reveals, it is a stilted speech, but the irritation we may feel
that Godwin should give a dying mother such abstract and impersonal words to address to her only son subsides when the author's
overall strategy is considered: this noble woman is given to an ideal
which, mercilessly, has made her an enemy of emotional sincerity
and spontaneity.

But some of Godwin's virtues as a novelist are badly impaired in
the special situation in which he found himself when he was writing
a Gothic novel. The genre does not give him proper scope for one of
his finest gifts – the ability to portray the human mind in a change
from security and comfort to a crisis in which all hope of occupying a
happy middle ground seems lost. The road to extremes, social and
psychological, is one that Godwin has considerable knowledge
about. It is a double portrait of this kind which informs *Caleb Williams*;
another gives nerve to the last volume of *Fleetwood*; and a similar
development gives an uncommon intensity to the fate of the main
character in *Mandeville*. *St Leon*, too, offers some good examples of
such development, for instance in the chapter about St Leon's last
evening in Paris and in the description of his awakening in Switzerland after his economic ruin (pp. 79–85). St Leon's debate with
himself whether he ought to accept the stranger's gift (pp. 136–8) is
another example of Godwin's somewhat ungainly strength: the discussion is longwinded and stilted at times, but its urgency and
psychological precision make it a moving turning-point. However,
once St Leon has accepted the philosopher's stone and the *elixir vitae*
he knows himself to be unique and alone; and we are reminded of
this more than often enough to remember it all the time. All the
crises in the second half of the novel have an empty ring.

This result of Godwin's Gothicism is the more unfortunate since
moments of emotional intensity in the first half of the story have

sometimes been moments of irritation for the reader. When St Leon has lost most of his fortune gambling in Paris, his wife comes to see him and finds that she can still believe in him. The great crisis of St Leon's early life has arrived:

> Every word of this speech was a dagger to my heart. What were my feelings, while this admirable woman was taking shame to herself for her suspicions, and pouring out her soul in commendation of my integrity! I looked inward, and found every thing there the reverse of her apprehension, a scene of desolation and remorse. I embraced her in silence. My heart panted upon her bosom, and seemed bursting with a secret that it was death to reveal. I ought, in return for her generosity, to have given up my feigned engagement, and devoted this night at least to console and pacify her. But I could not, and I dared not. The wound of my bosom was opened, and would not be closed. The more I loved her for her confidence, the less could I endure myself in her presence. (p. 68)

"Every word a dagger to my heart", "a scene of desolation and remorse", "the wound of my bosom was opened" – these metaphors are sadly melodramatic, and the allusion to Shakespeare does not at all improve Godwin's case. But at this stage Godwin's hold on the reader is not lost: one reason why these phrases sound hollow is the contrast which the paragraph itself establishes between these images and an overall psychological insight which rings true and which does not depend on the most pathetic phrases Godwin makes use of here. The result is a certain bafflement; a reader is irritated at a style whose chastity seems irretrievably lost; at the same time the paragraph as a whole commands assent. St Leon's reaction is a result precisely of that mistaken idea of honour which is exposed throughout the novel.

But in the second half this firm basis of social and psychological verisimilitude founders. St Leon and his family can be forced to flee from a happy valley; he may have to leave the surviving members of his family; he can be imprisoned for months and years. But by the acceptance of the stranger's gift he has placed himself absolutely outside ordinary humanity, and the psychological interest in his further development is correspondingly limited. He can flounder, but he cannot fall in the second half of the novel.

Another of Godwin's virtues which is endangered by his use of Gothicism is his sense of the interaction between individuals and society. Normally one cannot accuse Godwin of underestimating the power of history in the lives of his characters. No *dei ex machina*, no sudden interventions by rich relatives or returning friends, save Godwin's protagonists. There are coincidences – and some few of them quite striking – in Godwin's fiction, but most often they intensify rather than counteract social forces, as does, for instance, the chance meeting between Caleb and Collins in the last volume of *Caleb Williams*. However, in *St Leon* the hero's gifts of eternal youth and unbounded wealth exempt him from historical necessity. Therefore his never-ending appearances in new societies, obviously meant to give us a comprehensive survey of social and political wrongs, never quite suit this purpose. Whenever he enters a society, with him comes something which is foreign to economics and labour as we know them from all other countries and ages. Even when thought of as an experiment in economics, St Leon's intervention in Hungarian trade fails to make sense; the venture depends on something supernatural from beginning to end; and therefore the improvements it is meant to illustrate are not applicable to any society that the author of *Political Justice* cares about. The later parts of *St Leon* do illustrate certain isolated statements in Godwin's political philosophy, but they lack the force that social criticism can have when it describes plausible action in recognisable societies.

In the strange story of *St Leon* Godwin explores, probably without being fully aware of it himself, his attitude to his own position as a political and religious outsider. Though St Leon is no forerunner of late eighteenth-century radicals, his life story does illustrate themes that Godwin had a personal interest in: why does a man seek fame? What are the effects of ostracism on a sensitive mind? And to what extent can the world, when it is experienced by a suffering human being, really serve as an illustration of what *Political Justice* says about man's capacity for clear, consecutive thinking? The novel offers no simple and clearcut attitudes to these problems. It includes, for instance, an element of regret: there is nostalgia in some of Godwin's portraits of honest and kind pillars of society. Moreover, the novel examines the psychological need for a cult (a need whose existence is not denied by *Political Justice*) and our attitudes to what is thought of as holy. The truly noble Marguerite and the evil stranger – not interesting as individuals – acquire new meaning in this larger context of Godwin's development. They give us glimpses of the author as a liberal Tory *manqué* and a believer *manqué* (in the Devil more than in God).

After *St Leon* the stark opposition in Godwin's fiction between two ways in which life can be experienced and understood is modulated. His stories are still ambiguous, but less violently so; and his language becomes more homogeneous, more psychological, and less strongly marked by a restless search for analogies that can explain the whole of life. But Godwin's later heroes, and notably Fleetwood in the first novel after *St Leon*, all try in vain to master life by means of calm philosophy and all find themselves overwhelmed by pain and despair and guilt. One of Godwin's last works is a compilation called *Lives of the Necromancers* (1834). It is of no great value in itself, but it can serve as a reminder of how permanent his interest was both in the social outsider and in the opposition between superstition and religion on the one hand (one of the "necromancers" is St Dunstan, another Pope Silvester II) and rationalism on the other. A reader is destined to moments of gloom, but not necessarily to disappointment as Leslie Stephen feared, when he ventures to study Godwin's later novels.

V

Fleetwood:
Sentimentality in a
New Key

There is more tolerable writing and more common sense in the
minor novel than is usually supposed.

J. M. S. Tompkins, *The Popular Novel in England 1770–1800*

Fleetwood: Or, The New Man of Feeling[1] appeared in 1805, six years
after *St Leon*. Godwin's daily life had changed radically in the course
of these years. After two or three unsuccessful approaches to single
literary women in the late 1790s, he had married in 1801. On
Godwin's part the new marriage was probably based more on
expediency than on romance. He had Mary and Fanny to look after,
and obviously felt that they needed a proper home. Mrs Mary Jane
Clairmont, a widow with two children, was not a perfect woman.
Kegan Paul portrays her as a quarrelsome wife, a fairy-tale step-
mother and a sheer disaster to Godwin's literary friendships. But the
letters actually printed by Kegan Paul modify this picture; and Don
Locke's new biography gives an admirably balanced (and fascinating) account of the marriage. Though touchy (who wouldn't be if
married to a rather pedantic man who had made an idol of his first
wife?), the new Mrs Godwin was a conscientious help-mate in
domestic and financial affairs. They both struggled courageously to
support the family. In 1805, when Godwin had finished *Fleetwood*,
the two founded the "Juvenile Library". Mrs Godwin was in charge
of the business side of the venture and translated French stories for
the library; he wrote a number of history books for children. They
did quarrel quite often; and in an autobiographical sketch Godwin

grumbles at the strain which marriage is to a "temper . . . of a recluse and contemplative cast" like his own. But he sounds sincere in letters written to the seaside resort which Mrs Godwin visited annually when he wishes for her speedy return to London. In one of the letters there is a little sentence, apparently not appreciated by Kegan Paul, which suggests that both enjoyed the marriage bed.[2] A son was born in 1803.

The political climate had changed, too, since the nineties. There were no longer any revolutionary societies that threatened the constitution. Some people still thought of themselves as radicals and the *Anti-Jacobin* continued to live high on anti-revolutionary sentiments; but the intensity of the political warfare had abated. Godwin could earn a living in the children's books market only by using a pseudonym, but the very fact that he was able to hide for some years behind "Edward Baldwin" reminds us that the outright intellectual war of the nineties had entered a new phase. A striking example of the change in atmosphere is found in the *Anti-Jacobin* itself; its review of Godwin's *Life of Chaucer* in September 1804 is almost consistently laudatory.[3] Godwin could now hope to find a market for history books even though Mr Baldwin presented himself as the constant defender of liberty.[4]

Fleetwood was written in this new situation. It is not surprising that the book has been classified as a Jacobin novel[5] – it contains a fair sprinkling of anti-establishment criticism; but it is even more noticeable that Godwin writes under reduced pressure from political events. He now feels at liberty to consider more fully areas of life not directly relevant to the urgent issues raised by the French Revolution. He turns to domestic life with new vigour. In *St Leon* the description of family life had been a simple, straightforward tribute to an idealised Mary Wollstonecraft. His life in 1804–5 gave him other experiences that made it impossible to repeat the portrait of a marriage which he had given in the previous novel.

The novel begins with a description of Fleetwood's childhood and youth. He lives with his invalid father at their family seat in Merionethshire; he is lonely, but not unhappy; and he loves long hikes in the mountains surrounding his home. Chapter II relates an heroic incident. In great danger himself, Fleetwood saves the life of a young farmer. On this occasion he behaves with the courage, resourcefulness and generosity of countless heroes in fiction, but he never returns to this role. When he leaves home to go to Oxford he finds himself in circumstances in which he becomes a different man. His sheltered background has not prepared him for undergraduate life: "once I feared not the eye of man, except as I was reluctant to give him pain; now I was afraid of ridicule" (p. 21). Chapter IV relates the story of the student who went mad and drowned himself after having been the object of a practical joke. This incident, which begins in hilarious comedy,[6] foreshadows Fleetwood's blindness in the third volume, and it serves as an emblem for Fleetwood's new situation. He, too, is stunned by the cruelty and the vanity of his surroundings, and he, too, loses heart. His own position at Oxford is so precarious that he cannot risk standing out against the bright, young rakes who set the tone. After Oxford Fleetwood goes to Paris where his adventures of the heart begin pleasantly enough, but he is soon tormented and jilted, first by a vivacious marchioness, then by a soft, languid countess. On the Continent he receives news of the death of his father; it is broken to him in an exquisitely romantic setting on the Lake of Uri.

The second volume begins in the middle of a long interpolated tale which contains the life story of his father's friend Ruffigny. It is a tale in which Fleetwood might have found counsel and support, but his later life, though more sober, does not become happy or creative. He returns to his home in Wales where he is agreeably occupied in lamenting the death of his father for a long time. Later, he examines the pleasures of London but they prove to be much like those of Paris. Brief periods of enthusiasm are followed by disappointment, first in a literary club, later as a member of Parliament. Then, after some years spent mostly on the Continent in vain attempts to relieve his misanthropy, he meets the good Macneils, but this friendship ends suddenly in the death at sea of all but one of that charming and wise family. In the last pages of this volume Fleetwood marries the daughter who had stayed behind, a girl who is just awakening from the grief she had been plunged into. Here there is a note of happiness. At first, marriage is a source of great pleasure and content to Fleetwood.

The third volume contains the history of Fleetwood's marriage. When the happy pair return from their honeymoon, Fleetwood soon finds it difficult to accept his wife as a woman with a will, and a sensibility, of her own. He is easily jealous; and she suffers a recurrence of grief now that she lives near the sea. In fits of madness she visits the shore at night to find the dead bodies of her parents. In an attempt to improve her spirits Fleetwood takes her to Bath. She rallies, but he succumbs to jealousy. An evil nephew works on his suspicions so that in the end Fleetwood believes that his wife, though far advanced in a pregnancy, is on the point of eloping with another nephew. He repudiates his wife and leaves for the Continent where he goes virtually insane, driven to despair and cruelty by the machinations of his nephew. Finally, he is saved, and all misunderstandings cleared up by the intervention of good friends of his wife; and in a sober mixture of regret and content he can sit down to write "the record of my errors".

The beauties and dangers of delicacy

The full title of the novel indicates one of Godwin's main concerns: "Fleetwood: Or, The New Man of Feeling" points to Henry Mackenzie's *The Man of Feeling* (1771), a novel which had appeared in nine editions by the year 1800 and of which there were more than thirty re-issues in the first quarter of the new century.[7] Mackenzie conducts his hero through a number of scenes in which the engaging young man's sensibility can be properly exercised. Regularly, at the climax of each episode, the hero dissolves into tears at the plight of those in need. He is naïve. but always likeable; he is indeed a character whose blend of sentiment, charity and whimsicality most readers even today may find irresistible. Godwin did resist the young Harley. Or rather, he accepted in *Fleetwood* one of Mackenzie's premises, the insistence that man is an emotional creature, and rejected another, the view that an emotional involvement in life must lead to charity.

The popular tradition which Godwin related to, and wanted to exploit, gave him suggestions for story as well as character. Mackenzie's novels are heavily indebted to Richardson, and both Mackenzie and Godwin owe something to Rousseau's *La Nouvelle Heloïse* in which the main character's mind is influenced by a romantic landscape and in which his *éducation sentimentale* is a central theme. Like Mackenzie's Harley, the young Fleetwood leaves a home in the country to be exposed to the wiles of the world. Mackenzie's *Julia de Roubigné*, a novel that Godwin knew well,[8] had added a refreshing element of jealousy to Rousseau's husband-wife-younger-man story; and Godwin builds the third volume of his novel on jealousy and on a similar, triangular set of misunderstandings, but his debts to these earlier novels are not massive. In sharp contrast to Rousseau and Mackenzie, he does not include a young man who makes a deep impression on the wife. This, of course, is to court failure. For both earlier writers depend for interest on an engrossing conflict in the young wife, torn between two men. Godwin cannot have been blind to what he risked, but his centre of interest is all the time the middle-aged husband; and, as we shall see later, there are good reasons why he makes the husband suffer from jealousy even though his wife is faithful in heart, word and deed.

Behind the novel of sensibility lies the belief that benevolent feelings are the hallmark of man. Latitudinarian divines had preached this, often in reply to Hobbes's less sanguine view of man's nature, from the Restoration onwards. Tillotson, who was never deaf to the whisperings of the *Zeitgeist*, told his Whitehall congregation on 8 March 1689:

> So far is it from being true, which Mr *Hobbes* asserts as the fundamental *Principle* of his *Politicks*, *That Men are naturally in a State of War and Enmity with one another*; that the contrary *Principle*, laid down by a much deeper and wiser Man, I mean *Aristotle*, is most certainly true, *That Men are naturally a-kin and Friends to each other*.[9]

Donald Greene has recently shown that the "doctrine of benevolence" had been preached before the Restoration[10]; and it can thus in itself scarcely be responsible for the growing importance of sensibility in the eighteenth century. What happened was, I think, that old ideas about man's capacity for goodness and sympathy were then able to fill a vacuum created by Locke's and Hume's ideas about reason. The beginnings of this movement can be seen in Shaftesbury, who finds a "moral sense" in man which is neither the result of a God-given faculty of inspired reason nor of man's capacity for consecutive thinking.[11] In Hume the ideas behind the sentimental novel find their full expression. In a chapter of the *Treatise* which he calls "Moral distinctions deriv'd from a moral sense", Hume says:

> since vice and virtue are not discoverable merely by reason, or the comparison of ideas, it must be by the means of some impression or sentiment they occasion, that we are able to mark the difference betwixt them. Our decisions concerning moral rectitude and depravity are evidently perceptions; and as all perceptions are either

impressions or ideas, the exclusion of the one is a convincing argument for the other. Morality, therefore, is more properly felt than judg'd of . . .[12]

This moral sense is aided by the imagination: "'Tis remarkable, that the imagination and affections have close union together, and that nothing, which affects the former, can be entirely indifferent to the latter. Wherever our ideas of good or evil acquire a new vivacity, the passions become more violent" (p. 471). In "On the love of relations" Hume argues that our love is very easily excited by relations such as family, nationality, neighbourhood, and occupation: "*Acquaintance* . . . gives rise to love and kindness" (p. 401). "'Tis remarkable", says Hume towards the end of his discussion of morality, "that nothing touches a man of humanity more than any instance of extraordinary delicacy in love or friendship" (p. 654).

These quotations outline the respectable trend of thought behind the flow of tears in *The Man of Feeling* and *Julia de Roubigné*. Two phrases in the last quotation from Hume are revealing: a *man of humanity* is particularly susceptible to instances of *extraordinary delicacy* in love or friendship. To be able to give or receive, or appreciate as spectator, instances of such delicacy is a sign of belonging to the species, of being properly human. The whole of the *Treatise* argues that the reason which man is capable of is even more limited than Locke thought. *Rationis capax* is therefore no longer a particularly attractive or useful definition of the nature of man. Hume does not attempt a systematic redefinition; he seems to think that philosophy is not capable of such tremendous tasks. But his incidental hints of what "a man of humanity" is, stress the importance of a moral sense which is excited by family feeling and friendship, and which finds its crowning glory in instances of "extraordinary delicacy". We have, in other words, a brief recipe for a sentimental novel.

Godwin was acquainted with this line of thinking behind the literary genre. His work on political philosophy had necessitated a thorough study of Locke, Shaftesbury, Hutcheson and Hume. There are a number of direct references to Hume in *Political Justice*, and in the library Godwin left behind at his death there was a copy of the *Treatise*.[13] Godwin's startingpoint in moral philosophy was different from Hume's.[14] The first edition of *Political Justice* testifies to a belief in reason not only as a means to "the discovery of truth or falsehood" (Hume), but as an active, moral force. Later Godwin realised that he had underestimated the power of the affections, and he approached Hume's idea that "reason is wholly inactive, and can never be the source of so active a principle as conscience, or a sense of morals".[15] In a memorandum from 1798 Godwin says that he wants to correct certain ideas in *Political Justice*, one part of which "is essentially defective, in the circumstance of not yielding a proper attention to the empire of feeling". Godwin proceeds to give a paraphrase of ideas that owe a great deal to Hume:

> The voluntary actions of men are under the direction of their feelings: nothing can have a tendency to produce this species of action, except so far as it is connected with ideas of future pleasure or pain to ourselves or others. Reason, accurately speaking, has not the smallest degree of power to put any one limb or articulation of our bodies into motion. Its province, in a practical view, is wholly confined to adjusting the comparison between different objects of desire, and investigating the most successful mode of attaining those objects.[16]

The change in Godwin's attitude is brought out in the preface to *St Leon*, too, when he argues that though he has not changed his mind about the basic principles in *Political Justice*, he now wants to stress that the "domestic and private affections [are] inseparable from the nature of man".[17]

These modifications in Godwin's thinking naturally led him towards the novel of sentiment. There is abundant praise of domestic affection in *St Leon*, and *Fleetwood* is saturated with feeling. In one place there is an outright defence of tears:

> We reached Merionetshire, and found a desolated mansion, and a tenanted grave. In the one, and over the other, we united our tears. . . .
> And here I beg leave to protest against the doctrine too commonly promulgated in the world, that we ought to call off our thoughts, as speedily as possible, from the recollection of our deceased friends, and not waste our spirits in lamentation for irremediable losses. The persons from whom I have often heard this lesson, have been of the class of the hard-hearted, who have sought in such "counsels of prudence" an apology for their own unfeeling serenity. He was a wiser man than they, who said, "It is

good to dwell in the house of mourning; for by the sadness of the countenance the heart is made better." (p. 150)

Other feelings, also, are described in slow motion sequences typical of the sentimental genre. Misgivings about an insignificant mistress, "This woman, so frivolous, so fickle, so uncertain, could she love?" (p. 53), are given a page and a half of earnest meditation; and his response to a worthier subject, his own honeymoon, takes up a whole chapter in which the story is allowed to stand still.

But in spite of the obvious relish with which *Fleetwood* makes use of the sentimental mode, it presents a *new* man of feeling. The reviewers were quick to note Godwin's originality, and most of them disliked it. In Scott's words in *The Edinburgh Review* "we humbly think Fleetwood merits any title better than that of a man of feeling".[18] Scott is right. Fleetwood is not a man of feeling like Mackenzie's Harley. The reason for this difference is not, I think, found in any wish on Godwin's part to debunk a form that had been ridiculous, though with a great many redeeming traits, in Mackenzie and that had deteriorated afterwards. Godwin is a writer who subverts earlier literature in a number of ways, but he was not an author for whom it was natural to satirise colleagues.[19] *Fleetwood* is strikingly different from the mainstream of sentimental fiction for another reason: Godwin wants to present a main character in whom there are no longer any absolute and sacred ties between sensibility and benevolence.

The novel does not flatly deny the possibility of an alliance between feeling and goodness. Two elderly gentlemen, Mr Macneil and M. Ruffigny, illustrate this beautiful union. But Fleetwood himself does not. His sensibility is great, his feelings deep and intense, but he is not charitable. On the contrary, his sensitivity is at its most acute in bouts of cruel jealousy, and even in more sober moments it contributes to his isolation from his wife. His first misgivings about his wife's feelings can be seen as a consequence of his extreme delicacy, which has made him an ardent lover of the very chamber his young wife appropriates as her own when they move to his family seat:

"This is an enchanting closet!" said she.
"It is." – My heart knocked at my bosom, my very soul was full of its little history, as I spoke.

"Do you know, Fleetwood, I shall take this closet for mine? I will have all my drawings brought here, and arrange my favourite flowers in the window. Will you give it me?"

"Surely, my love! I am glad it pleases you so much."

My sensations at this moment were of a singular and complicated nature. I had been on the point of employing all my eloquence to describe to Mary how I loved this closet – how unalterably it had fixed its hold upon me as my favourite retreat. For this purpose I had recollected in rapid succession all the endearments that made it mine, all the delights which, almost from prattling infancy, it had afforded me. (pp. 238–9)

Fleetwood masters his feelings and he even has moments in which he is happy that she is gratified; but his generosity recedes as tender memories about this room return:

"Mary, Mary," said I sometimes to myself, as I recurred to the circumstance, "I am afraid you are selfish! and what character can be less promising in social life, than hers who thinks of no one's gratification but her own?" It was true, I could not tell her, "This, which you so inconsiderately desire me to give up, is my favourite apartment." But she could have enquired of my servants. The housekeeper or the steward could have informed her. (p. 241)

This is typical of Fleetwood. Together, his tenderness and his egocentricity lead him up emotional blind alleys: he cannot tell his wife that he wants his room back (she would certainly have understood him, and given up the room with good grace), nor can he be happy in renunciation.

When the two are invited to a dance in the neighbourhood, his feelings reach a new climax of tortured intensity. In an attempt to relieve his pain he manoeuvres his wife into a situation in which, sweet though she is, she becomes exasperated:

"I try every way to please you, but in vain. I ask you for your company; you refuse it. I offer to stay at home; you reproach me with my youth. In the innocence of my heart I name to you a gentleman as my partner, and you insult me. My dear parents! Is my happiness for ever sunk with you in the caverns of the ocean?" (p.251)

Briefly, Fleetwood repents; but he does not really change. He needs to bolster his own ego by placing his wife in a situation in which she is to blame both if she accepts the invitation and if she does not. He is himself in a similar, and worse, emotional *impasse*. Traditional male assertiveness could have offered him a way out, but his sensibility is much too delicate even for mild outbreaks of straightforward aggressiveness. On the other hand, he is completely unable to assume the role of the patient, good-natured husband who is happy to see his wife please herself. His sensibility is, in fact, his prison. He cannot escape from it into a more liberal and better-balanced appreciation of the moral demands of his surroundings; and the oppressiveness of his situation – in his weakness he feels that he must have a complete hold on his wife – makes him a neurotic despot.

A number of minor characters contribute to this discussion of sensibility. The villain, Fleetwood's nephew Gifford (named after the editor of the *Anti-Jacobin*), is far from being insensitive. He is quick to grasp the emotional implications of what he sees; but his psychological acuteness does not make him kind and considerate; it becomes, instead, a tool in his evil designs. Conversely, characters such as Gifford's half-brother Kenrick and the harsh Mr Scarborough can be insensitive or unimaginative, but they are described as basically good.

Altogether, Godwin uses, and examines, the sentimental novel in such a way that ultimately *Fleetwood* moves well beyond this genre. This is due not only to the straightforward discussion of the moral nature of sensibility which the portrait of Fleetwood himself brings out. Mr Scarborough, for instance, is clearly a descendant of Commodore Trunnion; and by including him, Godwin is able to relate the concept of "feeling" to a world like Smollett's. More important are the links which are established between *Fleetwood* and the kind of sensibility explored by Wordsworth in the *Lyrical Ballads*. Godwin had looked hard at this new emotional climate and made up his mind about it.

Not so much on story

Henry Mackenzie reveals an awareness of a problem which was Godwin's, too. In *Julia de Roubigné* Mackenzie is in no doubt about the price he has to pay for sentiment. The alleged editor says about the letters which make up the body of the book: "I found it a difficult task to reduce them into narrative, because they are made up of sentiment, which narrative would destroy."[20] He loves to "read nature in her smallest character", and thinks it best to break up the chronology of the tale in order to keep

> the correspondence of Julia, which communicated the great train of her feelings on the subjects contained in them, as much undivided as possible. . . . I was aware of some advantages which these papers, as relating a story, might derive from an alteration in that particular; but . . . I resolved to give them to the public in the order they were transmitted to me from France. Many of the particulars they recount are anticipated by the perusal of the foregoing letters; but it is not so much on story, as sentiment, that their interest with the reader must depend.[21]

Not so much on story. Mackenzie realises that author and reader alike must accommodate their expectations to a type of novel in which the tempo is slow. From *Fleetwood* onwards, Godwin's fiction cries out in a loud voice for a similar reconsideration. *Fleetwood*, said the crusty reviewer in *The British Critic*, "seems to have been constructed . . . merely to be a vehicle of moral and prudential reflections".[22]

The main story of *Fleetwood* is impeded by two kinds of additions. One, outlined above, is the result of a willingness to describe sentiment at length, a heritage from Richardson, Rousseau, Mackenzie and Sterne (though Godwin fights shy of the whimsical in Sterne which a great many other writers tried to imitate). The other feature that makes for slow reading is a result of Godwin's philosophical bent: he stops to consider intellectual and moral responses not only to domestic crises as in the sentimental novel, but to social, political and psychological issues as well.[23] Such responses cannot simply be classified as "asides". Godwin's fiction is consistently philosophical; the generalising tendency isn't one which is allowed to slip in, perhaps with implicit excuses, here and there. It is an important part of the stuff of which his fiction is made, and though it slows down the narrative, it does add a special intellectual strength to his novels. These are Fleetwood's thoughts about the period in which he surrendered himself "with the best grace I could" into the hands of his fellow students:

As soon, however, as I had chosen my part in the dilemma before me, I became instinct with a principle, from which the mind of ingenuous youth is never totally free, – the principle of curiosity. I was prompted to observe these animals, so different from any that had been before presented to my view, to study their motives, their propensities, and their tempers, the passions of their souls, and the occupations of their intellect . . .

It happened in this, as in all cases of a similar nature, that familiarity annihilated wonder. As the hero is no hero to his *valet-de-chambre*, so the monster is no monster to his friend. Through all the varieties of the human race, however unlike in their prominent features, there are sufficient chords of sympathy, and evidences of a common nature, to enable us to understand each other, and find out the clue to every seeming irregularity. (pp. 20–1)

These paragraphs invite us to be philosophical, to consider this part of the story in the light of our own generalisations about life. But Godwin's commentary may have another function, too: here, for instance, Fleetwood's reflections are motivated by his philosophical tendency, but also by his need to offer an excuse for having been drawn into a behaviour of which he is profoundly ashamed. Quite often, Fleetwood's ruminations on men and manners turn out to be attempts to convince us of the truth of what are in fact vicarious motivations of various kinds; and in this way the commentary adds important shades to the portrait of the hero.

The chapter in which Fleetwood engages in an election can serve as an example of Godwin's excursions into political commentary. There is no Hogarthian emphasis on the actual events. The campaigning is brushed aside in two or three sentences, nor do we follow Fleetwood in his daily work as a Member of Parliament. Godwin concentrates almost entirely on what Fleetwood thinks and feels about political life in England. These reflections may come as a surprise to readers of Godwin's earlier work. Instead of the attack on an aristocratic mode of government which is implicit in the portraits of Falkland and Tyrrel, we now find Fleetwood – who is an authoritative political commentator throughout the novel – echoing Burke:

I saw that the public character of England, as it exists in the best pages of our history was gone. I perceived that we were grown a

commercial and arithmetical nation . . . Some measures in which
I had a part, were of immediate importance to the welfare of
thousands. Some struggles in which I had joined were arduous;
some victories, in which I was one among the conquerors, carried
transport to my heart. I witnessed situations like that which
Burke describes upon the repeal of the American Stamp Act . . .
But these occasions were of rare occurrence; we soon fell back into
the shopkeeping and traffic-trained character I deplored . . . (ii,
pp. 173–4)

This should really give little occasion for surprise. Though Godwin's
basic theories about the principles of government are radically different from Burke's, his practical conclusions are not. When it comes
to day-to-day political decisions, Godwin's cast of radicalism may
sometimes not be very different from the flexible conservatism which
Burke outlines in the *Reflections*.

There is a marked change in political temperature from *Caleb
Williams* to *Fleetwood* and the new kind of commentary is less fervid,
but it is far from being insipid. There is still considerable energy in
Godwin's attempts to show his readers what the duties and rights of
men are; and in one of his insets he breaks new ground as a social
critic. The life story of Fleetwood's elderly friend Ruffigny includes
three chapters on child labour in a silk mill. They represent, says
Professor Kovačević, "the first occurrence in prose fiction of social
criticism directed against the factory system".[24]

These chapters are not great imaginative literature as corresponding scenes were to be in Dickens, who may have taken a hint or two
from *Fleetwood*.[25] Godwin is unable to capture the idiom of a child;
and little Ruffigny's stilted phrases and pedantic behaviour almost
destroy the impact of the scene. What saves it is the ironic structure
of the presentation. Godwin gives us both the sound common sense
of the elderly Ruffigny as he considers his sad childhood and the
extravagant praise which M. Vaublanc, the owner of the mill,
lavishes upon his enterprise. M. Vaublanc is our guide:

"You cannot think," pursued M. Vaublanc, "what an advantage
these mills are to the city of Lyons. In other places, children are a
burthen to their poor parents; they have to support them, till they
are twelve or fourteen years of age, before they can do the least
thing for their own maintenance; here the case is entirely other-

wise. In other places they run ragged and wild about the streets: no such thing is to be seen at Lyons. In short, our town is a perfect paradise. We are able to take them at four years of age, and in some cases sooner. Their little fingers, as soon as they have well learned the use of them, are employed for the relief of their parents, who have brought them up from the breast. They learn no bad habits; but are quiet, and orderly, and attentive, and industrious. What a prospect for their future lives!" (pp. 94–5)

Ruffigny then gives us a description of the place. There was nothing "very cheerful or exhilarating in the paradise we had entered". In bare rooms filled with stunning noise children are employed for nearly twelve hours a day:

There were about twenty on each floor, sixty in all. Their chief business was to attend to the swifts; the usual number being fifty-six which was assigned to the care of each child. The threads . . . were of course liable to break . . . The affair of the child was, by turning round the swift, to find the end, and then to join it to the corresponding end attached to the bobbin. The child was to superintend the progress of these fifty-six threads, to move backward and forward in his little tether of about ten feet, and, the moment any accident happened, to repair it. (p. 96)

By my soul, I am ashamed to tell you by what expedients they are brought to this unintermitted vigilance, this dead life, this inactive and torpid industry! (p. 98)

This factual description serves Godwin's purposes well enough. Nothing is left of Vaublanc's eulogy. But the novel then proceeds to give us a view of childhood which serves as a background for a more theoretical indictment of child labour, too:

Every boy learns more in his hours of play, than in his hours of labour. In school he lays in the materials of thinking; but in his sports he actually thinks: he whets his faculties, and he opens his eyes. The child, from the moment of his birth, is an experimental philosopher: he essays his organs and his limbs, and learns the use of his muscles. . . . But the whole process depends upon liberty.

110

Put him into a mill, and his understanding will improve no more than that of the horse which turns it. (p. 98)

If this is objected to as being an essay in child psychology, and not fiction, Godwin can at least be defended as having given us what, in the England of 1805, was an unorthodox and pioneering account of learning.

Other chapters in *Fleetwood* embody long reflective passages on the vices of undergraduate life, on the dangers and possible benefits of the Grand Tour (Godwin had not made this himself), on Rousseau's life, on the marriage of a "fallen" woman (the admirable Mrs Macneil is one of his many portraits of Mary Wollstonecraft), and on Swiss republicanism. His praise of republicanism is carefully linked with Swiss history so as not to make it obnoxious in England. An evaluation of a literary club has a special interest since Fleetwood's own keen sensibility is of an artistic or literary kind:

I saw also, contrary to the received opinion, that the men of real genius, and who were genuine ornaments of the republic of letters, were always men of liberal tempers, of a certain nobility and disinterestedness of sentiment, and anxious for the promotion of individual and general advantage, however they might sometimes be involved in petty and degrading altercations and disputes.

On the other hand, I must do myself the justice to say, that I discovered many real blemishes and errors in these conversations. The literary men whose acquaintance I could boast, were frequently as jealous of their fame and superiority, as the opulent men, their neighbours, were of the preservation and improvement of their estates. This indeed is but natural: every man who is in any way distinguished from the herd of his species, will of course set no small value upon the thing, whatever it is, to which he is indebted for this distinction. No one who has tasted of honour, would willingly be thrust out among the ignoble vulgar. The only thing which can defend a man against this pitiful jealousy and diseased vigilance, is a generous confidence in his own worth, teaching him that it will find its place without any dishonest and clandestine exertion on his part. The individual who is continually blowing the fire of his own brilliancy, who asserts and denies, is direct or artificial, serious or jocose, not attending to the inspirations of truth and simplicity of heart, but as he thinks may best

111

contribute to advance his reputation, if he can at all be acknowledged for a pleasant companion and associate, is so at least with a very powerful drawback. Such men form to themselves an art in conversation by which they may best maintain the rank in intellect they have acquired. They think little of the eliciting truth, or a conformity to the just laws of equal society, but have trained themselves to a trick, either by an artful interruption, a brutal retort, a pompous, full sounding, and well pronounced censure, or an ingeniously supported exhibition of sarcastic mockery, to crush in the outset the appearance of rivalship, and to turn the admiration of bystanders entirely upon themselves.

. . . I am inclined to believe that no one ever uniformly maintained, in various companies, the first place in subtlety and wit, who has not cultivated this character with dishonest art, and admitted many unmanly and disingenuous subterfuges into the plan by which he pursued it . . . (pp. 167–9)

This shows Godwin both at his best and at his worst as an essayist in fiction. The syntax is sometimes wobbly, and the vocabulary lamely latinate in places. The first paragraph reads like a poor imitation of Johnson. But altogether, this description of literary men is readable and quite convincing in tone: there is a fine balance here between indignation and calm reasoning. On the one hand we find phrases that bring out Fleetwood's emotional involvement. The club is seen through a vulnerable temperament – "dishonest and clandestine exertion", "brutal retort", "sarcastic mockery". On the other, an impression of accuracy and fairness to all is conveyed by the many sub-clauses that refine the main points.

Many of Godwin's digressions can be seen as existing in a kind of magnetic field between sound, generalised commentary and complex, baffling life. But it is necessary to stress again the fact that, by most standards for fiction, Godwin is dangerously fond of generalisations. He is a pleasant essayist; his commentary reveals a writer who is humane, commonsensical, sympathetic to the underdog, independent, well informed and able to find striking examples to bring out his main points. But the essays are too many and too long to leave the reader of a novel at ease. In Godwin's earlier fiction this uneasiness is not felt with the same acuteness. *Caleb Williams* can carry the reader along on a wave of suspense; the moral lessons of *St Leon* are wrapped in horror and thus at one remove from the sober atmosphere of an essay; and in the later *Mandeville* the relationship between teller and tale invites the reader to the kind of exercise which Joyce implies when he makes his Stephen say that in fiction the author, "like the God of creation, remains within or behind or beyond or above his handiwork, invisible". In common with *Rasselas* or *Tom Jones*, *Fleetwood* embodies elements that were not gaining ground in the English novel; but it is interesting to note that another nonconformist, George Eliot, is also a lover of asides in which life can be considered more philosophically than it can in terms of incident and metaphor. Both George Eliot and Godwin were writers who considered "good society" from a distance, and who realised that their main themes were too urgent and too novel to be embodied in traditional stylistic ideals. George Eliot's observation in *The Mill on the Floss* describes Godwin's approach, too:

> In writing the history of unfashionable families, one is apt to fall into a tone of emphasis which is very far from being the tone of good society, where principles and beliefs are not only of an extremely moderate kind, but are always presupposed, no subjects being eligible but such as can be touched with a light and graceful irony. (Book IV, Ch. 3)

The generalising tendency in these two writers can be seen as a result of their development. Protestant nonconformity entails belief in the efficacy of abstract formulations: the right doctrinal profile can only be presented to the world in words. And when nonconformists leave their spiritual home, it is only natural that they feel the need to formulate their new view of life in an analogous style. Moreover, both George Eliot and Godwin became what one can call positivist artists – they wanted their readers to draw conclusions about life on the basis of concrete observations, and for the conclusions to be brought home the cumulative effect of the evidence had to be strong. The philosophical commentary is meant to ensure that the readers relate their reading of the story to their experience of the outside world, which – so both George Eliot and Godwin hope – provides a great many further illustrations of the points made in the novels. The effect is similar to that of Brecht's *Verfremdung*. The spell of fiction is briefly broken by the commentary: the reader's intelligence is exercised; and he can less easily than before compartmentalise the experience of reading so as to reduce it to the level of innocent entertainment.

113

Finally, it must be asked whether Godwin could have saved himself at least half the trouble he took over the reflective passages in *Fleetwood*: isn't the sentimental novel anti-establishment anyway since it always tends to extol the emotional life of an individual who suffers because of the customs and rules of society? Marilyn Butler has suggested that *Julia de Roubigné* is "strikingly radical"; and the *Anti-Jacobin* would agree – in 1798 it published a cartoon in which a personified Sensibility weeps over a little bird and at the same time tramples on the severed head of a king.[26] But Godwin could not build on this view of the genre. For one thing, he probably realised that the sentimental novel in England is not politically subversive at all (the *Anti-Jacobin* does not always aim well in its attacks on potential enemies); the emotions which this genre praises above all others are the meek and mild ones – submission, long-suffering, forgiveness and self-abasement. It therefore makes more sense to see the sentimental novel as an attempt to come to terms, emotionally, with suppression than to read it as an attack on authority. Moreover, since he negates absolute links between sensibility and benevolence, Godwin gives us a sentimental protagonist who cannot possibly serve as an ideal. In fact, stolid conservatives come off better than Fleetwood in the final chapters. Godwin the radical commentator is therefore right when he allows Fleetwood to expatiate on specific political issues; he could not rely on any built-in radicalism in the sentimental features of the story he wrote.

The novel inside the novel

So far, the discussion of *Fleetwood* may have left the impression that Godwin might just as well have written a volume of essays to bring out his main concerns. But the book contains insights which could not have found adequate expression in discursive prose. It embodies a view of life – a dark vision – which the daylight language of moral and political reflection could not attempt to describe. The reader actually finds himself in a world which is not unlike the Congo of Conrad's *Heart of Darkness*. Its nature is suggested by an atmosphere of death and other losses; and its challenge to man is overpowering and sickening. Though the movement of Godwin's tale is slow, it has a poignant rhythm, created by a repetition of shocks to which the hero is exposed. Appropriately, his story begins with the death of his mother and ends with the execution of the young relative in whom he had put his trust. Fleetwood is intelligent and no weakling, but still a prey to the darkness and uncertainty that surrounds him and invades him.

Some of Godwin's digressions acquire a new perspective when related to this theme of deprivation and failure. Fleetwood's account of verbal wit and the art of conversation can now be seen as a pathetic search for a peaceful, intellectual Arcadia and also as an indirect, but urgent defence of his own style of life. It is important for him to give an *apologia pro vita sua* because he somehow knows that his life is not easy to defend.

The tension between the essays on various topics and the actual story of *Fleetwood* should cause no surprise. In this novel, too, God-win is willing to let the sad fate of his hero develop with its own logic, even though the tale may then clash with certain aspects of the commentary on life with which the story is studded. On a number of occasions Godwin may himself have been unaware of the strength of emotional emphases that give his generalities an air of irrelevance. At times I suspect that Godwin knew very well what he was doing, but found comfort in what he had argued in *Political Justice*: in complex civilisations like those of Northern Europe life is too mud-dled to yield easily to philosophical analysis. In any case, this battle between rational reflection and recalcitrant life engenders a special vitality which is one of the basic virtues of Godwin's fiction.

One sentence in Fleetwood's comments on literary clubs is par-ticularly interesting in relation to the rest of the novel: "The only thing which can defend a man against this pitiful jealousy and vigilance, is a generous confidence in his own worth, teaching him that it will find its place without any dishonest and clandestine exertion on his part." This seemingly sound comment is intriguing, for Godwin's fiction insinuates that its wisdom is almost completely beside the point. His characters are not in a position in which they can profit from this advice; either they are flatly incapable of a generous confidence in their own worth, or they find, sometimes to their surprise, that such a confidence does *not* "find its place" in the world. There are only two characters in *Fleetwood* who enjoy a generous – and justifiable – confidence in their own worth, Mr Mac-neil and M. Ruffigny; and of these two, only M. Ruffigny finds that it secures him an honourable place in society. Mr Macneil is happy in his home life, but for all his uprightness he cannot find social acceptance for himself and his family in England. The most memorable characters in Godwin are men who lack a generous belief in their own worth, and its absence is crucial to their fates. Caleb, Falkland, Tyrrel, St Leon, Mandeville, and Fleetwood torture themselves and others because they cannot find this confidence in themselves.

Such studies in pain and defeat lend themselves easily to melodrama, and Godwin is sometimes rather too fond of apostrophe. Fleetwood's soliloquy when he hears that his father is dead can serve as an example:

> My father! my only friend! Where have I been? Losing myself when you stood in need of my consolation! Breaking through every plan that was arranged, loitering away my time among the frivolities and licentiousness of Paris, while you laid down an aching head in solitude, while your pulses failed, and your eyes were closed in darkness! Would to God it were in my power to recal a few past months! – No matter! – My prospects and my pleasures are finished; my life is tarnished; my peace is destroyed . . . (pp. 75–6)

I can find no good excuse for such attempts at the emotional sublime. But Godwin's heroes do not always express their agony in monotonous groans. He is also capable of other approaches to the intense; he can, for instance, bring out emotion indirectly, and forcefully, when he allows his narrator to stand back and give what is apparently a dispassionate account of his own situation. Fleetwood has this to say about his experience of marriage:

> It is human nature, that a man should retain some resentment against the instrument that has often wounded him, however valuable the instrument may be, and however innocent of any purpose to harm. The man, who has repeatedly crossed me in my desires, and has constantly stepped before me in the objects of life, it is morally impossible I should not come to consider as a bad man. It was thus with Mary. Every time she did any thing that jarred with my propensities, – and by some accident or other no day passed without something, greater or smaller, of this kind, – my favourite theory about the female sex revived . . . (p. 263)

The attempt at calm generalisation here and in particular the submerged metaphor by means of which Fleetwood calls his wife an "instrument" bring out the intensity of his egocentricity with greater force than could any number of exclamation marks.

The emotional poverty of Godwin's heroes is linked with a set of circumstances which is important in all his novels – the death or disappearance, actual or metaphorical, of a father. Fleetwood is let loose without guidance in a world which he is not properly prepared for. He says about his life story: "The proper topic of the narrative I am writing is the record of my errors. To write it, is the act of my penitence and humiliation" (p. 7). He *has* been a rash youth, a licentious young man, a misanthrope and a husband blinded by jealousy, but the reader can see that forces outside Fleetwood rushed him towards defeat. In the world of the novel the good people are, on the whole, unable to help. Fleetwood's father was an invalid; M. Ruffigny, who becomes a second father to him, has greater strength of body and mind, but not enough to give Fleetwood an idea of how he could form for himself a rich and creative life. Mr Macneil, his later friend and mentor, is both wise and good, but he is drowned at sea at a time when the daughter he leaves behind and Fleetwood are in desperate need of the kind of advice which he might have given.

The insistence in the novel on loss and bewilderment is not as monotonous as the bare outlines of the story may suggest. Fleetwood is very happy for one month of his life; and Ruffigny's story is one of at least qualified success: he is saved by the combined effects of his own resourcefulness and the intervention of a kind, rich father-figure. But his life is also an illustration of the rapacity of the world. His rightful inheritance is embezzled by an uncle; he has to work in the silk mill; his money is stolen from him on the road; and when he returns from abroad as a rich, middle-aged banker, he finds that his benefactor's family are bankrupt.

Throughout, Fleetwood's situation is made more acute by the absence of any conception of God or nature that might support him. This is surprising. We know that Godwin had been "converted" from atheism to theism in conversations with Coleridge,[27] and the opening of *Fleetwood* makes it clear that Godwin had read Words-worth. The hero's fine sensibility is not only tested and developed among friends and family as in the sentimental novel in the tradition of Richardson. Young Fleetwood responds with equal intensity to his natural surroundings. The first chapter sounds like a prose imitation of Wordsworth. Fleetwood's "earliest years were spent among mountains and precipices, amidst the roaring of the ocean and the dashing of waterfalls" (p. 2). And this is what he remembers:

> Often have I climbed the misty mountain's top, to hail the first beams of the orb of day, or to watch his refulgent glories as he sunk beneath the western ocean. . . . I had a presentiment that the crowded streets and the noisy mart contained larger materials for constituting my pain than pleasure. (p. 2)

He finds, almost in the words of "Tintern Abbey", that "the clouds, the winds, and the streams present us with the image of life, and talk to us of that venerable power which is operating every where, and never sleeps" (p. 3). This is insipid, almost painful, if taken simply as an attempt to emulate Wordsworth. But the passage comes to life when it appears that Godwin in fact launches an attack on the idea of nature which we find in Wordsworth's early poetry. For Fleetwood is not chastened and subdued; his raptures in the mountains are not "matured/Into a sober pleasure". His hikes give rise to day-dreams that are pleasant, but dangerous. This is what happens on his solitary rambles:

> While thus amused, I acquired a habit of being absent in mind from the scene which was before my senses. I devoured at first with greedy appetite the objects which presented themselves; but by perseverance they faded on my eye and my ear, and I sunk into a sweet insensibility to the impressions of external nature. . . . the day-dream . . . is the triumph of man; our invention is full, our complacency is pure; and, if there is any mixture of imbecility or folly in the fable, it is a mixture to which the dreamer at the moment scarcely adverts. The tendency, therefore, of this species of dreaming, when frequently indulged, is to inspire a certain propensity to despotism, and to render him who admits it impatient of opposition and prepared to feel every cross accident, as a usurpation upon his right, and a blot upon his greatness. (pp. 4–5)

In the early Wordsworth the maturing of sense impressions into an harmonious adult mind is often presented as a natural process, inevitable whenever man is placed in the right surroundings. This Hartleyan optimism informs "Expostulation and Reply" and "The Tables Turned":

> 'The eye it cannot chuse but see,
> 'We cannot bid the ear be still;
> 'Our bodies feel, where'er they be,
> 'Against, or with our will.
> . . .
> Let Nature be your teacher.
>
> She has a world of ready wealth,
> Our minds and hearts to bless –
> Spontaneous wisdom breathed by health,
> Truth breathed by chearfulness.[28]

Wordsworth is wise enough to place these rather bald statements in a dramatic situation that gives them an air of playfulness. But similar thoughts can be found in the completely serious "Tintern Abbey":

> . . . Nature never did betray
> The heart that loved her: 'tis her privilege,
> Through all the years of this our life, to lead
> From joy to joy: for she can so inform
> The mind that is within us, so impress
> With quietness and beauty, and so feed
> With lofty thoughts, that neither evil tongues,
> Rash judgements, nor the sneers of selfish men,
> Nor greetings where no kindness is, nor all
> The dreary intercourse of daily life,
> Shall e'er prevail against us, or disturb
> Our cheerful faith that all which we behold
> Is full of blessing.   (ll.123–35)

These lines need not be taken entirely at face value. There is a persistent undertone of sadness and uncertainty in "Tintern Abbey" which modifies the insistence on nature's healing influence. The poet's sadness is so ingrained that nature *disturbs* him with her joy. Still, the optimistic belief in the good influence from vernal woods and Welsh mountains in the early Wordsworth is so insistent that Godwin's reaction becomes understandable and refreshing.[29]

When Fleetwood leaves Wales for Oxford, Paris and London, the "forms of beauty" among which he grew up do *not* remain with him; he does *not* owe to them,

> In hours of weariness, sensations sweet,
> Felt in the blood, and felt along the heart,
> And passing even into my purer mind
> With tranquil restoration. . . .

Godwin's commonsensical attitude to the relationship between youthful country hikes and later life agrees with the sombre view of man's possibilities in his fiction; no benevolent influence from hills and flowers leads man "from joy to joy", as nature is said to do in "Tintern Abbey". Godwin does not attempt to give any philosophical answer to Wordsworth's view of nature; the early chapters of *Fleetwood* find their place not so much in a debate of ideas as in an exploration of climates of feeling. Here an intense meeting between a sensitive youth and the landscape of Wales fails to produce moral strength and joy. Instead, it fosters a tendency to moral solipsism. Here, as elsewhere, Godwin can envisage no useful education outside society, outside that little circle of sympathetic friends in which the young can be given the advice and support they need. But most often, of course, young people in Godwin's novels find themselves in Master Fleetwood's social situation – there is no such society in which they can grow up.

Godwin's psychological insight is limited. The sunny regions of the mind, represented in Walter Scott by upright young men who behave honourably in various conflicts of allegiances, have no geographer in Godwin. The regions that Godwin can describe are those in which promising young men are caught in conflicts which threaten their very selves, not only their first engagement, their inheritance or their chances of a long life. He can describe delicately the twists and turns of this kind of precarious existence. It is interesting to note that Scott reacted against Godwin's view of man. When the Macneils die at sea, their fortune is in the hands of a Genoese banker who, finding that the appropriate documents sank with the family, steals the fortune for himself. Fleetwood helps his future wife in long and difficult proceedings against this man. Scott has this to say about what follows:

It is even hinted, as a reason for which he pressed his marriage with the deserted orphan, that he at length became afraid that, since the question rested on a trial of character betwixt himself and the Genoese, he might himself be suspected of having embezzled her fortune. This is one of the instances of coarseness and bad taste with which Mr Godwin sometimes degrades his characters. . . . Fleetwood, a man of feeling, in soliciting an union pressed upon him by love, by honour, and by every feeling of humanity, is influenced by a motive of remote and despicable calculation, which we will venture to say never entered the head of an honest man in similar circumstances.[30]

In this particular case it is easy to see Scott's limitations and Godwin's shrewd consistency. The world of *Fleetwood* is one in which nearly all motives are mixed simply because the characters lack confidence in themselves. This insecurity creates desperate secondary needs, and one of these is the wish to be thought well of by others which influences Fleetwood at this moment.

Another is possessiveness. In the pages that precede those which Scott mentions in his review there is another twist which he must have disliked. Fleetwood considers the fact that he has experienced "the successive images of my mistress as the possessor of an ample property, and a beggar", and he is honest enough to realise that this has influenced him:

Had Mary entered into my alliance a distinguished heiress, this, in spite of my philosophy, would have commanded from me a certain deference and homage. As she was pennyless, a mere pensionary on my bounty, – I swear I did not value her less, – I felt more tenderness, more humanity, a more religious kind of forbearance towards her. But the sentiment was of a different sort; her first claim was upon my pity. . . . When I waited upon her as an heiress, I approached her with a certain submission; I looked at her as an independent being . . . (p. 223)

Fleetwood reveals more here than he realises himself.[31] There *is* no flagging of tenderness and there is more intimacy when she belongs to him also economically, for what he really wants is not "an independent being" as a wife, but somebody who can be his other self because he has, in one sense, none himself. His thinking about

121

her fortune is of a piece with the jealousy which features so prominently in the action of the third volume. It makes sense that Godwin avoids a situation in which Mrs Fleetwood is torn between two men. If she had been placed in Julia de Roubigné's predicament, Fleetwood's jealousy would be seen as justified by the divided feelings of his wife; but Godwin presents a situation in which the husband's misgivings are a result only of his own sad lack of inner security.

Fleetwood's total inability towards the end of the novel to see for himself and act on his own is another indication of his hollowness. That he should go almost mad is natural in that his wild ravings make up a frantic attempt to assume another, and bolder, personality than the tortured but honest and well-meaning one which is never completely forgotten, and which enables him to survive.

Godwin's next novel, *Mandeville*, examines more closely the relationship between individual breakdowns and large-scale cruelty and injustice. In *Fleetwood* there are only a handful of rather bald indications of such an awareness. The story takes us to France where Fleetwood becomes a victim of *ancien régime* frivolity; later, a stay in Switzerland gives him a chance to recuperate and to admire Swiss freedom, industry and common sense; and the hero's name combines references to a protégé of Cromwell and to an early eighteenth-century Bishop of Ely who preached forbearance and tolerance;[32] but the novel does not really establish any close links between the fortunes of the hero and the history of Europe at the time.

Fleetwood is a novel in which the emphases change in the course of the reading. What looks like a fairly straightforward attack on the "old" man of feeling, an attack enlivened by a brisk commentary on social conditions and manners, becomes a story which evokes a destructive world in which moral commentary is largely beside the point. Godwin's preface suggests that he was himself aware of a change in the course of his work on the novel. He began in social realism: "the following story consists of such adventures, as for the most part have occurred to at least half of the Englishmen now existing" (p. xv). He prides himself that he describes common incidents which, though of daily occurrence, have not previously been within the range of fiction. But he himself realised that he did not follow this plan to the end, as we see in a curious footnote to the preface: "I confess however the inability I found to weave a catastrophe, such as I desired, out of these ordinary incidents. What I have here said therefore, must not be interpreted as applicable to the concluding sheets of my work" (p. xv).

Happily, this change is not just a result of Godwin's "inability". The tempo rises and uncommon things happen, but the reader can take this in his stride without feeling that the unity of the narrative is impaired. For without realising this fully himself, Godwin releases pressures in the last volume which have been built up earlier. The violent and uncommon events towards the end are proper images for the kind of life – brutal, predatory, and often unpredictable – which we have been acquainted with all along.

There is, ultimately, a contradiction implied in this story, but not one which destroys novels: like *Caleb Williams*, *Fleetwood* suggests two ways in which life can be perceived and considered. One is suggested by the material which Godwin's preface insists that he presents. Daily life must be observed closely; and what you observe can then be used as material for commonsensical, rational thinking. The results are shown to be encouraging – you can suggest improvements in university life, in sexual morality, in intellectual exchanges, and in politics.[33] But, and this is what the last volume in particular brings out with considerable force, in important crises this process of careful observation and rational thinking is felt to be completely irrelevant. Life does not always place us in situations in which we can assess our surroundings in this clear and commonsensical way. We are sometimes blind to facts, even though they may loom large in the landscape, as well as to the moral rules which we should have been able to extract from our observations. And we do not always think of ourselves as responsible moral and intellectual beings.

This is a question not only about the immediate feel of life, but also about language. In the last chapters of the third volume Fleetwood's disorientation, his intense pain and bouts of madness, or near-madness, necessitate another style than that of calm reflection. When the writing of his memoirs takes him to the nadir of his fortunes, Fleetwood re-experiences how completely he failed, and as a consequence his tendency to generalise disappears almost completely. Instead, the story proceeds in terms of violent action and ritual. In his loneliness and misery he has wax models made of his wife and of the man he believes to be her seducer; and on the aniversary of his wedding he sits down with these two in his room:

I gazed at the figure of Mary; I thought it was, and it was not,

Mary. With mad and idle action, I put some provisions on her plate; I bowed to her in mockery, and invited her to eat. Then again I grew serious and vehement; I addressed her with inward and convulsive accents, in the language of reproach; I declaimed, with uncommon flow of words, upon her abandoned and infernal deceit; all the tropes that imagination ever supplied to the tongue of man, seemed to be at my command. I know not whether this speech was to be considered as earnest, or as the Sardonic and bitter jest of a maniac. But, while I was still speaking, I saw her move – if I live, I saw it. She turned her eyes this way and that; she grinned and chattered at me. I looked from her to the other figure; that grinned and chattered too. Instantly a full and proper madness seized me; I grinned and chattered, in turn, to the figures before me. It was not words that I heard or uttered; it was murmurs, and hissings, and lowings, and howls. I became furious. . . . I rent the child-bed linen, and tore it with my teeth. I dragged the clothes which Mary had worn, from off the figure that represented her, and rent them into long strips and shreds. I struck the figures vehemently with the chairs and other furniture of the room, till they were broken to pieces. (pp. 334–5)

There are echoes of the Last Supper here, and hints of cannibalism; and the language of the whole incident is that of fetishism. Fleetwood offers "his wife" food, reproaches her; she "grins"; he breaks her to pieces. She does not eat; he digs his teeth in the "child-bed linen". It is important to realise that Fleetwood has not really become a different man; indeed, this scene very neatly summarises his emotional development in the last months. But the experience of this anniversary – both the immediate taste of gall and wormwood, and Fleetwood's bitter memory of hellish violence as he writes this part of his memoirs – could only be brought out in a new style. And there is no immediate return to the old: the rest of the novel is told in curt summary, in dialogue, and in a report by the blunt Mr Scarborough. The attempt to render life in a sophisticated blend of sensibility and reflection has broken down. This earlier style reappears only in a brief glimpse on the very last page when Fleetwood has been brought back to his family. Then, it reminds us that the old Fleetwood is not completely destroyed; he may be able to rebuild a new existence on the ruins of the old.

It is possible to make sense of this last scene only when the narrative point of view is thought of as three-fold: we listen to Fleetwood as he goes virtually mad, to the older Fleetwood who writes about the incident, and to Godwin as author. But the novel does not consistently offer its readers such exciting richness in perspectives. In Godwin's next novel the reader knows where he is all the time: *Mandeville* invites – and rewards – a search for a meaning which can be found only when tale and teller are consistently judged against each other by a reader who takes neither for granted. But in *Fleetwood* the role of the narrator is sometimes confusing. Quite often, there is an interesting interaction between commentary and story, and between immediate experience and the writing down of the memoirs; but other parts of the book are simpler and can be read only on the flat assumption that there is no distinction what-soever between protagonist, narrator and author. This kind of flat-ness does not affect the last chapters. In these we find another powerful manifestation of what was the central ambiguity in God-win's fiction from the nineties. Throughout the book Godwin the philosopher has joined hands with the Fleetwood who tries, albeit unsuccessfully at times, to master life by means of rational cerebra-tion; then, in the last volume the personality of what I have called the other Godwin appears, and the language of strange ritual be-comes the only one in which his insights can be rendered.

This ambiguity is less persistent in this novel than in *Caleb Wil-liams*; and an important reason is surely Godwin's interest in an area of life which is not immediately metaphysical in its implications – domestic troubles. *Fleetwood* gives us a particularly fine account of a marriage; the episodes in which Fleetwood's intelligent and fragile sensibility clashes with the demands of a good young wife seem to me to be just as shrewd and moving as a great many studies of marriage that have become famous in literary history. But in God-win's own interest one's praise of these chapters should perhaps be guarded. In his whole career as a novelist this kind of excellence represents the exception rather than the rule. Generally, his fiction relies on other things than domestic realism for its stories to come alive.

VI

Mandeville:
History and Madness

HAMLET: I am but mad north-north-west. When the wind is
southerly, I know a hawk from a handsaw.

Mandeville, Godwin's third novel after *Caleb Williams*, appeared in
the autumn of 1817. Godwin, who was then sixty-one, felt that this
would be his last novel: "Approaching, as I now very rapidly do, to
the period when I must bid the world an everlasting farewel, I am
not unwilling to make up my accounts with it, as far as relates to this
lighter species of composition".[1] His life gives an ironic perspective
to this presentiment; he lived to a ripe eighty and wrote two more
novels. But in one way he was right in his feelings about the future;
Mandeville is the last novel from his pen which impresses by its
originality. It was written in a troubled period of his life. The
Juvenile Library was bankrupt; and Shelley, who had eloped with
Mary in 1814, decided in 1816 that he would no longer support this
father-in-law who denounced the elopement and asked for money at
the same time. In late 1816 there were two suicides, first that of
Fanny Wollstonecraft Imlay. Fanny had been a kind stepdaughter
who got on well even with the second Mrs Godwin whose maternal
feelings rarely reached beyond her own children. Then, a month
later, Harriet Shelley, who was well known to the Godwins,
drowned herself in the Serpentine. The year ended with the marriage, in a London church, of Shelley and Mary. Godwin "appeared
to feel no little satisfaction", said the bridegroom in a wry letter to
Claire Clairmont.[2] But although it must have been a great relief
(even to a father who had expressed radical views on marriage) to
see Mary made an honest woman, the wedding probably reminded
Godwin of what he had lost. This daughter was the issue of what he

thought of as an intensely happy marriage, and the ties between father and daughter had always been strong. Now she had definitely left him. It is not difficult to see that this period in Godwin's own life could provide energy to the description of the way in which Mandeville clings to Henrietta who, to his despair, marries a brilliant young man.

The full title of the novel is *Mandeville. A Tale of the Seventeenth Century in England.* The Mandevilles are an old English Protestant family, and the story begins in Ireland in 1641 when Charles Mandeville is three years old. His parents (his father, a younger son, is an officer) are among those massacred by Sir Phelim O'Neile's troops in the rising of that year, but the child is rescued by a faithful Irish maid. He is later torn from her kind arms by another survivor, the chaplain of his father's regiment. This clergyman is a man of principle who would rather see the child slaughtered than nursed by a Roman Catholic. Mandeville then lives for nine years on the south coast of England with an uncle to whose immense estates he is heir presumptive. The uncle is a feeble valetudinarian; the chaplain who had brought him to the country of the faithful becomes his tutor; and little Mandeville is never allowed to live the natural life of a young boy. At the end of this period the tutor dies and Mandeville is sent to Winchester. On his way there he spends a delightful week with his sister Henrietta, who has been brought up by a friend of their mother's, a lady richly endowed with the warmth, sensibility and commonsense that have been so conspicuously absent in Mandeville's own upbringing. At Winchester Mandeville meets Clifford, who shines like a sun over the other boys. Clifford comes from a very poor branch of an old family, but he never complains; he is always honest, kind, active, articulate, happy, and popular. Mandeville feels, correctly enough, that his own intellectual resources are greater than Clifford's – why should he then be outshone? His dislike of Clifford grows into hatred when some years later they meet in an insurrection against Cromwell in which Mandeville acquires a largely undeserved reputation as a traitor to the royalist cause. From time to time Mandeville's mind now becomes seriously disturbed and he suffers a dangerous shock when he finds that Henrietta, his only friend, is engaged to Clifford, who now, in addition to all his other good qualities, has acquired the indispensable one of wealth. He has also become a Roman Catholic – a fact which enables Mandeville to complete his picture of him as a Lucifer. When Mandeville learns that the marriage is about to take place, he endeavours unsuccessfully to forestall it. His defeat is final; he spends the rest of his life in embittered solitude, his only relief being the writing of his gloomy memoirs.

Mandeville was only a moderate success when it appeared. The first edition was followed by two editions in America and a translation into French, but there are no editions after 1818.[3] The notices reveal a kind of bafflement conspicuous also in the case of Godwin's earlier novels. Nearly all the reviewers find moments of successful intensity and great strength, but a number of them are nevertheless exasperated. Some complain about monotony of tone; a great many find fault with Godwin's morality. The reviewer in the *Quarterly* summed up his impression by calling *Mandeville* "a very dull novel and a very clever book".[4] Shelley read his father-in-law's novel as soon as it appeared. He did not find it dull and sent Godwin an enthusiastic thank-you letter (the glibness of which was probably unintentional and unconscious):

> I have read Mandeville. . . . the interest is of that irresistible & overwhelming kind, that the mind in it's influence is like a cloud borne on by an impetuous wind, like one breathlessly carried forward . . . Caleb Williams never shakes the deepest soul like Mandeville. . . . In style and strength of expression Mandeville is wonderfully great . . .[5]

It is not difficult, even for a reader who can appreciate Shelley's eulogy, to see some of the reasons why dust has been allowed to settle on the book. Its seriousness is monotonous, the story is often slow-moving, and Godwin's style has not become livelier over the years. But both style and events are given a special twist by the fact that the narrator, who is also the main character, is only partly sane. A case can be made for seeing *Mandeville* as a novel which unites political commentary, a sense of history and a *vae victis* theme in a story of considerable complexity and compassion.

Scott and Godwin

As usual, Godwin gives an account of his debts in the preface:

> Every author, at least for the last two thousand years, takes his hint from some suggestion afforded by an author that has gone

before him . . . and I do not pretend to be an exception to this rule. The impression, that first led me to look with an eye of favour upon the subject here treated, was derived from a story-book, called Wieland, written by a person, certainly of disting-uished genius . . . who calls himself C. B. Brown. This impression was further improved from some hints in De Montfort, a tragedy, by Joanna Baillie. Having signed these bills against me, I hold myself for the present occasion discharged from all claims of my literary creditors, ... (pp. ix–x)

Godwin is true to his habits as a novelist also in making these acknowledgements something of a red herring. His private papers reveal the fact that there is a glaring omission in the list. In the Abinger MSS (Bodleian microfilm reels nos. 72–3) we can follow Godwin on a visit to Sir Walter Scott at Abbotsford in April 1816. He then read both *Guy Mannering* and *The Antiquary* in the next month, on the last day of which he began the writing of *Mandeville*.[6] On April 30 he had written to his wife: "Would you have the indulgence for me to have the first volume of 'Guy Mannering' in the house against my return, to serve me, if God so pleases, in the nature of a muse?"[7]

The early Waverley novels did serve Godwin in the nature of a muse. Indeed, this kind of historical fiction was a real windfall. Godwin had himself written historical works in which he had taken pains to describe the relationship between an individual and his age (as in the *Life of Chaucer*); and his sense of history, and knowledge of history, had been further developed in the course of the years in which he had written history books for the Juvenile Library. *St Leon* and *Fleetwood* had both been historical at least in the sense that the setting was not Godwin's own day, and in the former the Reforma-tion is described as a period which in certain ways resembles the 1790s.[8] In Scott he now found a kind of fiction which strengthened his belief that he could project the political problems of the second decade of the nineteenth century into an earlier period where they could be treated with great freedom. Scott showed the way; it was possible to give a trustworthy and comprehensive account of a period in the history of your own country inside the covers of a novel. It is ironic and sad that this idea of a realistic – a non-Gothic and English – historical novel matured in Godwin's mind as late as it did. It would have been the best form, it seems, in which the political philosopher might have been able to go on writing fiction in the troubled period after *Caleb Williams*.

However, Godwin makes good use of it in *Mandeville*, which is set in a period of Civil War. Scott's method – to link the fortunes of the characters with the rises and falls of political groups – becomes Godwin's, too. From the early nineties Godwin had been a keen student of the seventeenth century;[9] and Charles Mandeville is formed by the Irish Rising of 1641, by the heated religious controversies in the 1640s and by the Civil War. No lives are private in *Mandeville* in the sense that they can be lived unaffected by historical movements. Like Scott, Godwin creates a main character who is neither a prince nor a poor man. By birth and fortune Mandeville is placed in a position in which he must very soon be enmeshed by the political struggles of the time. But he is not a figure that we can read about in history books. As in Scott, it is only the minor characters that are historical in this literal sense.

Godwin's account of mid-seventeenth century England focusses on the contention between Presbyterians and Roman Catholics. Scott's *Old Mortality* appeared in 1816, too late to influence Godwin's choice of subject for *Mandeville*, but Godwin must have noted with great interest that the new novel from Scotland could be read as a large-scale examination of religious and political bigotry and zeal. Not that Godwin needed help on this score. He is always authoritative and precise when he describes the growth of political and denominational extremism, and *Mandeville* gives a subtle and forceful account of the ways in which religious zeal, and even mania, provide fuel to civil outrages of various kinds. Mandeville himself is driven into a situation in which, in order not to be completely overpowered by despair or hysteria, he must think of himself as one of the righteous few, a Presbyterian who must never compromise in the all-important, good war against Rome. On one occasion both Mandeville and Clifford are guests in the same house; and when Clifford, much against his inclinations, is pressed by the host to tell the party how he rescued his commanding officer after a defeat in the Civil War, Mandeville is tortured with envy and with memories of his own humiliating dismissal by the same commander. This is how Mandeville winds up his reflections on Clifford afterwards:

> I see the falseness of his eye, personating all softness, all tenderness, all consideration for another . . . I see the insidious curl of

that lip, that to a discerning eye expresses volumes. The sound of his voice makes me start again with the hollowness and treachery of its cadences. Yes, I feel an instinctive antipathy to the wretch: but it is the voice of God, warning me of my danger; it is founded upon reasons and indications as infallible as the pillars of creation. He has indeed a superficial grace, well adapted to ensnare the thoughtless and unwary, that thinly veils his Satanic soul. (ii, pp. 206–7)

Godwin's novel, which is not rich in minor characters, includes a number of studies in analogous situations. Hilkiah, the tutor, is the greatest bigot of all, but honest according to his lights, while Holloway and Mallison, who are hollow and evil, use bigotry for their private ends. We find models of tolerance and benevolence in Henrietta, Mrs Willis and Clifford. In those who fight for the King in the West of England Godwin gives us further studies in degrees of dogmatism, portraits that remind us how complex the relationship between abstract principles and muddled, real life can be.[10] Godwin is aware of the fact that bigotry and fanaticism do not make up absolute entities, but express defence mechanisms and protests varying from group to group and from period to period.

Parallels between English history from 1630 to 1660 and Godwin's own day are conspicuous in *Mandeville*. Godwin had experienced the hardening of the political climate in the 1790s. He had been forced to realise that there was no quiet corner to be found for the philosopher; the political thinker who strenuously advocated evolution was denounced as a dangerous revolutionary. Even his chances to earn a living by his pen were drastically reduced; fewer than before had the courage or the inclination to buy a book by Godwin for their library. Godwin was thus in a situation in which he could appreciate at close quarters the ways in which political combatants become bigoted or find it expedient to make use of bigotry to gain their ends. The political situation in 1815–16 looked like a repetition of the nineties. Radical clubs were formed again in England after the fall of Napoleon; strikes occurred in the new industry, and machinery was destroyed here and there in the North. The government answered in 1816–17 by suspending the Habeas Corpus Act and by forbidding "seditious meetings".[11] It was in this political climate that *Mandeville* was planned and written.

Scott had seen that the unscrupulous and clever often thrive on civil struggles in which their own greed can pass unnoticed or be disguised as political zeal. The Waverley novels offer a number of examples of this kind of astuteness. In *Guy Mannering* the thriftless old laird, Mr Bertram, is cheated of his land by his cunning agent. Godwin takes up the idea of the faithless steward and lets Mr Holloway ingratiate himself with old Mandeville and then with his nephew by weaving a net of lies around these invalids. In Scott and Godwin alike, these agents destroy the domestic happiness of their employers.

However, in spite of these obvious similarities between Scott's first novels and *Mandeville*, Godwin can defend himself against the imputation of an unacknowledged debt to his Scottish colleague. He did take over the idea – and hoped to share in the popularity – of the historical novel, but Godwin is too English to care for the particular clash of cultures that informs the Waverley novels. And what is more important, the whole movement of *Mandeville* is different from that of Scott's novels. An early nineteenth-century reader who jotted critical comments in the margin of my copy of Godwin's novel was exasperated when he read the last page: "instead of *ending*, it breaks off in the middle, why are not the two lawyers exposed and punished – ". This reader expected the kind of rounding-off which Scott very carefully provides. In the Waverley novels the villains are properly punished and reward distributed according to desert. There is something communal about the concluding chapters in Scott: the main characters are established in their proper places in relation to public categories such as nation, rank, party and wealth. In contrast, Godwin's broad picture of seventeenth-century England leads up to a study of one single individual who is being maimed by the march of history. This movement is epitomised in the fact that the book ends with Mandeville's description of his own disfigured face:

> The sight of my left eye is gone; the cheek beneath is severed, with a deep trench between. My wound is of that sort, which in the French civil wars got the name *une balafre*. I have pleased myself, in the fury and bitterness of my soul, with tracing the whole force of that word. It is *cicatrix luculenta*, a glazed, or shining scar, like the effect of a streak of varnish upon a picture. *Balafré* I find explained by Girolamo Vittori, by the Italian word *smorfiato*; and this again – I mean the noun, *smorfia* – is decided by "the reso-

lute" John Florio, to signify "a blurting or mumping, a mocking or push with one's mouth." The explanation of these lexicographers is happily suited to my case, and the mark I for ever carry about with me. (iii, p. 365)

The hideous grin on the face is reflected in the style, in the sickly jocularity of this interest in lexicography. The whole description is the product of a mind partly diseased; and it would have been entirely out of character for this narrator to give us the calm survey of the histories of heroes and villains normally found in Scott's concluding chapters.

Godwin's independence and honesty (and perhaps his masochism as well) are seen also in the way in which he places himself in relation to his novel. As George Lukács has noticed, Scott's novels consistently approve of the developments which resulted in the political climate in which Scott himself throve.[12] It is not difficult to see the close links between the commonsense, decency, kindness and flexible conservatism of Colonel Talbot, Colonel Mannering and Mr Pleydell on the one hand and Scott's own ideals on the other. Godwin was not a successful professional man and author. He was looked upon as an outsider, and he makes an outsider the centre of interest in his novel. Mandeville must not be thought of as Godwin's *alter ego* in any simple or straightforward sense, but it is not difficult to imagine the ways in which Godwin's isolation gave him experiences out of which he could fashion Mandeville's loneliness and envy. Against this background we can see Godwin as having paid with his own tears for the considerable victory which this novel is: we are given a disturbingly convincing and original portrait of a loser.

The fact that Godwin narrows down his novel so that in the end it becomes a study of the mind of one person only, does not make the book less historical. It might even be argued that Godwin is more true to history than Scott in that *Mandeville* does without the network of influences which Scott's *dei ex machina* – his imitable and fascinating, but not always plausible, beggars and gypsies – represent. To include characters functioning in the same way as Meg Merrilies and Edie Ochiltree would be for Godwin to accept a frequency of coincidences and a pattern of justice and benevolence which to him would seem unhistorical. The characters in *Mandeville* who are caught up by great political events are not saved from the inexorable movement of history, nor from their private follies, by Colonel Talbots or by noble and friendly beggars. This is not to say, of course, that Scott's novels falsify history and Godwin's do not. The thing to note is that Godwin remained true to *his* conception of the relationship between history and individuals when he imitated the broad outlines of the form which Scott had made popular. It is unfortunate that Lukács did not read *Mandeville*. If he had, he might have found a highly appropriate object for much of the praise which *The Historical Novel* lavishes on *Ivanhoe*.

The teller and the tale

Most readers of Godwin's preface to *Mandeville* will be surprised to find no mention of Scott, but it is equally surprising that the first book Godwin does mention as a source is *Wieland*, Charles Brockden Brown's novel about mysterious and marvellous incidents that are finally shown to have been the results of electric discharges and ventriloquism. Brown was an admirer of *Caleb Williams* and *Political Justice*; and Godwin may have like *Wieland* because he found some of his own thoughts reflected in it;[13] but Brown's horror is not of Godwin's kind. In *Wieland* a fair maid hears strange and menacing voices in her lonely room (behind which there is a dark closet); and footsteps are heard on the landing in the night. Godwin had used elements from this kind of Gothicism in the very early *Imogen*. But Radcliffean terror, experienced by a beautiful, noble and virtuous young lady, is not an ingredient which Godwin makes use of in his later books. At sixty-one he found *Wieland* fascinating because of the other centre of interest in it: the last chapters make up a study in religious mania. The noble and erudite Wieland hears the voice of God, commanding him to kill his beloved wife and children. Against his better feelings he must obey this summons; and he exults afterwards that he has been obedient to his master. *Wieland* does not observe madness from the inside as Godwin's novel does, and the account it gives of its development is sketchy; but the link Brockden Brown establishes in his story between religious belief and fanatical outrage as well as his incidental hints about a psychological explanation of madness must have seemed particularly useful to Godwin.

The close connection which Godwin creates between *envy* and madness was not suggested by *Wieland*, but by the other source Godwin mentions, Joanna Baillie's *De Montfort*.[14] The brother-sister-antagonist situation in *Mandeville* echoes Joanna Baillie's tragedy; and Godwin copies the ironic situation in which what looks like a disinterested plea for friendship becomes suspect in the eyes of the protagonist. (Shelley disliked this irony in *Mandeville*. In the letter quoted above he wishes that Henrietta's angelic plea for love and friendship had remained unquestioned.) Moreover, there is a fierce egotism in both De Montfort and Mandeville which flavours both stories. Neither character has a moral sense strong enough to save the mind from being overwhelmed by envy. Godwin probably called his main character Mandeville to remind us of another writer who had little belief in man's essential benevolence, Bernard Mandeville, whose *The Fable of the Bees* was thought of as a misanthrope's answer to Shaftesbury. But Godwin goes beyond *De Montfort* in letting the sister actually fall in love with the antagonist; and in *Mandeville* the portraits of all three characters are contained in the memoirs written by one of them. This change in perspective is important: Godwin is primarily interested in how one character experiences life, not in an analysis of envy presented in a dramatic mode.[15]

What Godwin realises very clearly in *Mandeville* is the fact that envy, as well as madness, cannot be presented simply as a way of feeling or thinking, it is inseparable from a certain way of *seeing*. Therefore, he chose a narrative technique in which he could avoid the objectivity of a stage presentation.[16] In this novel we are placed in a situation in which we see with Mandeville, who is the writer of the story, all the time; but we are not asked to accept his vision of life. The novel invites the reader to experience a basic and consistent tension between the actual incidents and the *way* the story is told.

This tension – recognised, no doubt, by most readers – is also indispensable. Looking back, Mandeville has this to say about his house on the south coast of England:

The whole situation was eminently insalubrious. . . . we had to the west a long bank of sand, and in different directions various portions of bog and marshy ground, sending up an endless succession of vapours . . . For a great part of the year we were further involved in thick fogs and mists, to such a degree as often to render the use of candles necessary even at noonday. (i, pp. 49–50)

The reviewer who, in the name of truth, objected to this description of the pleasant coast of Devonshire,[17] missed a vital point: Mandeville is no unbiassed witness, and is not meant to be. It is for the reader to sift the evidence which he provides.

This is a task which Godwin has not made at all easy. There is an uncertainty in the novel for which the author is clearly to blame: he could at times forget that the story comes to the readers through Mandeville's pen. The criticism of the clergy on page 39 in the first volume is Godwin's; it jars as a part of Mandeville's memoirs. Only one page earlier the moral commentary had come indirectly and therefore naturally when Mandeville calls the chaplain, that truly destructive character, "a man of the utmost integrity and purity of heart". But the occasional slip on Godwin's part does not destroy his strategy: he manages to establish Mandeville as a trustworthy narrator in the first pages and then by degrees to force the question of Mandeville's sanity on the reader.

As he writes his story down, Mandeville is never stark mad. It is important that he should not be, for the novel as a whole is an exercise in awareness of how sanity and madness can coexist in the human mind and of how blurred the line between the two can be. The following is taken from a relatively calm period in Mandeville's life:

> One thing I determined on, – that I would see Clifford no more. The world was wide enough for both of us. Let him, the beggar! hide himself in his hovel; let him keep far from the terrace, where I mean to tread! I was in some degree improved, from the latest feelings I experienced at Winchester School. No; I would do him no harm! I retained still so much of Henrietta's philosophy. The world was stored with a thousand blessings! The splendours of prosperity offered themselves to my acceptance. What would not wealth purchase? What might not talents achieve? All I asked was, that Clifford would stand out of my sun. That surely was a small matter. If by fair means he would not yield to this, I might obtain it by force. (ii, p. 211)

Is this madness? One simple answer is that this trend of thinking on Mandeville's part is a clear indication of his morbid paranoia. A man in his right mind would not believe that his happiness depended on the removal of *one* man from the country. As early as in

Caleb Williams Godwin shows how false and dangerous such a belief can be: both Tyrrel and Falkland find themselves in situations when they cannot rise above this kind of delusion. But in *Mandeville* another and equally important point is brought out by the story as a whole: Charles Mandeville's scheme is not unlike certain political and private strategies commonly used by non-certified (and by ordinary standards non-certifiable) people. Mandeville's uncle believes that he can exist in total isolation from mankind, but he is not mad. Similarly, the carnage in Ireland that opens the first volume was an inhuman attempt on the part of O'Neile and his followers to remove those who stood in their way, but historians would call these men ruthless politicians, not madmen. In the novel their cruelty is shown to be the natural consequence of large-scale ideological and military warfare. Mandeville is at his most lucid and convincing when he tries to explain the slaughter of English prisoners:

> The British, circumstanced as they were, were hated as heretics, and despised, because they were in the power of their enemies, and could make no retaliation to any contumely that might be heaped upon them. Insult went first, and plunder speedily followed. The Irish took from the fugitives the valuables they were carrying away with them; they next stripped them of their clothes. . . . The unhappy wretches, who were suffering every species of privation and inconvenience, could not always help, in the bitterness of their hearts, reproaching their conductors with perfidy, who had first disarmed them on the faith of the most solemn engagements, and now took advantage of their helpless condition to rob them of all that remained to them. The Irish, in the topics of heresy, and the assured damnation of their victims in another world, found copious matter for recrimination. From words they proceeded to blows. (i, pp. 24–5)

The novel thus makes it quite clear that though Mandeville may have to be censured as bigoted, envenomed, unstable, and, for at least one particular period, completely crazy, his outrages and his hatred are insignificant compared with certain atrocities committed by the "sane".

A general interest in madness was, of course, widespread in Godwin's own day, and he could scarcely avoid thinking about some of the important issues that were raised. The King, George III, was insane when Godwin wrote *Mandeville*; and his condition had been an important public issue both at the time of his first attack in 1788–9 and after 1811 when his insanity became permanent.[18] Dr Willis's successful treatment of the King in 1789 contributed to a new interest in psychiatry. Samuel Tuke's influential *Description of the Retreat* appeared in 1813; in 1815 a Parliamentary Committee was set up to investigate alleged abuses in mental hospitals.[19] Godwin may have found food for thought in Tuke's treatise which refuses to see the insane person as utterly irresponsible:

> Insane persons generally possess a degree of control over their wayward propensities. Their intellectual, active, and moral powers, are usually rather perverted than obliterated; and it happens, not unfrequently, that one faculty only is affected. The disorder is sometimes still more partial, and can only be detected by erroneous views, on one particular subject. On all others, the mind appears to retain its wonted correctness.[20]

Godwin had of course seen similar questions asked about madness in *Hamlet* and *King Lear*; and Brockden Brown's *Wieland* illustrates this point, too: Wieland himself is a model of reasonableness, kindness and responsibility; it is only in his one paranoiac idea that God wants him to kill his family that his insanity manifests itself. But Godwin's picture is less clear-cut than Brown's for the very reason that Godwin presents more complex situations in which any *simple* classification of actions as either sane or insane becomes impossible. Therefore he gives us a series of thoughts and incidents in *Mandeville* that we can range from stark frenzy to calm rationality without telling us exactly where the line is to be drawn between normal and abnormal.

In the Retreat which Samuel Tuke describes the superintendents tried to reason with the patients whenever their condition made this possible. The patient was told that as long as he was tolerably successful in controlling his symptoms, he would be treated with respect and kindness. Tuke's "moral treatment", as he called it, marks a great step towards mildness and humanity in the care of mental patients.[21] Tuke is insistent that lunatics must be treated, not as animals or criminals, but as human beings who, even in their illness, may be able to consider appeals to their rationality and feelings of responsibility. In this kind of treatment there may, however, be a subtle torture which patients who are treated as stark mad do not experience. In *Madness and Civilization* Michel Foucault describes the new therapeutic situation:

> Here fear is addressed to the invalid directly, not by instruments but in speech; there is no question of limiting a liberty that rages beyond its bounds, but of marking out and glorifying a region of simple responsibility where any manifestation of madness will be linked to punishment. The obscure guilt that once linked transgression and unreason is thus shifted . . .
>
> We must therefore re-evaluate the meanings assigned to Tuke's work: liberation of the insane, abolition of constraint, constitution of human milieu – these are only justifications. The real operations were different. In fact, Tuke created an asylum where he substituted for the free terror of madness the stifling anguish of responsibility; fear no longer reigned on the other side of the prison gates, it now raged under the seals of conscience. Tuke now transferred the age-old terrors in which the insane had been trapped to the very heart of madness. The asylum no longer punished the madman's guilt, it is true; but it did more, it organize that guilt; it organized it for the madman as a consciousness of himself, and as a non-reciprocal relation to the keeper . . .[22]

Godwin and Brown could not express their ideas about the nature of madness in a twentieth-century existentialist language like Foucault's, but they tried to express an insight which is related to his. In *Wieland* the wise Mr Cambridge listens to his niece who wants to visit her brother in prison after the murder of his wife and children:

> "If it be a mere fit of insanity that has seized him, may not my presence chance to have a salutary influence? The mere sight of me, it is not impossible, may rectify his perceptions."
>
> "Ay," said my uncle, with some eagerness; "it is by no means impossible that your interview may have that effect; and for that reason, beyond all others, would I dissuade you from it. . . . Has he not destroyed the wife whom he loved, the children whom he idolized? What is it that enables him to bear the remembrance, but the belief that he acted as his duty enjoined?"[23]

That the worst possible torture for Wieland would be a full awareness of his own insanity – to feel responsible for his violent acts – is
shown later when the poor maniac is disillusioned: then his despair
is unbearable, and he commits suicide. Brockden Brown's treatment
of this situation is melodramatic (and quite successful as such);
Godwin's approach is different: he shows us the protagonist torn
between two interpretations of himself. At times Mandeville can
realise his own unreasonableness and the decency and kindness of
Clifford; on other occasions Clifford is thought of as nothing but the
Devil's tool while Mandeville presents himself either as one of the
few who stand out against the Whore of Babylon or as a man
hopelessly in the clutches of his enemy. Mandeville is not fully aware
of these shifts in his own narraitve. He proudly reminds the readers
that as he is now an old man he can give an objective account of his
own youth.[24] He insists on being truthful although he realises that a
candid memoir will entail a painful picture of himself as at least
intermittently insane. But he is not consistent. As he writes, he again
enters into "the free terror of madness", that state in which he is
fully and happily convinced that everything he fears is found in
Clifford, not in himself.

There is bitter relief in these passages. The style rises from the
factual or reflective to the passionate: Mandeville may begin a
passage in his calm, conscientious mode, in which the style seems to
reflect the scrupulousness of a writer who has a bird's eye view of his
medium:

> I know that fiction is a very ingenious thing; but I defy fiction in
> all its luxuriance to equal that, which I cannot yet tell that I can
> hold my pen to relate. I was wounded in every point where my
> soul most lived along the nerve; in religion, in frustrated ambition,
> in the hatred of disgrace which pervaded my every muscle, and
> most of all in love . . . (iii, p. 314)

As he continues writing, Mandeville works himself into a state in
which he can blame somebody else for all his misfortunes:

> Would to God, when I quitted Winchester, I had lost sight of
> Clifford for ever! But it was not so. He was born to thwart my
> ambition; and ambition perhaps never burned more fervently in
> any human breast than in mine. The evil did not stop here. He not

only kept me down in all my hopes to rise; in addition to this he overwhelmed me with disgrace. No, I felt that I was not born to the inheritance of disgrace. Never was a creature more innocent, more honourable, more plain and direct in all he did, more stranger to the crooked dealings of a corrupt world. How therefore did I bear disgrace? It made me mad! I have said it repeatedly, but I must say it once more; it was Clifford, that reduced me to the state of a beast, that added weight to all the chains I endured, and a rowel to every lash I received from my inhuman keepers . . . (iii, pp. 316–17)

The tactics in this war against pain may change for a moment, but the underlying strategy does not, when Mandeville envisages Clifford as God's enemy who will be rightly punished:

One thing only occured to console me under these accumulated sufferings. Clifford turned Papist. Now it came to my turn to triumph. God had smitten him with his thunder. God had made him 'an astonishment, and a hissing, and a perpetual desolation, to the nations round about.' (iii, p. 318)

A more lasting relief is found not in this kind of righteous joy, but in the idea of martyrdom.

I viewed my murderers, Clifford and Henrietta, trampling on my lifeless limbs with looks of scorn. I never saw such looks. Diabolical triumph sat on the lips of each. Inhuman laughter flayed and mangled my ears like a hundred lancets. (iii, p. 322)

Even in periods like these, Mandeville may have glimpses of Clifford's innocence, but he is dominated by his deep psychological need to see those who thwart his wishes as overpowering and diabolical. The novel ends on a note like this, too. In the last pages Mandeville presents himself as a man who is not responsible for his own life, a man whose very self has been invaded by something alien to him:

The sword of my enemy had given a perpetual grimace, a sort of preternatural and unvarying distorted smile, or deadly grin, to my countenance. . . . Before, to think of Clifford was an act of the mind, and an exercise of the imagination; he was not there, but my thoughts went on their destined errand, and fetched him; now I bore Clifford and his injuries perpetually about with me. . . . Clifford had set his mark upon me, as a token that I was his for ever. (iii, pp. 366–7)[25]

We are now in a position where the discussion with the reviewer who objected to Mandeville's description of the Devonshire coast can be continued. This reviewer might have argued that even though he could, on consideration, agree that the narrator is not meant to be trustworthy, the novel would still have to be condemned. For the narrative weaves in and out of truth in such an absurd way that the story becomes incomprehensible. The account of Mandeville given above answers this criticism: the narrator and his narrative both make sense when the novel is seen as a study in the various strategies a desperately insecure man resorts to in order to create a view of himself and his surroundings which can make his fear and pain less agonising.[26]

Godwin makes it quite clear that these strategies must be seen as a result of what we may call Mandeville's weak hold on his identity. In *Fleetwood* we were reminded that "the only thing which can defend a man against . . . pitiful jealousy and diseased vigilance, is a generous confidence in his own worth".[27] Both the vivid description of little Mandeville's fortunes in Ireland and the slow-moving passage about his boyhood in his uncle's gloomy house contribute to establish the sad conditions against which Mandeville's weakness must be appreciated. Mandeville is deprived of those contacts with others that could have given him a definite and secure idea of his own self. There is sharp irony in Mandeville's tribute to the memory of his tutor:

Never did man receive so religious an education as I did, sanctified by the tall and solemn figure of my instructor, his colourless cheek, his inflexible muscles, his face, every feature of which spoke consecration and martyrdom. Solomon says, "The words of the wise are as nails, fastened by the master of assemblies." Every one of these nails, in my case, was driven to the head, and clenched again on the other side, by means of the impenetrable solitude and wild desolation, amidst which all my early years were passed. (iii, p. 314)

The unpleasant metaphor tells the reader what Mandeville cannot openly admit: by hammering iron tenets right through his head Hilkiah has tortured and "killed" a scared and lonely orphan.

The feelings of Mandeville for his sister must also be seen against this background. Godwin's treatment of the theme of incest, or potential incest, makes a welcome change from the she-was-not-his-sister-or-mother-after-all version of the motif. Godwin must have taken hints from *Wieland*, in which a warm friendship between brother and sister provides the only possible psychological explanation of the protagonist's delusions. Godwin gives a more consistent psychological account of Mandeville, who never acquires enough buoyancy to think in concrete terms of a sexual relationship with anybody, but whose attitude to Henrietta, the "dearest half" of his soul (i, p. 168) is nevertheless incestuous. He wants the two of them to live one life, inseparable and separated from the rest of the world. To begin with, Henrietta is as eager as he is: "Charles, . . . we must be all in all to each other" (i, p. 173). In his more sober moments Mandeville realises that Henrietta must be allowed to live her own life; but he is never really in a position in which he can think of giving her away to another man. She is his better self and his main link with the society of his equals. Without her his isolation would be total and there would be nobody who could support his idea of himself as sane. It is thus only natural that his last desperate action is an attempt to steal Henrietta away from Clifford, who has become her husband.[28]

Morbid, said Hazlitt

When a novelist suggests close links between social forces and mental disease, he cannot completely avoid a question which has considerable interest, it seems, in our own day: a number of philosophers and psychiatrists have asked themselves whether madness should be seen as a natural, understandable, "sane" response to social situations which inflict unbearable pain on man. R. D. Laing has suggested that "in the context of our present pervasive madness that we call normality, sanity, freedom, all our frames of reference are ambiguous and equivocal".[29] In the writings of his contemporaries Godwin could find different attitudes to this problem of the possible soundness of insanity, two extremes being represented by William Cowper and William Blake.[30] To Cowper madness is a condition for which society cannot be thought of as responsible. It is linked with man's sinful nature, and only God in his grace may lift the awful burden of such a disease from a repentant sinner:

> Me thro' waves of deep affliction,
>   Dearest Saviour! thou hast brought,
> Fiery deeps of sharp conviction
>   Hard to bear and passing thought.
>   . . .
> Food I loath'd nor ever tasted
>   But by violence constrain'd.
> Strength decay'd and body wasted,
>   Spoke the terrors I sustain'd.
>   . . .
> But at length a word of Healing
>   Sweeter than an angel's note,
> From the Saviour's lips distilling
>   Chas'd despair and chang'd my lot.[31]

God finally heals him, but no relief – no sense of a natural reaction to a grotesque world, no creative energy, no valuable insight – may be gathered from this "deep affliction" itself. In Blake we find a radically different view of madness. Blake, who was never insane in a medical sense, knew that friends and critics who heard about his visions sometimes called him mad.[32] His answer is very different from Cowper's humble acknowledgement of sin and disease. Blake hit back: the kind of commonsense represented by the intellectual *milieu* of the London of his day is really arid nonsense. *The Marriage of Heaven and Hell* illustrates this attitude: the world has become such that "the just man rages in the wilds" because he had been expelled by the "sneaking serpent" which "walks/ In mild humility". Any sensible man threatened by this serpent of conventionality must turn his ear to "The Voice of the Devil" and learn from the "Proverbs of Hell":

> The road of excess leads to the palace of wisdom.
> Prudence is a rich, ugly old maid courted by Incapacity.
>   . . .
> The tygers of wrath are wiser than the horses of instruction.[33]

Blake's position is related to that of the early Wordsworth. In the *Lyrical Ballads* the wisdom of the Idiot Boy is at least equal to that of those around him. Moreover, insanity is shown to be natural and understandable: in "The Female Vagrant" the young woman is "robb'd of [her] perfect mind" by the greed of a North of England landowner and by the large-scale madness of the American War.

At the time when Godwin wrote *Mandeville* Wordsworth had revised "The Female Vagrant" so that the close connection between politics and mental strain had disappeared. Godwin would certainly have disapproved of these revisions. Indeed, it is tempting to think of Godwin in 1817 as a writer who doggedly defends attitudes to madness which we find in Blake and the early Wordsworth. This, however, is not quite the case. I hope that the discussion above has shown that Godwin gives a sympathetic account of a madman, sympathetic in the sense that madness is described as an understandable reaction to a certain kind of life. Moreoover, *Mandeville* places private madness and communal outrage ironically side by side, the implicit suggestion being that political atrocities are far more dangerous than the violent actions of the insane. But Godwin never suggests that Mandeville's insanity is creative or that it becomes a source of insight (except that is, in the limited sense that the protagonist learns how to use his madness so as to lessen his mental agony). On the contrary, it is in the pleasant parlour where Henrietta was brought up and in the sober circles in which Clifford moves, that understanding can be shared and reasonable solutions to moral problems be approached through conversation and discussion. Henrietta and her friends illustrate an idea which is central in *Political Justice*: by reasoning on a basis of generally shared knowledge man can come closer towards a realisation of what his duties are. Though the road to political and social justice may be long and narrow, there is no doubt about the direction. The road is not one of visions, of Blake's kind of "madness", but of calm discussion in which evidence can be sifted and standards of social behaviour clarified. Therefore, the author of *Mandeville* can scarcely agree with Laing that "all our frames of reference are ambigious".

Mandeville is Godwin's most homogeneous novel. The radical ambiguities in style and story that can be traced from *Caleb Williams* to *Fleetwood* give way to a narrative which is almost consistently psychological. Whereas Fleetwood's evening of madness constitutes an attempt by him, and by the author, to explore a new language,

Mandeville's report of his weeks in an asylum is kept firmly inside the style of the whole story. What he has experienced is simply an intensification of earlier crises:

> A thousand hideous visions had perpetually beleaguered me. All that had ever occurred to me of tragic in the whole course of my existence, had beset me. Ireland, and its scenes of atrocious massacre, that one might have expected to be obliterated from the tablet of my memory, presented themselves in original freshness. My father and my mother died over again. . . . Then came Penruddock and Grove, and the many victims that had fallen by the sword of the law. . . . I saw their heads roll on the scaffold . . . (ii, pp. 113–14)

A faint reflection of the dialogue in the earlier novels between rational philosophy and religious sensibility may be found in the picture of some of the other characters. The few happy and good men and women in this novel acquire a special lustre. Since the novel is Charles Mandeville's memoirs, these portraits are distorted; but the distortions are intriguing. Mandeville hates Clifford the more because he cannot help thinking of him as a perfect human being, an angel on earth. And Henrietta, too, though Mandeville distrusts her, is revealed to us in such a way that we may well think of her as truly angelic. An interesting development has taken place: in the earlier novels, the eruptions of a metaphysical language were generally associated with moments of pain, loss and guilt; in *Mandeville*, the small glimpses we have of supernatural agents are fleeting visions of angels, not devils.

Hazlitt summed up *Mandeville* in one word – "morbid".[34] And in one important sense he was right. The novel is limited, and more so than Godwin's other novels, in that it is throughout a study in morbidity. It is not a pleasant theme, and Godwin has not enlivened it by incidental merriment. But this concentration is the novel's best defence. It also gives it a curiously modern taste. Godwin's tale has quite a number of features in common with Doris Lessing's *The Golden Notebook*, for example. Both authors see madness as a reaction to war, either the more conventional atrocities of a seventeenth-century campaign or the threat of the Bomb in the Cold War; both describe madness from the inside, with empathy and compassion and without sentimentality; the point of view is that of the character who suffers, but nets of ironies enable the novelist to give the reader more than simply the sufferer's perspective; both stories give us, though in different ways, a narrative which is disjointed because the narrator does not experience his or her self as unified.

But Godwin's Modernism should not be exaggerated. He is not willing, as Doris Lessing to some extent is, to see madness as a world from which man can emerge richer and better equipped to deal with his fears. More emphatically than Doris Lessing, Godwin presents the case for rational normality. Indeed, the homogeneity of the language of *Mandeville* can be read as a sign that Godwin himself can more easily than before master his own fears. His position can be compared with Lukács's well-known account of Modernism:

> With Musil – and with a great many other modernist writers – psychopathology became the goal, the *terminus ad quem*, of their artistic intention. . . . The protest expressed by this flight into psychopathology is an abstract gesture; its rejection of reality is wholesale and summary, containing no concrete criticism. It is a gesture, moreover, that is destined to lead nowhere; it is an escape into nothingness.[35]

This criticism of Modernism (in which Lukács's insensitivity to certain kinds of literature may be more in evidence than his formidable critical intelligence) does not affect *Mandeville* at all. For all its narrowness, Godwin's novel is one in which there is a lively interaction between society and individuals, between fragile rationality and madness which is made understandable, between different states of madness, and between determinism and freedom. The very form of the story, ending as it does without the sense of completion that we find in Jane Austen's or Walter Scott's last chapters, highlights the inclusiveness of Godwin's design.

VII

"A Tottering King": *Cloudesley* and *Deloraine*

A reviewer of one of Godwin's last novels called him "a tottering king".[1] This phrase sums up, I think, the only approach to *Cloudesley* and *Deloraine* which is at once generous and just. These last two novels mark a decline: Godwin's weaknesses as a novelist are more obvious than earlier; and the painful exploration of defeat which is his strength is now often completely drowned in the copious reflections on life which flow freely in almost every chapter. But it is a *king* who totters: a sovereign independence is seen in the aged writer who had the perseverance and courage to write two more novels about insecurity and guilt, and who was still young enough to see some few new complexities in his great theme.

Cloudesley: A Tale[2] appeared thirteen years after *Mandeville*. The novel is narrated by a servant called Meadows, who begins his narrative by describing his long stay in Russia; the main story takes us to Central Europe where the two Alton brothers fight for the Emperor of Austria against the Turks. One day they rescue a delectable Greek maiden, and the elder brother marries her. After a year he dies in a duel fought to vindicate the honour of his wife's country. Overwhelmed by grief she dies in childbirth a few days later. The younger Alton, who was the kindest and most considerate of brothers, has always been painfully aware of his own inferior position. To his great disappointment he now finds that the baby is a boy and that the child seems to be a strong and well-made little heir. In desperate envy Alton arranges for the boy to be passed off as the child of his brother's confidential servant. They produce the corpse of a baby which is then placed in Lady Alton's coffin; and attestations are drawn up to show that Lord Alton died without issue and that the baronial title must devolve upon his younger brother.

148

– Cloudesley, the confidential servant, could not resist the temptation of the comfortable income he was promised if willing to take care of the baby; but he is really no scoundrel and gives the boy an excellent education in Switzerland and Italy. At home in Ireland, and later England, the new Lord Alton is tortured by his conscience. He marries, but not even a happy marriage can alleviate his remorse. Cloudesley appeals to him to reveal the truth, but is successful only when Alton's wife and children have died one by one of a mysterious atrophy. Learning that the true heir has disappeared, Alton appoints a new confidential servant, Meadows, tells him the whole story, and sends him to Italy to find the young man and help him if necessary: Alton has never wanted him to suffer bodily harm. The young man is found in prison where he awaits execution together with other members of the band of outlaws with whom he has been living. When the Neapolitan authorities realise that he is an English nobleman, he is set free. Consumed by his feeling of guilt, Lord Alton dies; and the fine young man who has been known as Cloudesley can assume his rightful title and estate.

Cloudesley leaves no doubt that Godwin is still a great admirer of Scott. Godwin's story is set in the early eighteenth century; and his preface argues convincingly that historical textbooks cannot give us anything like the whole truth about the men of the past.

> The folds of the human heart, the endless inter-mixture of motive, and the difficulty of assigning which of these had the greatest effect in producing a given action, the desire each man has to stand well with his neighbours, and well with himself, all render the attempt to pass a sound judgement upon the characters of men to a great degree impossible. (Preface, pp. ix–x)

Godwin proceeds to praise historical novels, which, he believes, can come closer to a sound judgement of the men of the past. Godwin also follows Scott in acknowledging that he has used an earlier story as a framework for his narrative. This source, the *Memoirs of an Unfortunate Young Nobleman, Returned from a Thirteen Years' Slavery in America*,[3] is an account of one of the famous legal cases which haunted the eighteenth-century imagination; Smollett had treated it in *Peregrine Pickle*. The case features an uncle who cheats a young boy of his inheritance. As the title indicates, the boy finally comes back and successfully asserts his rights. Godwin has not copied any portraits from these "Memoirs", in which the uncle, for instance, is an out-and-out villain, whereas Lord Alton, for all his envy and ambition, is not without kindness. The parents of the "Unfortunate Young Nobleman" are largely to blame for his fate – his father is profligate and weak; his mother immensely superior in strength and morality, but dangerously temperamental. Cloudesley's real parents are ideal. Any marriage in Godwin's novels in which a little child is left an orphan is perfect; he never tired of paying Mary Wollstonecraft (and himself) this tribute. Altogether, the use Godwin made of the "Memoirs" is so sketchy that he might just as well have mentioned a Scott novel as the source for his story. For in *Guy Mannering*, too, a young heir is sent abroad by a villain in such circumstances that the family believe the boy to be dead. But it does not really matter greatly from which particular source Godwin has the story of a child who is deprived of its rights and sent abroad, for he is not interested in the details of such tales, but in their emblematic meaning. They outline a situation which can be seen as an image of human life as Godwin thought of it in his novels. In *Cloudesley*, it is not only the young nobleman who is cheated of his proper place. Godwin takes pains to show us that his uncle, the villain, has suffered a symbolic abduction in that his parents never considered him as a valuable addition to the family and never cared about him. And in the case of Meadows economic necessity steals a child away from home; the novel begins with the narrator's account of his miserable exile in Russia.

It is not only evil parents and uncles that threaten the young. Godwin describes at very great length the history and the political climate of Russia, Austria and Italy in an attempt to show us the various ways in which politics invades private life. St Elmo, the respectable robber, sounds like a man who has read certain chapters in *Political Justice*: he regards "what is called civilised society as a conspiracy against the inherent rights of man" (iii, p. 109). In the denouement Cloudesley himself is saved from the executioner's platform by the mere fact that his noble birth is revealed. Earlier, Lord Alton has commented in passing that in a court of law "money is every thing" (ii, p. 142); and the usurpation around which the story is organised illustrates the destructiveness of that idea of wealth and honour which drives Lord Alton to his crime.

But in spite of this interest in political history, Cloudesley can scarcely be called an historical novel in Scott's sense. It differs from

Waverley or *Old Mortality* – or *Mandeville* – in that it does not really examine complex relationships between individuals and historical forces. The first chapters give a detailed account of Russia after the death of Czar Peter; but, vague generalities apart, we are not shown how the various political forces at work in St Petersburg relate to the main issues of Godwin's story. The lengthy expositions of the history of Greece, Austria and Italy are relevant only to the crude outline of the action. There are few attempts to reveal conflicts of allegiances of the kind in which Scott's heroes are caught, conflicts that give depth and liveliness to heroes and history alike. And the awareness which Godwin had revealed in *Mandeville* that history shapes the present is virtually absent in *Cloudesley*.

The most important literary influence in this novel comes from Godwin's own *Caleb Williams*: a crime is perpetrated because of an overwhelming love of honour; a young man is not given his proper chance in life; there is a visit to a Robin Hood-like band of robbers; and we follow the workings of guilt at close quarters. This paucity of new incidents in *Cloudesley* reminds us that Godwin has not gained in inventiveness in the course of his career. But he has also retained some of the outstanding virtues of his younger days. His will to write in a conscientious, straightforward and unpretentious way is the same. He still has the engaging habit of saying something which sounds true and then proceeding to refine on it so as to come even closer to the truth. Meadows returns to England after sixteen years in Russia:

> I knew no one; I belonged to no one. The soil of England was before me, where to chuse my place of rest. I might wander as I pleased, uncontroled by any foe, unaided by any friend.
>
> This is not exactly true. The forlornest creature that lives, especially if he returns, as I did, to the place of his birth, finds some one that knows him (though, God knows, with indifference enough), and can scarcely fail to find some one that is bound to him by the ties of kindred. (i, p. 94)

The style of *Cloudesley* is not always marked by this admirable restraint: he goes to great lengths when he describes Italian land-scapes that he has never seen,[4] and Godwin's attempts to describe female beauty are sometimes painful.[5] But England, as well as the north of Europe generally, can emerge in little glimpses that do justice to the kind of experience in which view and viewer merge. When he has consigned his nephew to forgetfulness, Alton travels to England to be installed in his new position:

> I travelled in my route many extensive forests, and many sandy and dismal plains. My journey was made in the bleakest and most naked season of the year. Dark clouds were perpetually hurried along the horizon; and the air was nipping and severe. I seldom slept in my carriage, but was left to the uncomfortable communion of my own thoughts. I slept not, but was lost in long and vague reveries, unconscious how time passed, but feeling that it was insupportably monotonous and tedious. My mind was in that state in which a man has an undefined feeling that he exists, but in which his sensations rarely shape themselves into any thing that deserves the name of thoughts. (ii, pp. 45–6)

It is not fortuitous that Godwin's style is quietly authoritative in descriptions of Lord Alton. He is the emotional centre of the book; no stylistic gimmicks are needed to reveal the bleak chambers of *his* soul. The chapters on young Cloudesley make up a rather facile little *Bildungsroman*, interspersed with declamatory essays on education; and Meadows's own story, the novel's most important commentary on public government, suffers because the style is drab and dull. It is Lord Alton's story as he reveals it to Meadows which gives life to the novel.

Godwin does not simply imitate *Caleb Williams* in his description of guilt. Alton sins, much like Falkland, because of an exaggerated love of honour, but his later life illustrates other complexities than Falkland's. Lord Alton has married an admirable lady who loves and respects him; they have lovely children, two boys and two girls. Sensitive as he is, Alton realises that he cannot escape from the awful prison in which his guilt keeps him until he confesses his crime and restores young Cloudesley to his rightful position. But his innocent family, for whose happiness he is also responsible, makes a confession virtually impossible. He feels that he must weigh their happiness against Cloudesley's: isn't the young man happy where he is, thinking himself the son of a kind and upright English yeoman? The utilitarian thinking which invades certain parts of *Political Justice* is reconsidered here. Alton might argue that he added more to the world's total sum of happiness by saving his family than by giving Cloudesley a status he had not even dreamt of. Isn't the law after all a terribly abstract principle? And wouldn't it really be selfish of Alton to destroy his family in an attempt to relieve his own private pain? But the novel does not support Lord Alton in this line of thinking. Though we are made to realise that some of his motives are honourable, we are in no doubt that the course of action he adopts destroys him. The overall structure of the story endorses straightforward honesty: the narrative can rest only when Lord Alton has confessed his crime and Cloudesley's real identity is established.

We might have wished Godwin to pursue Alton's conflict further: the third volume of *Cloudesley* solves it summarily, and in the language of melodrama. Too conveniently, Alton's wife and children have died one by one in rapid succession, and he is himself a dying man when he makes his confession. But this denouement does not blur the sharpness with which Lord Alton's situation as a married man is delineated.

Deloraine (1833)[6] is sharply divided in the middle. The second half continues Godwin's analysis of guilt. Deloraine, who has lost an admirable wife, marries a young woman who has been engaged to marry a fine young man who was lost at sea. Both are wasted with grief. There is no great passion in this union, but mutual friendship and consideration. Then, contrary to all expectation, the young man who was reported to have been drowned turns up. He meets his former fiancée; Deloraine happens to see them and kills the young man in a fit of anger and jealousy. His wife dies the next day of a broken blood vessel. With his sweet and loyal daughter from his first marriage Deloraine tries to hide from the law. Godwin still knows how to give intensity to a pursuit and this last part of the novel is exciting. Deloraine's situation is similar to Alton's: he has committed a crime, is tortured by remorse, and realises that he can find no peace until he gives himself up. But he has a daughter for whom he is responsible; and he also feels that though he has sinned, he does not really deserve the sentence of death which awaits him in England.

It is the old story of Eugene Aram which Godwin here returns to. At a time of legal reform it was only natural that this eighteenth-century murder case would be in people's minds. Godwin's memory of it may have been refreshed by Thomas Hood's "The Dream of

Eugene Aram" (1829); and at this time, probably just after he had finished *Cloudesley*, he jotted down notes about Aram, in form and arrangement, says Kegan Paul, "precisely like the drafts which Godwin made and left behind him of other books, both those which were afterwards completed, and others only planned".[7] Godwin did not write a novel on the unfortunate Aram; instead, he probably encouraged his young friend Bulwer Lytton, whose novel *Eugene Aram* appeared in 1832. But in *Deloraine* Godwin considers some of the moral and legal questions which Aram's life illustrates: does an otherwise exemplary man deserve capital punishment for a murder committed in a moment of violent and understandable jealousy? And if an escaped criminal lives a good life for many years after the crime, ought he then to be forgiven by the law? In *Cloudesley* we have seen how ironic any conception of a good life for an undetected criminal must be. Deloraine, too, realises that there is no peace to be found for a murderer; but unlike Alton, he still thinks of himself as a virtuous man and can turn with aggressive criticism against the very paragraphs of the law which would commit him. He is quite sure that he is not a common murderer.

Deloraine's life after the murder is not simplified by the death of his daughter or by his own health giving way. He has to live on and face the natural consequences of his new life – fear, disguise, exile, and the heaviest burden of all, a loving daughter being deprived of her birth-right. The best parts of the novel are given to an account of the degrees of misery which he experiences. Godwin scores his last point as a novelist when, towards the end of the novel, Deloraine goes about the streets of London in disguise. This disguise – false teeth, minor plastic surgery and a talent for mimicry – is so perfect that he can even meet the man who has headed the search for him without being detected. The meeting itself is a piece of buffoonery, but Deloraine's thoughts afterwards are intriguing. He then finds that in this success lies his greatest pain: he can only escape the law by destroying his old self – an identity he may hate at times, but whose virtues he also believes in. Nobody can accuse Godwin of inconsistency here; the last pages of his last novel agree with *Political Justice*, published forty years earlier, both that no man must be allowed to take the law into his own hands and that the legal code of a country presupposes grotesquely simplified categories of action.

The first part of the novel is a study in marriage, and another obvious tribute to Mary Wollstonecraft. Deloraine and his first wife,

Emilia, had been absolutely happy in each other. Emilia had "a truly original mind", "you were sure to hear from her something new" (i, p. 83). In the rather engaging words of the middle-aged Deloraine, "she was without a fault: at least I can remember none" (i, p. 53). In parts, it is a tribute which would have enraged Mary Wollstonecraft. Echoing the language of Milton in *Paradise Lost*, Book IX, Deloraine has this to say about the nature of the sexes:

> Man is the substantive thing in the terrestrial creation: woman is but the adjective, that cannot stand by itself. A sweet thing she is; I grant it: no one has a greater right to say this thing than I have. But she is a frail flower; she wants a shelter, a protector, a pioneer. She is all that omniscience, that principle of divine meditation (so far as we can understand it), could produce, for the best consolation, the entire repose and good of the stronger sex; and, in forming his happiness, she forms her own. (i, p. 70)

We can only hope that Mary, had she lived, would have read on. She would then have found a conception of sexual roles closer to her own. For Godwin describes this marriage as essentially the union of equals. Each is active in promoting the happiness of the other; and though Deloraine on one occasion calls Emilia a "pupil", there is more stress on the fact that in this marriage there is a steady *interchange* of ideas.

That Godwin had not forgotten the *Vindication of the Rights of Woman* is even more apparent in later parts of the novel. Before the fiancé of Deloraine's second wife was lost at sea, she was for a time forced into an engagement with a rich relative. The engagement is arranged by the prospective father-in-law, an inveterate collector of art who looks upon the beautiful Margaret as one more object to be added to his collection. When despair has made her thin and pale, he is more than willing to have the engagement broken off. This straightforward example of sexual discrimination is followed, after a happy interval, by the marriage of Margaret and Deloraine. It is a marriage of equals in the sense that both are convalescents; each is sensitive to the happiness of the other; neither is a fiery young lover. But after a time Deloraine wonders whether the marriage is a mistake: his wife thinks of her relation to him as a duty; she is essentially passive, and always reserved. Then, when he kills her former fiancé and, indirectly, Margaret herself, this rash act is seen not only as the murder of a rival, but as the result of a marriage built on an insecure foundation. A feminist would probably have liked Godwin to be more explicit about Deloraine's ideal: does he long for an even more devoted servant, or does he fret because Margaret is too servile? The novel does not explore these possibilities in depth, but Deloraine's feelings of guilt about the murder are coloured by these misgivings. And the bare outlines of the story remind us that if he had been wise enough to avoid a marriage which was not a union of equals, he would not have become a murderer.

VIII

Conclusion

The variety in Godwin's work is striking. He makes use of a considerable number of different types of fiction; in turn, he attempts the Pastoral, the Epistolary, the Jacobin, the Gothic, the Sentimental, and the Historical. This continual search should be given a positive construction: this is no amateurish sampling of virtually all available modes of narrative, but a serious artist's persistent search for appropriate form. Godwin tried to express a constellation of feelings and ideas that could not easily be accommodated in any further developments of eighteenth-century fiction; there was no ready-made form which he could make his own and develop gradually from novel to novel.

Despite this great formal variety in Godwin's work, there is a marked unity in themes and mood – in an underlying sensibility which is recognisably the same throughout, but in which there is also a slow growth. Central elements in this awareness of life are summed up by Godwin himself in a moving note which he wrote in his late seventies. He considers the blank pages of his journal in which he had as yet only written the dates; and it is the novelist in him who speaks when he considers the ways in which the future will fill these pages:

With what facility have I marked these pages with the stamp of rolling weeks and months and years – all uniform, all blank!   All this at present is mere abstraction, symbols, not realities. Nothing is actually seen: the whole is ciphers, conventional marks, imaginary boundaries of unimagined things. Here is neither joy nor sorrow, pleasure nor pain. Yet when the time shall truly come, and the revolving year shall bring the day, what portentous events may stamp the page! what anguish, what horror, or by possibility what joy, what Godlike elevation of soul! Here are fevers, and excruciating pains 'in their sacred secundine sleep.' Here may be the saddest reverses, destitution and despair, detrusion and hunger and nakedness, without a place wherein to lay our head, wearisome days and endless nights in dark and unendurably monotony, variety of wretchedness; yet of all one gloomy hue; slumbers without sleep, waking without excitation, dreams all heterogeneous and perplexed, with nothing distinct and defined, distracted without the occasional bursts and energy of distraction. And these pages look now all fair, innocent, and uniform. I have put down eighty years and twenty-three days . . .

Everything under the sun is uncertain. No provision can be a sufficient security against adverse and unexpected fortune, least of all to him who has not a stipulated income bound to him by the forms and ordinances of society.[1]

"The forms and ordinances of society", "sufficient security", "destitution and despair, detrusion and hunger and nakedness". Though Godwin had at this time accepted a sinecure office, the social critic in him is alive; he is still moved by the misery he witnesses in London and is quick to link the uncertainty of life with the "forms and ordinances" of a society which does not help those in need. This combination of ready compassion with the poor and of hard-headed thinking about society constitutes a remarkably stable element in all Godwin's work. In his fiction this stability is reflected in the choice of narrators. Like the note I have just quoted, Godwin's stories consistently consider society from the point of view of an insecure man in whose misery the shortcomings of the English political system are reflected.

As he grows older, the urgency with which Godwin advocates political renewal becomes less intense, and concrete criticism of political institutions occurs less frequently. After *St Leon* a nostalgic note can at times be heard in descriptions of comfortable conservative preserves. The society that his later heroes dream of, and that readers can glimpse on the outskirts of the action, is described not only as comfortable, but as good. The country house that Mandeville briefly visits in the New Forest is the home of tolerance, moderation and good will; and there is reason to believe that the younger generation in *Cloudesley* will be both happy and virtuous in the possession of the enormous Alton estates. Godwin avoided concessions of this kind in the 1790s. Then, the insinuating power of "government" made life a sad prison for all, rich and poor alike. A radical reader must find this change a sign of weakness in the ageing Godwin; all readers will probably feel that a certain kind of poignancy has been lost.

"Without a place wherein to lay our head", "excruciating pains" – the late journal entry quoted above also reminds us of another unifying factor in Godwin's career as a novelist. The rational politician and psychologist does not hold the stage alone. In the rhythm and diction of Godwin's prose the language of the Bible is heard, too; and the biblical echoes evoke a world other than that of social criticism. It is impossible to assess accurately the degree of consciousness with which Godwin handles this tension. Quite often it is obvious that he begins a novel in the spirit of an essayist who wants to illustrate certain general propositions, and then, as his work proceeds, he seems to stumble on complexities that make his stories more than simple illustrations and his heroes more than types. It is in these later stages of the planning and writing of fiction that the contradictions, doubts and despairs that give life to his novels are realised. He had to think for some time in terms of story before he could admit insights – conscious or otherwise – besides those of his political philosophy. *Caleb Williams* was obviously intended to teach the message of *Political Justice* to those who had no taste for long, abstract theses; but when Godwin was writing the story we soon find him working at a considerable distance from the emotional and intellectual climate of his own treatise.

This kind of distance is nowhere as remarkable as in Godwin's attitude to evil. It has been argued that Godwin "never seemed able to recognize the power of evil. He saw and exposed to the gaze of his contemporaries the operations of evil in government. He recognized this political evil as so pervasive and invincible that only the dissolution of government itself could end the evil. But he seemed quite unable to see evil as an integral and continuing part of the nature of man, not to be reasoned gently away, but lived with realistically to the end."[2]

This may perhaps be a tenable summary of the view of evil in *Political Justice*, but as an account of the novels it is wide of the mark. Of course, since man is a social being in fiction as well as in life, government represents a potent evil force in Godwin's stories. But this is not the only framework within which evil is found. His characters are threatened by other forces, for instance by a hollowness in their own minds (which need not be the result of social pressures) and by the elements.[3] The weather and the landscape often reflect the psychological development of Godwin's heroes, and sometimes their social milieu: Caleb finds a moment of happiness in a deep valley in which there is a sheltered village; and the misery of his flight from the law is epitomised in the scenes where he is drenched in cold rain. But there are other interventions by natural forces – more sudden and more violent – that lead the reader's thoughts in another direction. In *Fleetwood* the Macneils are lost at sea; in *Deloraine* a storm separates the lovers, and a gale on a lake results in the death of Deloraine's first wife. Mandeville tells his readers that as a boy he was tossed about for more than three months in the Irish Sea before the boat, the only one afloat of a fleet that left Dublin at the same time, reached the shores of Wales. In the early *Imogen*, too, a violent storm overtakes the young couple and enables an evil spirit to carry away the heroine. Even when Godwin called himself an atheist, incidents such as these stand out as "acts of God" or, more precisely, perhaps, of the Devil; they cannot be "reduced" to psychological or political symbolism, and serve as forceful reminders that Godwin could conceive of what is destructive in terms other than those of his philosophical theories. There is a change of emphasis after 1800 when he was converted to theism by Coleridge. From the point of view of his own early Calvinism, this conversion must be seen as inefficient, but it did lay some ghosts in his mind. The radical ambiguities in *Weltanschauung* that we find in *Caleb Williams* and *St Leon* are modified in later novels. In *Fleetwood*, too, an attempt to consider life in a calm, philosophical spirit breaks down, but the tension between two different views of life is not as sustained as it had been; and in Godwin's last novels this tension occurs only in a burnt-out version. This is natural; no mind can be expected to work for a whole lifetime so near an intellectual break-ing-point as did Godwin's in the nineties.

Loss, failure and guilt remain a central theme throughout his career. Man is a fallen creature; and a dark Old Testament atmos-phere prevails: Godwin's stories leave man to atone for his faults himself. There is no Christ, no offer of salvation which man can receive purely as a gift, in any of the novels. This is sad, because Godwin's protagonists are individuals who, though gifted, suffer from the most painful sense of their own weakness and insigni-ficance. In its turn, this pain makes them envious and tyrannical, and even paranoiac. The novels do not contradict readers who may find that all this suffering stems from evil systems of government; in *Caleb Williams* and *Mandeville* in particular Godwin traces a number of subtle connections between political struggles and individual lives. But the experience of evil in the novels transcends his theories. Evil is not considered philosophically. At his best, Godwin concentrates his stories so as to bring out what it feels like to be a human being tossed about in an incomprehensible world, and doomed by an oppressive sense of emptiness and guilt to do harm to others.

Godwin does not invest this fate or doom which overwhelms his characters with a theology. It is, of course, possible to see a reflection of a painful, inverted Sandemanianism in his stories, but it is equally important to realise that systems of belief or logic do not explain these insights into pain and defeat. The nearest Godwin comes to an intellectual organisation of the darkness in which his protagonists find themselves is the extended Old Testament analogy in *Caleb Williams*. But this analogy is itself ambiguous and, as I have tried to show, it should not be taken to present a final evaluation of Caleb's situation. Those aspects of Godwin's response to life which fall outside his relatively straightforward political philosophy are terribly vague. And their power is, as in Kafka, a result of the vagueness.

This experience of vagueness is pointed, not flaccid. Godwin's philosophy can break down in his fiction, but the sensibility which informs his stories is unified, though tense and complex. It is this sensibility which lies at the heart of the concentration which Hazlitt noticed as being characteristic of Godwin:

Mr. Godwin, in all his writings, dwells upon one idea or exclusive view of a subject, aggrandises a sentiment, exaggerates a character, or pushes an argument to extremes, and makes up by the force of style and continuity of feeling for what he wants in variety of incident or ease of manner.[4]

This appreciation balances praise and blame. All readers of Godwin will probably share what must have been Hazlitt's occasional wish for wit, gaiety and speed in action and dialogue. But, as Hazlitt seems to realise, Godwin's limitations are inseparable from his strength. Without them he could not have achieved the dark troubled intensity which makes his novels memorable.

Godwin's novels foreshadow important trends in nineteenth-century fiction, but it is only in the case of some very few writers that an important direct influence can be traced. One of these is his daughter. Mary Shelley's *Frankenstein* is dedicated to Godwin; and in the first preface, written by Shelley for his wife, the basic plan of the novel closely resembles Godwin's recipe for *St Leon*.[5] The monster's life story is obviously indebted to Godwin's philosophy: had the new being only been given an adequate education, the catastrophe could have been averted. Indeed, if Frankenstein himself had been a better psychologist, and if the society in which the monster grows up had been a just and benevolent one, the ugly giant would have been a model of kindness. But Godwin has also influenced the overall design of his daughter's book. *Frankenstein* tries to unite a completely rational theory of education with a metaphysical, Faustian or Promethean problem. Mary Shelley is much more explicit about this latter theme than her father ever was: in her 1831 preface she describes the creation of the monster (in Godwin's life the analogous creation would be the establishment of a philosophy which challenges the wisdom of the Almighty) in the following way: "supremely frightful would be the effect of any human endeavour to mock the stupendous mechanism of the Creator of this world. His [the artist's] success would terrify the artist; he would rush away from his odious handy-work, horror-stricken."[6] This metaphysical perspective dominates the last pages of *Frankenstein*. The monster and his creator both stand as warnings against hubris; Frankenstein dies; and Walton returns to England, having realised that the price one pays for the exploration of dangerous and unknown lands may be too high. Mary Shelley's explicitness highlights the tension between rationality and the mysterious, and for this very reason the story becomes clumsy in places. A novelist who is too explicit about his or her ambiguities robs them of a great part of the power they may exercise on readers. Mary Shelley's language, though more flexible than her father's, fails to support a consistent, half-hidden ambiguity of the kind that we find in *Caleb Williams*. But one of the great virtues of her novel is related to her father's work too: like him, Mary creates memorable portraits of characters baffled and defeated by forces they cannot control. Without being in any sense an unimaginative imitation of *Caleb Williams*, Frankenstein's story parallels that of Caleb from beginning to end. In both novels a fine young man is spurred on by a thirst for knowledge, in both he releases a chain of actions which he had not really foreseen and cannot master, and in both the young man becomes terrified, bewildered and cruel. Both stories portray complex and painful father-son relationships, and both end in internecine struggle.[7]

The other novelist who knew Godwin and his novels well was Edward Bulwer Lytton; and, as literary historians have noted, he was influenced by Godwin in a number of ways. In Lytton's first novel, *Falkland*, the name of the eponymous protagonist comes from *Caleb Williams*; and the beautiful young woman loved by the hero is Lady Emily Mandeville. Another pointer to *Mandeville* is found in a later novel: Godwin's fine young man lends his family name to the hero of *Paul Clifford*. But Lytton is much too versatile to be a docile disciple. In the story and style of *Falkland* the mixture of ingredients is amusingly extravagant. Lytton models the first half of his story on Godwin's *Fleetwood*, then allows his hero to change from being a respectable misanthrope to becoming an adventurous rake whom we are obviously meant to admire in spite of perfunctory warnings. Finally, Falkland is sent off to Spain where he dies an appropriately Romantic death. The style is a boyish attempt to combine philosophical seriousness with Silver Fork gracefulness and Byronic grandeur. Godwin is not forgotten in all this: his radicalism and willingness to philosophise about life are reflected throughout. But I have sometimes wondered whether *Falkland* should be read as a joke on Godwin. If the Master's heroes could only stop being sad and bitter and instead begin to love the neglected wives of their neighbours, life would smile on them; these delectable young women would give them moments of exquisite sensual pleasure, and then save them from embarrassing entanglements by dying at the right moment; and there would be fields of glory on the outskirts of Europe to which the heroes could rush off to fight and die for freedom. A skit like this at the expense of the Master's glumness would have been understandable, but Lytton's other novels militate against this interpretation of *Falkland*. The younger man was obviously an earnest admirer. His work is modelled on Godwin's to such an extent that Godwin becomes what is perhaps the most important unifying influence in Lytton's rather shapeless career as a writer. In *England and the English* he presents himself as a radical political essayist with a particular dislike of aristocratic institutions. His early novels expose the wrongs of the legal system and probe the minds of different kinds of losers. The theme of *Eugene Aram* was one that Godwin and Lytton had probably discussed. Some of Lytton's books combine political radicalism with an interest in the supernatural; in *Zanoni* and *A Strange Story* there are loud echoes of *St Leon*. Godwin's influence is thus pervasive, but it can scarcely be called profound. The tense unity that characterises Godwin's best novels is lost on the way. The Godwin who is present in Lytton's novels is one who has been dismembered and whose parts remain separate.

No other novelists have thought of themselves as Godwin's disciples.[8] In the letters of George Eliot there is not a single mention of him;[9] Dickens had read *Caleb Williams* and mentions it in 1842 in a letter to Edgar Allan Poe;[10] and Melville notes in his diary that he got hold of it in London in 1849;[11] but these two references are made in passing, and there is no mention of indebtedness in either. Godwin's importance lies not so much in direct influence as in the fact that in him we find early and sensitive reactions to the intellectual and emotional climate in which the Victorians found themselves. Sharply, his fiction outlines a number of problems and themes that were to occupy new generations of novelists.

The most obvious of these themes is the interest in the social underdog. Caleb who suffers under an unjust master and the young Ruffigny who slaves in the silk mill establish situations and attitudes reflected in a great many later stories. Godwin's willingness to relate his compassion with the poor to political theory foreshadows analogous attitudes not only in Lytton, but more importantly in Disraeli and Dickens. Godwin's analyses of minds in which hope gives way to a sickening experience of loss and humiliation make up a psychological companion theme to his political concerns; and this theme points forward, too. It can be recognised in writers like Conrad and Hardy, who probably never guessed that they could have learned something about the darkness of life from the novels of a philosopher who was generally considered absurdly optimistic.

At times, the defeats and despairs that Godwin studies in his novels resemble scenes from James Thomson's *The City of Dreadful Night*. But the theological, Dantean language of Thomson's kind of atheism is heard only intermittently in Godwin. What above all characterises him – and points forward to later literature – is a more radical exploration of stylistic problems; for what is interesting is not simply that Godwin the storyteller was caught between metaphysical and rationalistic interpretations of man, though this was to be the situation of a number of later novelists. Equally important in an historical perspective is his search – largely unconscious, it seems – for a language that might convey his experience of this dilemma. An awareness of this search can help us to see the texture of novels as different as *Moby-Dick* and *The Mill on the Floss* with greater clarity than before. Godwin's novels illustrate both the nonconformist's earnest attempt to communicate with readers blinded by conventions, and the bafflement of a writer overwhelmed by the complexity of the experience he wants to fashion in words, an experience he finds it impossible to embody in one clear and uniform style throughout the narrative. Godwin wanted to be consistent in all he wrote. His essays and treatises illustrate this ideal of rational coherence and unity, his novels succeed because they do not. In his house of fiction he is not able to shut the back door; and ghostly visitors, not invited by the philosopher, roam among the properly received guests.

Damon and Delia

Damon and Delia is Godwin's first novel. He wrote it when, twenty-seven years old, he had left the ministry for good to try his luck in Grub Street: "This was probably the busiest period of my life; in the latter end of 1783 I wrote in ten days a novel entitled Damon and Delia, for which Hookham gave me five guineas, and a novel in three weeks called 'Italian Letters', purchased by Robinson for twenty guineas, and in the first four months of 1784 a novel called 'Imogen, a Pastoral Romance'."[1]

Damon and Delia were reviewed in at least four journals,[2] and then lost sight of. *Italian Letters* and *Imogen*, also thought to have disappeared completely, were found in the 1960s and reissued. But *Damon and Delia* seemed to be irretrievably lost, and Godwin critics have had to make do without it. Then, on 2 October 1978, the library of Brodie Castle in Scotland, the property of Lord Brodie of Brodie, was sold at an auction in London. Lot 6 in Sotheby's Catalogue included: "Damon and Delia: a Tale. *calf, T. Hookham*, 1784 [Apparently not in B. M. C.]." The lot was bought by the British Library, and the novel added to its Godwin collection. *Damon and Delia* is a short novel, its 182 pages divided into two parts, each consisting of nine chapters.

In spite of what the title seems to promise, the novel is not set in a pastoral Arcadia. On the contrary, we meet the beautiful, innocent and lively Delia (whose favourite book is *Tom Jones*) in provincial Southampton, where she is admired by Squire Savage, Mr Prattle and Lord Martin:

> The celebrated Mr Prattle, for whom a thousand fair ones cracked their fans and tore their caps, was one of the first to enlist himself among her adorers. Squire Savage, the fox-hunter, who, like

Hippolitus of old, chased the wily fox and the timid hare, and had never yet acknowledged the empire of beauty, was subdued by the artless sweetness of Delia. Nay, it has been reported, that the incomparable Lord Martin, a peer of ten thousand pounds a year, had made advances to her father. It is true, his lordship was scarcely four feet three inches in stature, his belly was prominent, one leg half a foot shorter, and one shoulder half a foot higher than the other. His temper was as crooked as his shape; the sight of a happy human being would give him the spleen . . . (p. 3)

Her father, the widowed Mr Hartley, " – let the reader drop a tear over this blot in our little narrative – " (p. 5) has amassed a fortune as a tradesman, but is now retired.

When Damon – tall and elegant – suddenly appears at a ball, Delia is deeply stricken and dreams all night (and the better part of the morning: she gets up at twelve) about this unknown hero. When they meet two days later, he fervently kisses her hand, but talks incoherently and sadly about "her whose fate is surely destined to mix with mine" (p. 32). Delia doesn't quite know what to think, but concludes that he must love another girl.

Damon does not reappear; and Delia tries to hide her disappointment while she fends off the advances both of Lord Martin and a newcomer, the vain and foolish Mr Prettyman who spends two hours every morning at his toilette. Godwin's habit of turning to Shakespeare for stylistic support has already been formed: Delia "pine[s] in green and yellow melancholy" (p. 57). And she now learns that Damon, who is the son of a neighbouring lord, is engaged to a girl favoured by his father; the wealthy Miss Frampton was a charming girl at first sight, but Damon has now realised that she is frivolous and vain. Sir William Twyford, the fiancé of Delia's best friend, now sets out to help Damon and Delia. He accompanies Damon to Miss Frampton and is instrumental in accomplishing the longed-for breach. But happiness is still a long way off. The lovers are poor; Lord Thomas Villiers, Damon's father, is still against the match; and so is Mr Hartley, who has always favoured the claims of Lord Martin and his ten thousand a year. The first volume ends as Damon prepares to go to America as a soldier.

The second volume begins with a journey to Windsor, proposed by Delia's best friend for the benefit of her companion whose health is now "visibly decayed" (p. 88). The journey proves a marvellous antidote to love-sickness until they reach Windsor. There, walking with a friend, is Damon. The lovers cannot hide what they feel for each other, but Delia nevertheless encourages him to go to America: they cannot possibly marry on nothing, and against the wishes of their fathers. Damon has to leave for London the same evening, but his friend, Mr Godfrey, stays behind and tells them the story of his life. The author includes it "as we apprehend it will be interesting in itself, and as we foresee that he will make a second appearance in the course of this narrative" (pp. 101–2). It is, in fact, the thinly veiled – and idealised – story of Godwin's own life after he left college, to which is added wishful thinking about the future. After brief and disappointing spells as a curate and as a tutor, the noble Mr Godfrey becomes an author. He writes a book "fraught with fire and originality of genius". But it takes him a very long time to find a publisher, and his masterpiece is slaughtered by critics because it is not "written in the same cold, phlegmatic insupportable manner" (p. 108) as their own works. Damon, however, appreciates the book, and becomes the generous friend of Mr Godfrey.

The tide now seems to turn. An uncle of Damon's is willing to provide for them, and Mr Hartley is approached. But he still favours Lord Martin and threatens to shut his daughter up if she does not become more pliable. She is not intimidated, but decides, when Damon proposes an elopement, that a breach with her father is too high a price to pay, at least for the time being. Time, she decides, may work for her. And it does. Not long afterwards, when the Southampton circle spend an evening together, Lord Martin, abetted by Sir William, fastens a firework to the skirt of a lady Mr Hartley wants to marry. Miss Sophia, whose home ground is politics, is interrupted in a philippic against Fox, Burke and Lord North when the cracker goes off. As soon as she finds out who is the criminal, Delia is saved: Miss Sophia decrees that Delia shall be Mrs Villiers; if not, she herself will never be Mrs Hartley.

On the eve of the marriage, Delia is abducted by two ruffians hired by Lord Martin. After some anxious hours on the road her cries are heard by two walkers who happen to be Mr Godfrey and a thief-taker he has befriended. They stop the coach, and after a brief fight Delia is saved and escorted to Godfrey's sister whose husband is one of Lord Thomas Villier's tenants. The lord sees the fair girl, and swears that her beauty is such that if only his son had had the guts to choose her, he should have had his father's blessing at once.

The novel can now be rounded off, and Godwin does so in the same bantering, good-humoured style he has used throughout:

The next day the proposed weddings took place. It is natural perhaps, at the conclusion of such a narrative as this, to represent them all as happy. But we are bound to adhere to nature and truth. Mr Hartley and his politician for some time struggled for superiority, but, in the end, the eagle genius of Sophia soared aloft. Sir William, though he married a woman, good natured, and destitute of vice, found something more insipid in marriage, than he had previously apprehended. For Damon and his Delia, they were amiable and constant. (pp. 181–2)

To readers of *Caleb Williams* and other later novels, *Damon and Delia* must come as a surprise. Taken as a whole, Godwin's *oeuvre* demonstrates that he was not really at home in the tradition of Fielding. His sense of urgency made him fight shy of the flippant and made him search for modes of fiction in which the art and craft were transparent and the readers confronted, not with an artefact, but with a slice of life. This, however, does not mean that the serious was the only style within Godwin's reach. The preface to *Imogen*, the *Instructions to a Statesman* and the imitations in *The Herald of Literature* offer small, but interesting examples of his irony; and now, with the reappearance of his first novel, we have more decisive evidence that Godwin had in him a fund of wit and liveliness that might have served as the basis for a literary career different from the one he actually chose. His eventual choice of seriousness was a deliberate preference rather than the result of sadly limited gifts. For *Damon and Delia* is a lively attempt to write in Fielding's vein: the story follows a commonsensical and natural young girl through misunderstandings, uninvited advances from unpleasant men, quarrels with a crusty father, picaresque incidents, and an abduction, to the altar; the portrait-gallery is largely semi-allegorical; and the style light and witty, often at the expense of more pompous traditions that are briefly evoked.

Damon and Delia is presented to us by an author who does not hide in his narrative. He comes forward and smiles ironically at readers, reviewers and at himself. Godwin's story is loosely knit in places and he does not mind admitting it: he calls the first chapter of the second part "Chapter I. In Which the Story begins over again". When, two-thirds through the novel, he resuscitates one of two middle-aged spinsters he had mentioned in the first chapter, his satirical remarks include both readers and writer:

> We are now brought, in the course of our story, to the memorable scene at Miss Cranley's. "Miss Cranley's!" exclaims one of our readers, in a tone of admiration. "Miss Cranley's" cries another, "and pray who is she?"
>
> I distribute my readers into two classes, the indolent and the supercilious, and accordingly address them upon the present occasion. To the former I have nothing more to say, than to refer them back to the latter part of Chapter I., Part I. where, my dear ladies, you will find an accurate account of the characters of two personages, who it seems you have totally forgotten.
>
> To the supercilious I have a very different story to tell. Most learned sirs, I kiss your hands. I acknowledge my error, and throw myself upon your clemency. You see however, gentlemen, that you were somewhat mistaken, when you imagined that I, like my fair patrons, the indolent, had quite lost these characters from my memory.
>
> To speak ingenuously, I did indeed suppose, as far as I could calculate the events of this important narrative beforehand, that the Miss Cranleys would have come in earlier . . . (pp. 129–30)

Foreshadowing, which becomes more important in later novels, is not ominous in *Damon and Delia*. The cup of misfortune itself is shown for what it is – an element in the plan an author has to make to complete a novel of the right size: "The cup of misfortune, by which it was decreed that the virtue and constancy of our heroine should be tried, was not yet ended" (p. 58). The titles of chapters direct the irony more definitely at the expectations created by popular reading in the 1780s. Chapter II is called "A Ball" and the next "A Ghost", then follow "A Love Scene" and "A Man of Humour". Gothic tales and Sentimental novels are both visited in the promises contained in these titles. But these literary ironies are not sustained; Godwin makes no attempt to hide the fact that he reels off his little skits in a careless manner.

Nor does he aim at a consistent style of humour; and his literary burlesques sometimes give way to crude farce, as when the other girls at the ball are described:

The daughter of Mr Griskin, an eminent butcher in Clare-market, who had indeed from nature, the grace of being cross-eyed, now looked in ten thousand more directions than she ever did before. . . . Miss Gawky, who had unfortunately been initiated by the chamber maid in the art of snuff-taking, plied her box with more zeal than ever. Miss Languish actually fainted, and was with some difficulty conveyed into the air. (p.13)

The humour sometimes depends on well-knit threads in the story. In the course of the party that was finally enlivened by fireworks, Miss Sophia Cranley hauls Mr Prattle forward by the arm and shows him to the other guests as a placeman without courage and honour: "Good God", she says to him "what would you do, if a brother officer shook a cane over your shoulders, as he did over those of the divine Themistocles? What would you do, if the brutal lust of an Appius ravished from your arms an only daughter?" (p. 134). Humour is generated not so much by the ludicrous classical echoes as by cross-references; the cane was used by Lord Martin in a ridiculous and abortive reconciliation scene with Mr Prettyman; and the abduction of an only daughter will take place later. The novel abounds in classical allusions, which always set up simple contrasts between past greatness and present triviality. In farcical scenes they work well, but they never move beyond the obvious.

The political satire in *Damon and Delia* is also light-hearted. Sophia is allowed to thunder at length against Fox, Burke and North, whose coalition Godwin had defended in a pamphlet. And the proper names in the novel, that at first sight seem to work as simple allegorical epithets only, in fact make up an offhand commentary on public figures. Mr Prettyman has a name which rang a bell when the book came out: the younger Pitt's tutor, and his private secretary in the ministry that succeeded the Fox-North coalition which broke down in late 1783, was George Pretyman, who later became Bishop of Winchester and changed his name to Tomline. I have not been able to find out whether the real-life Pretyman was big and brawny and had a reputation for personal vanity; he may well have been modest and elegant. But this would not have undermined Godwin's approach. His satire is not meant to be precise and hard-hitting. It succeeds because it is so obviously the result of youthful exuberance, not of a spirit of meticulous fault-finding.

Damon's father is Lord Thomas Villiers. This is the name of a well-known diplomat and politician, the first Earl of Clarendon, who was Chancellor of the Duchy of Lancaster under Lord North from 1771 to 1782. The fictional Villiers is no hero – he wants his son to marry for money, and he has not himself been a kind husband. But towards the end he becomes more sympathetic: he is so charmed by the beauty of Delia that he wants his son to marry her, be she rich or poor. That the portrait of one of Lord North's men should be a mixture of black and white is only natural; Godwin had learnt to see North as the least of a great many political evils.

If the portrait of Mr Hartley, Delia's father, contains an allusion, it is to a man from Godwin's own political camp. David Hartley (son of the philosopher) was a supporter of Rockingham and served as plenipotentiary in Paris when the definitive treaty of peace between Britain and the United States of America was drawn up in 1783. The joke may be one on personality rather than politics. Godwin's dull, money-hoarding merchant is not unlike the diplomatist, it seems: Hartley, said a contemporary, "though destitute of any personal recommendation of manner, possessed some talent with unsullied probity, added to indefatigable perseverance and labour".[3]

Mr Prattle is summed up by Delia's friend: "He is so gay and so trifling, and so fond of hearing himself talk. Why, does he not say a number of smart things?" (p. 19). There may be an allusion in this name to the two Pratts in Shelburne's unpopular administration, one of whom, Charles Pratt, Earl Camden, the Dictionary of National Biography describes as "an indolent dilettante and a temperate epicure" and "an omnivorous reader of romances", though still no patron of authors.[4] The fictional Prattle can thus be a thrust at this member of a government Godwin had nothing but contempt for.

At first sight, Squire Savage seems to be the typical boorish squire and nothing else: a "fox-hunter, who chased the wily fox and the timid hare" (p. 3). But Savage is also the name of one of the three tutors at Hoxton College. He probably irritated Godwin, who was a strict Sandemanian in his student days, by his liberal views. According to Savage's first biographer, "his character united in it piety and benevolence, and a catholic, liberal spirit towards those who differed from him. His own religious principles were . . . free from the bigotry of the high Calvinists".[5] Liberal, catholic views can be most exasperating to young men of other persuasions. Moreover, Savage had become a Fox-hunter. In *National Reformation the Way to Prevent National Ruin. Considered in a Sermon* (1782) Savage denounces the

vices of public and private life; and among the worst are those for
which Fox was notorious (and which Godwin had tried to excuse in
A Defence of the Rockingham Party): "inordinate love of pleasure and
gaiety", "Vain Confidence", and "Carnal Security". Moreover, we
have "learned to despise *Government*". No reader of the sermon could
be in any doubt who had been the foremost teacher; and, to crown it
all, "we have been long *studying and adopting the atheistical principles and
loose manners of the French*".[6] Godwin's fox-hunting Savage chases the
"timid hare", too. And one of Fox's best friends was James Hare,
politician, diplomat, wit and gambler – obviously not a man after
Savage's heart. Hare was known in his day not least for his maiden
speech in the House of Commons. Having just scored a great success
with his own first speech in Parliament, Fox said, "Wait until you
hear Hare!" But Hare broke down when he tried to address the
House and in the course of twenty-five years as an MP never
repeated the attempt.[7]

This use of names in *Damon and Delia* is playful and casual; the
novel does not aim at the seriousness of consistent satire. Nor, in
spite of frequent visits to traditional sources of sentiment, does it aim
at the pathetic. Godwin throws off hackneyed descriptions of sentimental scenes for fun:

> Delia and her companion advanced towards the well known spot.
> The mellow voice of the thrush, and the clear pipe of the black-
> bird, diversified at intervals with the tender notes of the nightin-
> gale, formed the most agreeable natural concert. The breast of
> Delia, framed for softness and melancholy, was filled with sensa-
> tions responsive to the objects around her, and even the eternal
> clack of Miss Fletcher was still. (p. 23)

Damon's voice is then mingled with that of thrush, blackbird, and
nightingale:

> "Ah lovely mistress of my soul," cried he, "thou little regardest
> the anguish that must for ever be an inmate of this breast! While I
> am a prey to a thousand tormenting imaginations, thou riotest in
> the empire of beauty, heedless of the wounds thou inflictest, and
> the slaves thou chainest to thy chariot . . ." (p. 24)

What saves this passage, and in fact makes it quite enjoyable, is the
raillery which has been built into the style from the beginning – we

are not meant to read the passage as the author's best attempt in pathetic seriousness. Similarly, Godwin treats the seduction scene, the natural climax in his narrative, with amused detachment. Delia's hours of anguish are described in a perfunctory manner; it is only when Lord Martin swims in the mud by the roadside that Godwin writes with heartfelt gusto.

Delia herself is a refreshing creature, a grandchild of Sophia Western in which the family likeness is not lost. Though she goes into the obligatory decline and wants to die when her love seems hopeless, she is generally active, sensible and down-to-earth. The day after the ball Delia and Miss Fletcher come upon the flute-playing Damon by the sea ("The air was melancholy, but the skill divine", p. 24). He rushes away, but Delia is not at a loss: the next day she arranges for her evening walk to be taken alone and secures a tête-à-tête. During the abduction her courage, stamina, and vocal cords are all shown to be first-class.

Damon is a young man of sentiment, and he illustrates an uncertainty in the composition which Godwin does not overcome. In a book whose style, story and robust morality remind us of Fielding, Godwin gives us a passive and feeble hero. Left to his own resources, Damon does not even manage to extricate himself from his unfortunate engagement to Miss Frampton; and when the news of Delia's disappearance reaches him, he breaks down. His friends have to organise the search while he lies in bed feverish and raving. Since Damon is thus not only a man of exquisitely keen emotions like Mackenzie's Man of Feeling, but a positive weakling, the portrait is probably meant as a satire on the sentimental hero; but this satire is not properly developed. Damon is neither interesting enough nor entertaining enough as a butt of the laughing scorn Godwin employs elsewhere in the novel. As a result, the portrait is vague; and, what is more unfortunate, it disturbs the direction of the whole story. Damon is not a man strong enough to deserve the heroine; and his weakness is so central to the story that it undermines our belief in the poetic justice of the conclusion. In later novels Godwin's best effects are often the result of unexpected subversions of given patterns, but *Damon and Delia* is too slight a story for such a strategy to be developed in a satisfactory way.

The English Review suggested that Godwin's "talent lies in the pathetic".[8] It does in fact lie in a tortured intensity that *Caleb Williams* is a good example of; but it is difficult to see how the reviewer could guess this after having read *Damon and Delia* only. (Godwin wrote for the same journal; and the reviewer, who praised the novel, may have known Godwin personally and noticed a seriousness in the man – or in *Italian Letters*, published at about the same time – which he wanted to encourage.) It is only in brief glimpses that later themes, and the later sense of urgency, appear in *Damon and Delia*. The most important of these foreshadowings is the interest in politics. But it is a very long way from the boyish thrusts at politicians considered above to the later novels in which government has become a matter of life and death. Since Godwin sides with Fox in his first novel, it is possible to see his career as anti-reactionary from beginning to end, but the truly radical thinking about society which informs his later work is not even found in embryonic form in *Damon and Delia*, whose author is obviously a man happily at home in the political life of his own day.

The discussion of parental authority is closer to that of the later Godwin. Whereas Mathilda in *Italian Letters* (written in the same year) has an absolute belief in obedience, Delia trusts her own judgement. She does hope that "there is some secret reward, some unexpected deliverance in reserve, for filial simplicity" (p. 127), but her opposition to the idea of elopement is built more firmly on other considerations than obedience: her reputation might be injured, and her joy in marriage not as unmixed as she might wish. The author's own voice supports her: "the gentleness of Delia was not yet sufficiently roused by the injuries she had received, to induce her, to cast off all the ties which education and custom had imposed upon her" (p. 127). This remark is the closest *Damon and Delia* comes to the climate of opinion in Godwin's writings from the nineties.

The novelist whose forte is the exploration of despair and defeat is even less in evidence in this first novel. But Damon's breakdown and the seduction scene, though the first has an uneasy place in the novel as a whole and the second is presented consistently in a spirit of comedy, can remind us of the insistence in later novels that life is predatory and security is nowhere to be found. The theme of friendship, indicated in Damon's name, is not developed beyond the obvious, but it creates a link with *Italian Letters* in which friendship has become a complicated matter of trust, blindness and treachery.

The portrait Godwin gives of Mr Godfrey, his own *alter ego*, is fairly conventional. Moneyless and unrecognised, the young author is overcome by bitterness at times: however, he had still the same warmth in the cause of virtue, as in the days of the most unexperienced simplicity. He still dreaded an oath, and reverenced the divinity of innocence. He still believed in a God, and was sincerely attached to his honour, though he had often been told, that this was a prejudice, unworthy of his comprehension of thinking upon all other subjects. (pp. 112–13)

"Still" means "for all that" here; it is not used in a temporal sense to suggest that Mr Godfrey's position is a half-way house on the road to atheism. But Godwin's new attitude to sectarianism is reflected in his portrait of Miss Sophia's elder sister: the ridiculous Miss Cranley "delight[s] in the study of theology" (p. 8), quarrels with the curate, and pesters the cobbler with Mr Whitefield's sermons.

However, it would be beside the point to ask for a more penetrating discussion of the themes of later novels in *Damon and Delia*. In it, Godwin used for what it was worth a form to which he never returned. This first novel presupposes – as does all good-humoured satire – a world which the intellect can command. And the overall movement of the narrative, which takes us through the tribulations of respectable heroes and heroines to the traditional marriage, is reassuring: virtue will be rewarded. True, Godwin pokes fun at his own book, but this pleasant irony, which saves the novel from being sugary, does not point forward. It was only when Godwin left the platform of wit that he could develop a personal and more memorable style.

The English Review gives an excellent account of *Damon and Delia* and its author: "he appears evidently to play with his readers. He presents to us the image of a hero, buried in the mock engagement of a tournament, who sports with his weapons, and puts forth but half his strength. His composition may be characterised as politely gay, and elegantly trifling."[9] I question only the elegance. *Damon and Delia* is not without a certain urbanity, but its gaiety is above all that of an offhand style, that of a young author who writes hurriedly (the grammar is shaky in places) and without second thoughts, and who is perfectly aware of the fact that what he does is unfinished and light. The result is a disarming little story completely different from Godwin's other novels.

Notes

I. Introduction

1 "Tradition and the Individual Talent", *Selected Essays* (1948), p.15.
2 The British Library catalogue gives the author as Edward Dubois. The parody appeared in 1800.
3 *The Spirit of the Age*, ed. E. D. Mackerness (1969), p. 48.
4 *The English Novel* (Penguin, 1962), p. 151.
5 *Jane Austen and the War of Ideas* (1975), p. 74.
6 "Godwin's Later Novels", *Studies in Romanticism*, 1 (Winter, 1962), p. 79.
7 *The English Jacobin Novel 1780–1805* (1976), p. 249.
8 *The Language of Politics in the Age of Wilkes and Burke* (1963), pp. 207–49.
9 *Caleb Williams*, ed. David McCracken (1976), pp. 196–7.
10 *The Language of Politics*, p. 210
11 Godwin's own essay "Of English Style" in *The Enquirer* (1797) does not really help us to understand his own language. He praises the simplicity of eighteenth-century English, and says about "beauty of style" that it "consists in this, to be free from unnecessary parts and excrescencies, and to communicate our ideas with the smallest degree of prolixity and circuitousness". But such longwinded, self-defeating generalities apart, the essay comes to terms neither with the stylistic problems he had to struggle with in *Political Justice* nor with the question of style raised in his fiction by the fact that his narrators often do not know what kind of world their language ought to describe. See *The Enquirer* (1965), pp. 370, 480 and *passim*.
12 *Political Justice* has often been given short shrift by historians of ideas, but studies by F. E. L. Priestley ("Introduction", pp. 3–116, in Godwin, *Political Justice*, vol. iii, 1946), D. H. Monro (*Godwin's Moral Philosophy: An Interpretation of William Godwin*, 1953) and Don Locke (*A Fantasy of Reason: The Life and Thought of William Godwin*, 1980) suggest that when scholars read Godwin's treatise with some care, they emerge with portraits of the political thinker in which the absurdity is reduced, and in which Godwin's honesty and shrewdness are given conspicuous place.
13 "Godwin's Later Novels", p. 82.
14 *The Spirit of the Age*, p. 37.
15 *The English Jacobin Novel 1780–1805*, p. 251.

16 "Godwin's Later Novels", pp. 78–9.

17 A recent study of Godwin's thought, John P. Clark's *The Philosophical Anarchism of William Godwin* (1977), illustrates this point: Clark's Godwin lives in a climate of opinions and attitudes radically different from that of the novels. Don Locke's picture of Godwin (in *A Fantasy of Reason*) is more faceted than Clark's and closer to mine, but Locke, too, concentrates on the philosophy to such an extent that the novelist does not come into his own.

II. Early Writings

1 Charles Kegan Paul (vol. i, pp. 10–11) quotes from an unpublished autobiographical fragment. Kegan Paul's *William Godwin: His Friends and Contemporaries*, 2 vols. (1876) is referred to as "Kegan Paul" in later footnotes. Don Locke's *A Fantasy of Reason: The Life and Thought of William Godwin* (1980), hereafter cited as "Don Locke", is by far the best of later biographies.

2 Cf. Basil Willey's account of eighteenth-century nonconformist academies in *The Eighteenth-Century Background* (1950), pp. 185–6.

3 Godwin was to salvage a critical attitude to government when his Sande-manianism suffered shipwreck. A great many elements from his early faith can in fact be found dispersed in his later work. Those that are prominent in the novels are discussed in the course of this study.

4 See in particular Sandeman's *An Essay on Preaching* (1763) and a work by his forerunner John Glas, *A Plea for Pure and Undefil'd Religion* (1741).

5 Kegan Paul, i, p. 17.

6 See Don Locke, pp. 18–20, and Kegan Paul, pp. 14–20, for a more detailed account of these years.

7 See Burton R. Pollin's "Introduction", pp. vii–ix, in his edition of Godwin's *Italian Letters* (1965).

8 Kegan Paul, p. 19.

9 *Four Early Pamphlets*, ed. B. R. Pollin (1966), pp. 172, 200.

10 From an autobiographical sketch; Kegan Paul, pp. 16, 19–20.

11 See Robert Sandeman, *An Essay on Preaching* (1763), p. 8 and *passim*; and John Glas, *The Testimony of the King of Martyrs Concerning His Kingdom* (1776), *passim*.

12 Kegan Paul, p. 30.

13 Don Locke, p. 13.

14 See Pollin's "Introduction" to *Italian Letters*, p. xii. In *A Gathered Church: The Literature of the English Dissenting Interest, 1700–1930* (1978) Donald Davie reminds us that Sandemanianism could be liberal in some respects. Michael Faraday, for instance, was a theatregoer and an enthusiastic reader of Byron and Scott (p. 68).

15 Kegan Paul, pp. 17–18. The other three were Thomas Holcroft, Coleridge, and a friend called George Dyson.

16 *Italian Letters*, pp. xi–xxi.

17 Cf. early reviews of these novels, summarised in Burton Pollin's "Introduction" to *Italian Letters*, pp. xxxi–xxxiii, and Jack W. Marken's "Introduction" to *Imogen*, p. 17.

18 I shall quote in the following from Pollin's excellent edition of the novel. Pollin's "Introduction" is the only scholarly study of this novel I have been able to find.

19 Burton Pollin reminds us (p. xvii) that the story of *Italian Letters* owes some important features to Henry Mackenzie's most Richardsonian novel, *Julia de Roubigné*.

20 Pollin has a brief description of the melodramatic elements in the novel, p. xxviii.

21 For a somewhat different view of parent-child relations, see Pollin, pp. xxiv–xxv.

22 Kegan Paul, pp. 20–1.

23 There is an admirable account of this popular tradition in J. M. S. Tompkins, *The Popular Novel in England 1770–1800* (1969), pp. 70–116.

24 *Imogen* was considered a lost work until Professor Jack W. Marken found two copies of it – one is now in the Berg Collection of the New York Public Library, the other in the Salisbury Library of University College, Cardiff. In the following I quote from Professor Marken's edition, published by the New York Public Library in 1963. This edition includes a useful introduction by Marken, and brief essays by Martha Winburn England, Burton R. Pollin and Irwin Primer.

25 I am indebted in these paragraphs both to the influential discussion of allegory in C. S. Lewis, *The Allegory of Love* (1936) and to Gabriel Josipovici's suggestive *The World and The Book* (1971). Josipovici discusses what I have called the "double truth" of Biblical stories, and he sees certain literary works, such as *The Divine Comedy*, as containing only incidental allegory. They are really something more – not simply an illustration of ideas and ideals but a re-enactment of what can be called Salvation. Josipovici calls this experience (of author and reader alike) an *analogue* in that it is analogous to the Incarnation. In his early work Godwin must be seen as a writer who chooses an approach different from the great writers of analogues: he tries to avoid the metaphysical and sticks to the more limited role of a moral teacher.

26 It is interesting to note that as an ex-minister of the Gospel Godwin actually did turn to history, now of course secular history. He published a *Life of Chatham* in 1783, a *History of the Internal Affairs of the United Provinces* in 1787, a *Life of Geoffrey Chaucer* in 1803, a *History of the Commonwealth* in four volumes (1824–8), and, under the pseudonym of Edward

Baldwin, a number of history books for schools. See Don Locke, pp. 356–67.

27 Burton R. Pollin gives an instructive account of the primitivism of *Imogen*; pp. 113–17 in Marken's edition.

28 In Martha Winburn England's words, Godwin "needed a vocabulary that excluded the vocabulary of Calvinism", *Imogen*, p. 110.

29 Cf. Jack W. Marken, pp. 12–13.

30 Martha Winburn England mentions that the wand, which we traditionally find in the hands of heroes and gods, is the property of the villain in *Imogen*; p. 111.

31 There is a detailed account of some of these ironies in Marken's "Introduction", pp. 11–12.

32 Cf. Don Locke, p. 26.

III. Caleb Williams

1 Cf. Don Locke, pp. 26–30, and Kegan Paul, i, pp. 21–4.

2 Kegan Paul, p. 40.

3 Kegan Paul, p. 72.

4 Godwin's relief was great when he was finally able to rent a house of his own. See Kegan Paul, p. 77.

5 Cf. Don Locke, pp. 40–53, and Kegan Paul, p. 65.

6 See D. McCracken's "Introduction" to *Caleb Williams* (1970), p. ix. All later references to the novel and to Godwin's prefaces are to McCracken's edition. Don Locke, p. 60, gives a more detailed account of the Cabinet discussion.

7 Don Locke, pp. 64, 81–2.

8 The historian Alfred Cobban suggests that this period gave rise to "perhaps the last real discussion of politics in this country". Quoted from McCracken's "Introduction" to *Caleb Williams*, p. ix.

9 See J. M. S. Tompkins, *The Popular Novel in England 1770–1800*, pp. 296–320; and Gary Kelly, *The English Jacobin Novel 1780–1805*.

10 Vol. xxi, p. 166.

11 "William Godwin's Novels" in *Studies of a Biographer*, second series, iii (1902), pp. 139–50.

12 See references in the following.

13 (1969), p. 5.

14 See *A Rhetoric of Irony* (1974), in particular pp. 1–12, 253–76.

15 "The Novels of William Godwin", *World Review*, new series, 28 (1951), 38.

16 "Metaphors of Private Guilt and Social Rebellion in Godwin's *Caleb Williams*", *ELH*, 34 (1967), 189–90.

17 Three accounts of this aspect of *Caleb Williams* are particularly helpful: D.

H. Monro, *Godwin's Moral Philosophy* (1963), pp. 207–49; Gary Kelly, *The English Jacobin Novel 1780–1805*, pp. 179–208; and Marilyn Butler, *Jane Austen and the War of Ideas* pp. 57–75.

[18] True, important parts of Books III and V of *Political Justice* are not reflected in *Caleb Williams* (see A. D. Harvey's argument in "The Nightmare of *Caleb Williams*", *Essays in Criticism*, 26 (1976), 240), but this is because the novel does not attempt to establish a new system of government; it is not a novel about things as they may be or will be.

[19] See D. Gilbert Dumas's instructive "Things As They Were: The Original Ending of *Caleb Williams*", *Studies in English Literature*, 6 (1966), 575–97. The original ending is printed as an appendix in McCracken's edition of the novel.

[20] All references to *Political Justice* are to F. E. L. Priestley's edition. The later development of Godwin's ideas of truth and justice is discussed in detail in Don Locke's biography.

[21] Cf. Butler, pp. 61–2.

[22] There is a detailed discussion of these in Eric Rothstein's "Allusion and Analogy in the Romance of *Caleb Williams*", *University of Toronto Quarterly*, 37 (1967), 22–3. The article is included, with additions and alterations, in *Systems of Order and Inquiry in Later Eighteenth-Century Fiction* (1975), pp. 208–42.

[23] See Mitzi Myers, "Godwin's Changing Conception of *Caleb Williams*", *Studies in English Literature 1500–1900*, 12 (1972), 621.

[24] I am indebted to Lord Abinger for permission to consult microfilms of Godwin's diaries where his reading is recorded.

[25] See Kegan Paul, i, p. 17; and, for an account of discussions between Godwin and Holcroft, pp. 64–5.

[26] There is a brief discussion of Holcroft's possible influence on Godwin's political thinking in Virgil R. Stallbaumer, "Holcroft's Influence on *Political Justice*", *Modern Language Quarterly*, 14 (1953), 21–30. An enthusiastic account of Holcroft as a radical novelist is found in Allene Gregory, *The French Revolution and the English Novel* (1913), pp. 60–75. Miss Gregory dismisses Godwin as "The Sentimental Individualist", p. 114. See also Don Locke, pp. 30–2.

[27] *Anna St Ives* is not completely without awareness of the complexities of life. Anna herself is at times placed in an amusing struggle between ideals and human nature, and there are even characters in the novel who ridicule Frank. But these endearing features are not extended to the happy ending which reinforces the idea that Frank has been right all the time (except for a charming mistake about the strength of his feelings for Anna) and that Anna has now been completely won over to his side. It is interesting to note that Holcroft originally had a tragic ending in mind. See Kelly, *The English Jacobin Novel 1780–1805*, p. 123.

28 *Reflections on the Revolution in France* (Penguin, 1969), p. 280.

29 Cf. Kelly: "the novel's argument is not uncompromising enough" (p. 137).

30 The page references are to the London 1792 edition.

31 Cf. J. M. S. Tompkins's analysis, *The Popular Novel 1770–1800*, pp. 196–7.

32 Cf. Kelly, p. 16.

33 See J. M. S. Tompkins's "Introduction" in the 1967 Oxford University Press edition.

34 London: G. G. J. and J. Robinson, 1792, vol. i, pp. iii, viii.

35 *Systems of Order and Inquiry*, pp. 208–42.

36 Cf. A. D. Harvey: the novel "embodies the deeply tragic notion that the individual is not merely trapped by his environment, but that *he himself* is the trap". See "The Nightmare of *Caleb Williams*", p. 243.

37 See Ian Ousby, "'My Servant Caleb': Godwin's *Caleb Williams* and the Political Trials of the 1790s", *University of Toronto Quarterly*, 44 (1974), 47–55.

38 See Rothstein's 1967 article, p. 18.

39 *Studies of a Biographer*, vol. iii (1902), pp. 145–6.

40 "Introduction" to *Caleb Williams* (1966), pp. ix, xiv–xv.

41 Cf. Kelly, pp. 183–4; and Butler, pp. 58–9.

42 *The History of Mademoiselle de St Phale* appeared in many editions in the eighteenth century. I have consulted those in the British Museum, from 1702, 1738, and 1761.

43 David McCracken, "Godwin's Reading in Burke", *English Language Notes*, 7 (1970), 266.

44 In *The Language of Politics in the Age of Wilkes and Burke*, pp. 226–32.

45 *A Philosophical Enquiry into the Origin of our Ideas of the Sublime and Beautiful*, ed. J. T. Boulton (1958), pp. 39, 68–70.

46 "'Mad Feary Father': *Caleb Williams* and the Novel Form", *Salzburg Studies in English Literature*, 47 (1975), 3.

47 There is a fine analysis of Caleb's guilt in Robert Kiely, *The Romantic Novel in England* (1972), pp. 90–3.

48 *William Godwins Romane: Ein Beitrag zur Geschichte des englischen Romans* (1906), p. 28.

49 *Essay in Criticism*, 5 (1955), 215–16.

50 "Metaphors of Private Guilt and Social Rebellion in Godwin's *Caleb Williams*", 188–207.

51 Going further than Storch and Rothstein, James Walton presents *Caleb Williams* simultaneously as the story of Caleb's neurosis and as the swan-song of eighteenth-century middle-class fiction. His closely argued "'Mad Feary Father': *Caleb Williams* and the Novel Form" is rich in interesting analyses. For a defence of the novel's alleged determinism, see A. D. Harvey, "The Nightmare of *Caleb Williams*".

[52] Good accounts of the psychological and moral development of Caleb are found in Gerard A. Barker, "Justice to Caleb Williams", *Studies in the Novel*, 6 (1974), pp. 377–88; and in Mitzi Myers, "Godwin's Changing Conception of *Caleb Williams*".

[53] Kelly, p. 16. Kelly quotes from a manuscript in the Abinger Collection.

[54] Some critics of *Caleb Williams* have found rather more coincidences than they like to see in it. But though it does seem contrived that Laura should have heard of Falkland's young days in Italy, I have never found the chance meetings in the book very irritating. Godwin is sometimes careless: he does not place the meeting on the road between Collins and Caleb in a likely part of England, something which he could easily have done in a sentence or two; but throughout what may look like mere coincidence is always supported by the general tendencies in Godwin's world. It really does not matter much that Laura knew about Falkland from before. What does matter, and what does not smack of contrivance, is the fact that she has been brought up to believe in a code of honour which would have made it virtually impossible for her not to lend an ear to rumours of the kind spread by Gines anyway.

[55] *Systems of Order and Inquiry*, pp. 208–42.

[56] 4 (July–December, 1794), p. 71.

[57] The psychologist Ronald H. Forgus suggests that in the case of the vase-and-two-faces drawing "reversals of figure-ground are spontaneous and very difficult to control". *Perception* (1966), p. 107.

[58] As might be expected, a more a-historical study like Storch's, which is also concerned with basic ambiguities in the novel, yields different results.

[59] Rothstein, *Systems of Order and Inquiry*, p. 209.

[60] See Kelly, p. 205. Barnabas Tirrell is also the name of a villain in Henry Brooke's sentimental *The Fool of Quality*. See Rothstein, *Systems of Order and Inquiry*, and G. A. Starr, "Henry Brooke, William Godwin and 'Barnabas Tirrell/Tyrrel'", *Notes and Queries*, 25 (1978), 67–8.

[61] Cf. F. E. L. Priestley's "Introduction" to *Political Justice*, Vol. iii.

[62] Quoted from John Berryman's edition of *The Monk* (1959), p. 35.

[63] Cf. Peter Brook's shrewd analysis in "Virtue and Terror: *The Monk*", *ELH*, 40 (1973), 249–63.

[64] See *Political Justice*, vol. i, pp. 126–8; and Monro, pp. 9–35 for an intelligent defence of Godwin's view.

[65] This does not mean that *Caleb Williams* must be classified as a sexless novel. There are glimpses of love, and of the possibility of love, on the outskirts of the story (these contrasts sometimes remind us very forcefully of the grimness of Caleb's life). Moreover, given a wide definition of sex like Freud's, one can see the struggle between Caleb and Falkland in terms of basic instincts which, given another environment, would have led to marriages, not murders.

[66] Cf. Walter Jackson Bate, *Coleridge* (1973), pp. 70–3.

[67] Cf. Stephen Prickett's view of Coleridge in *Romanticism and Religion: The Tradition of Coleridge and Wordsworth in the Victorian Church* (1976), pp. 9–17.

[68] See Kegan Paul, ii, pp. 1–17, 77–84 and 222–6; and the note, quoted by Kegan Paul, in which Godwin reveals that as a result of conversations with Coleridge in 1799–1800, "I ceased to regard the name of Atheist with the same complacency I had done for several preceding years" (i, pp. 357–8).

[69] See in particular vol. i, pp. 79–84, in the 1749 edition. I have used the facsimile reprint, Gainesville, Florida, 1965.

IV. St. Leon

[1] Kegan Paul, i, p. 78.

[2] See Don Locke, pp. 87–9, 100–7, and Kegan Paul, i, pp. 117–37, 146–7. Cf. also Jack W. Marken's introduction, pp. xv–xvii, in Godwin, *Uncollected Writings* (1968).

[3] Gary Kelly, *The English Jacobin Novel 1780–1805*, pp. 196–8.

[4] Cf. Kelly, pp. 222–4.

[5] Coleridge's *Letters*, ed. E. L. Griggs, i (1956), p. 553.

[6] London: J. Johnson and G. G. and J. Robinson, (1798), p. 2.

[7] See the excerpts in Burton R. Pollin's *Synoptic Bibliography*.

[8] Kegan Paul, i, pp. 294–6.

[9] Kegan Paul, i, pp. 357–8.

[10] See Don Locke, pp. 139 ff.

[11] Kelly, p. 211.

[12] Kelly, p. 212.

[13] References in the following are to the "Standard Novels" edition – London: Henry Colburn and Richard Bentley, 1831.

[14] See André Parreaux, *The Publication of* The Monk (1960), p. 43.

[15] *St Leon* sold reasonably well. The first edition (London: G. G. and J. Robinson, 1799) was followed in Godwin's lifetime by translations into French and German and by three other London editions as well as Irish and American issues. See Burton R. Pollin's "Bibliography" in *Education and Enlightenment* (1962).

[16] Horace Walpole, *The Castle of Otranto* (Oxford Univ. Press, 1969), pp. 7–8.

[17] A more detailed account of this background is found in W. A. Flanders, "Godwin and Gothicism: *St Leon*", *Texas Studies in Literature and Language*, 8 (1967), 533–45.

[18] This does not mean that Godwin was unable to face the psychological effects of a revolt against the conventions of family life and social class.

Both *Caleb Williams* and *St Leon* explore the mixture of respect and hatred with which the outsider considers the bearers of traditional values.

19 In *Godwin's Moral Philosophy: An Interpretation of William Godwin* (1953), p. 7, D. H. Monro sums up Godwin's view: "we do not really understand a generalization unless we see in detail how it applies to a particular concrete instance. Since no one instance is quite like another, generalizations are only approximately true. Human beings in particular are each of them unique. We will, then, never understand each other so long as we judge each other by the facile conventions imposed on us by society."

20 The following passage from *Political Justice* can illustrate Godwin's attitude: "If the conduct I am required to observe be reasonable, there is no plainer or more forcible mode of persuading me to adopt it, than to exhibit it in its true colours, and show me the benefits that really will accrue from it. . . . Truth and falsehood cannot subsist together: he that sees the merits of a case in all their clearness, cannot in that instance be the dupe either of prejudice or superstition." Priestley's edition, vol. i, p. 307.

21 The rapid succession of deaths in Richard Alton's family in *Cloudesley* is improbable, but must not necessarily be considered due to supernatural intervention.

22 This interpretation is supported by Flanders, pp. 536–7, J. T. Boulton, *The Language of Politics in the Age of Wilkes and Burke* (1963), pp. 226–32, and by D. H. Monro, pp. 98–101. George Woodcock disagrees, finding in *St Leon* "the allegorical teaching that a man who attains wisdom and wishes to use it for the general good, must expect and be willing to forego the ordinary comforts of life, and the benefits of domestic affection and even friendship in the course of his efforts." *William Godwin: A Biographical Study* (1946), p. 159. Gary Kelly follows Woodcock: "the alchemist or 'old philosopher', like the English Jacobin or 'New Philosopher', is fated to be misunderstood by his fellow man, denied the social usefulness he craves, and driven forth to be a lonely exile." Kelly, p. 209.

23 See e.g. vol. ii, pp. 91–2.

24 *The Enquirer*, p. 276.

25 Flanders, p. 534.

26 See in particular reels 74–6 in the Bodleian microfilm copy of the Abinger MSS; and Don Locke, *passim*.

V. Fleetwood

1 All references in the following are to the second edition – London: Richard Bentley, 1832.

2 See Kegan Paul, ii, pp. 129, 150 and *passim*.

[3] See Burton R. Pollin's excerpt in *Godwin Criticism: A Synoptic Bibliography* (1967), p. 21.

[4] See e.g. the *History of Rome*. I have consulted the second edition – London: Printed for M. J. Godwin, at the Juveline Library, No. 41, Skinner Street, 1811.

[5] See Gary Kelly, *The English Jacobin Novel 1780–1805*, pp. 237–60. Throughout this chapter I am greatly indebted to Dr Kelly's informative account of the backgrounds of *Fleetwood*.

[6] I agree with the contemporary reviewer who said about this incident: "This is told with such humour, which pleased us the more as it was unexpected in the pages of Mr. Godwin. It is possible that he has rather disdained attempts of this kind, than felt unequal to them." *The Critical Review*, third series, 4 (1805), 384.

[7] See Brian Vickers's introduction to *The Man of Feeling* (1970), p. vii.

[8] See Kelly, pp. 244–5.

[9] John Tillotson, *Works*, i (1728), p. 305.

[10] See R. S. Crane's pioneering survey in "Suggestions Towards a Genealogy of the 'Man of Feeling'", *ELH*, 1 (1934), 205–30, and Donald Greene's "Latitudinarianism and Sensibility: The Genealogy of the 'Man of Feeling' Reconsidered", *Modern Philology*, 75 (1977), 159–83.

[11] Anthony Ashley Cooper, *Characteristics* (1900); see for instance i, pp. 216–17.

[12] *A Treatise of Human Nature*, ed. F. C. Mossner (Penguin 1969), p. 507.

[13] See *Political Justice*, iii, p. 10.

[14] Cf. Don Locke's discussion of the development of Godwin's philosophy, pp. 140–3.

[15] *Treatise*, p. 510.

[16] Kegan Paul, i, p. 294.

[17] *St Leon*, p. x.

[18] Vol. vi, p. 190.

[19] That the young Godwin *occasionally* could enjoy taking off other writers is shown by his *Herald of Literature*.

[20] *The Works of Henry Mackenzie* (1816), p. 399.

[21] Ibid., p. 471.

[22] 26 (1805), 194.

[23] In *The English Jacobin Novel 1780–1805* Kelly shows in some detail that Godwin was not alone in combining sentimental elements with social criticism. See p. 245 and *passim*.

[24] Ivanka Kovačević, *Fact into Fiction: English Literature and the Industrial Scene 1750–1850* (1975), p. 177.

[25] Ibid., p. 185

[26] See *Jane Austen and the War of Ideas*, p. 27. The *Anti-Jacobin* cartoon is discussed in J. M. S. Tompkins, *The Popular Novel in England 1770–1800*, p. 111.

27 See Kegan Paul, i, pp. 357–8.

28 The quotations from "Expostulation and Reply", "The Tables Turned" and "Tintern Abbey" are from the *Lyrical Ballads*, ed. W. S. B. Owen (1969).

29 Kelly has chosen Wordsworth's "Lines left upon a Seat in a Yew-tree" as a basis for comparison with *Fleetwood*; this choice must, of course, lead to conclusions somewhat different from mine. See *The English Jacobin Novel*, pp. 240–2.

30 Review of *Fleetwood* in the *Edinburgh Review*, 6 (April, 1803), 187.

31 In a fine analysis of this episode P. N. Furbank reminds us that Mrs Fleetwood, too, realises that her poverty has made a difference in the marriage. See "Godwin's Novels", *Essays in Criticism*, 5 (1955), 223–4. James T. Boulton aptly remarks about this situation that it is now that "the stage is set for the disintegrating effect of jealousy". See *The Language of Politics in the Age of Wilkes and Burke*, p. 248.

32 See Kelly, pp. 253–6.

33 E. E. Smith and E. G. Smith have suggested that Godwin tends to become another man as a writer of fiction: exit the dry philosopher, enter the sentimentalist (*William Godwin*, p. 103). *Fleetwood* shows that this is not what actually happens.

VI. Mandeville

1 "Preface", p. vii. All references are to the first edition – Edinburgh: Archibald Constable and Co., and London: Longman, Hurst, Rees, Orme and Browne, 1817.

2 20 Dec. 1816. *Letters of Percy Bysshe Shelley*, i, ed. F. L. Jones (1964), p. 525. There are detailed accounts of the relationship between Godwin and Shelley in Richard Holmes, *Shelley: The Pursuit* (1974), pp. 97–152, 223–327; and in Don Locke, pp. 246–308.

3 Cf. the bibliography in B. R. Pollin, *Education and Enlightenment in the Works of William Godwin* (1962) and the British Museum Catalogue.

4 *The Quarterly Review*, 18 (1817), 176. Brief summaries of all the reviews are found in Burton R. Pollin, *William Godwin: A Synoptic Bibliography* (1967).

5 By sheer necessity Godwin had learnt to make the most of a little publicity and a little praise. He copied Shelley's comments and sent them to the *Morning Chronicle* where they appeared as an "Extract from a letter from Oxfordshire". It is here quoted from *Letters of Percy Bysshe Shelley*, ed. F. L. Jones, i, pp. 573–4, 576–7. Shelley's review of *Mandeville* in *The Examiner*, 28 Dec. 1817, is more measured in its praise of the novel.

6 I do not know whether Godwin guessed that Scott was the author of the Waverley novels. But it would of course have been impossible for an

English novelist and a famous Scottish man of letters to meet and not discuss novels which were creating such a great stir.

7 Kegan Paul, ii, p. 237.

8 Cf. Gary Kelly, *The English Jacobin Novel 1780–1805*, pp. 220–1.

9 Cf. Kelly, pp. 202–4.

10 In his *History of the Commonwealth* (1824–8) Godwin returns to the 1655 insurrection against Cromwell. The moral assumptions are the same as in *Mandeville*. Godwin generally sides with Cromwell against the Stuarts, but the great moral enemy is fanaticism and bigotry. Godwin can praise the Royalist Colonel Penruddock for his "humanity": the Colonel is "inexpressably shocked" at the cruel measures suggested by his commanding officer. See iv, pp. 168–70.

11 See E. L. Woodward, *The Age of Reform 1815–1870* (1946), pp. 60–1.

12 *The Historical Novel* (Penguin 1969), pp. 58–9.

13 See Fred Lewis Pattee's "Introduction" in *Wieland, or the Transformation* (1958), in particular pp. xvii–xix and xxxv–xxxvi.

14 De Montfort's life becomes embittered by the rivalry between himself and Rezenvelt, a former friend and playmate to whom he feels inferior. Like Clifford, the antagonist is really a very kind young man. Nothing is more galling to De Montfort than the memory of a duel he has lost and in which his former friend nobly abstained from killing him. The action reaches a crisis when De Montfort is told that his sister, who warmly pleaded for a reconciliation, is engaged to Rezenvelt. De Montfort realises that this was empty gossip only after he has murdered Rezenvelt.

15 George Sherburn's survey, "Godwin's Later Novels", has a brief paragraph on envy in *Mandeville*; see *Studies in Romanticism*, 1 (1962), p. 71.

16 There may have been other reasons as well why Godwin wanted to write a novel and not a play. His two tragedies, *Antonio* (1800) and the unpublished "Faulkener" (1807) had not been well received. For Godwin's troubled relationship with the theatre, see Don Locke, pp. 185–93, 210–11, 222–3.

17 *The British Review*, 11 (1818), p. 115.

18 See Charles Chenevix Trench, *The Royal Malady* (1964).

19 See the "Introduction" by Richard Hunter and Ida Macalpine to their edition of Samuel Tuke, *Description of the Retreat. An Institution near York, for Insane Persons of the Society of Friends* (1964), pp. 1–19.

20 Tuke, pp. 133–4.

21 The chapter in Tuke's book which gives a detailed account of the new treatment of insanity is called "Moral Treatment", see pp. 131–87.

22 *Madness and Civilization*, tr. by Richard Howard (1965), pp. 246–7.

23 *Wieland*, p. 210.

24 See for instance i, p. 304; ii, p. 3; and iii, p. 55.

25 In this last sentence of the novel Mandeville feels that he does not belong

to himself. He has earlier had the related – and equally ominous – feeling that his body does not belong to him (i, p. 267).

26 George Sherburn has suggested that "Mandeville's extreme misanthropy is made unconvincing by Godwin's attempt to realize for us aesthetically Mandeville's irrational hatred of the amiable and brilliant Clifford" ("Godwin's Later Novels", p. 71). It follows, of course, from the argument above that Mandeville's "extreme misanthropy" as well as his "irrational hatred" is not only accounted for by the book as a whole, it provides an important key to an understanding of the novel.

27 *Fleetwood*, p. 167.

28 The desperate hope that man may acquire new strength, and a new sense of self, in an absolutely exclusive friendship is first found as a minor theme in *Fleetwood*: "Friends, in the ordinary sense of the word, . . . I had many; . . . But what sort of a friend is it whose kindness shall produce a conviction in my mind that I do not stand alone in the world? This must be a friend, who is to me as another self, who joys in all my joys, and grieves in all my sorrows, . . . (1832 ed., pp. 176–77).

29 *The Divided Self* (Penguin, 1965), preface.

30 My discussion of the attitudes of Cowper and Blake to madness is indebted to Max Byrd's admirable chapter on these two poets in *Visits to Bedlam* (1974).

31 From "A Song of Mercy and Judgement", *The Poetical Works of William Cowper*, ed. H. S. Milford (1911), pp. 290–1.

32 A typical response of the friendly kind is recorded by Crabb Robinson: "Southey had been with Blake & admired both his designs & his poetic talents; At the same time that he held him for a decided madman. . . . Landor S. Says [he] is by no means a madman in common life, but is quite descreet & judicious." Crabb Robinson's Diary for 24 July 1811. Here quoted from G. E. Bentley, Jr., *Blake Records* (1969), p. 229.

33 *Complete Writings*, ed. G. Keynes (1969), pp. 150–2.

34 *The Spirit of the Age*, ed. E. D. Mackerness (1969), p. 49.

35 *The Meaning of Contemporary Realism* (1963), p. 29.

VII. Cloudesley and Deloraine

1 *The Metropolitan Magazine*, 6 (1833), 114.

2 All references are to the British Library copy – London: Henry Colburn and Richard Bentley, 1830. According to Burton R. Pollin there were three other editions of the novel in 1830 – another London edition, a New York edition and a translation into French. See *Education and Enlightenment in the Works of William Godwin*, pp. 277–8.

3 London: J. Freeman, 1743.

4 See Florence A. Marshall, *The Life and Letters of Mary Wollstonecraft Shelley*

(1889), ii, pp. 241–3, for an account of the assistance Mary gave her father when he wrote the "Italian" chapters of the novel.

5 See, for example, this description of the first Lord Alton's wife: "the eyes . . . were full and round, the dark balls dilating with innumerable rays, and fixed in a liquid heaven of the deepest, purest blue. The sweeping arch of the upper lid gave a peculiar look of nobleness and openness to the countenance. There seemed, so to speak, full room for the thoughts to come forth, and display themselves. Her nose was broad at the root, and, descending straight from the forehead, terminated in due season in a rounded point" (i, pp. 143–4).

6 All references are to the London: Richard Bentley, 1833 edition. Pollin's Bibliography in *Enlightenment and Education* lists only one other edition – Philadelphia: Carey, Lea, and Blanchard, 1833.

7 See Kegan Paul, ii, pp. 304–5, where these notes are given in full.

VIII. Conclusion

1 Kegan Paul, ii, p. 331.

2 Elton Edward Smith and Esther Greenwell Smith, *William Godwin* (1965), p. 147.

3 Cf. Smith and Smith, p. 111.

4 *The Spirit of the Age*, ed. E. D. Mackerness, p. 37.

5 Cf. pp. 81–82 above.

6 *Frankenstein Or The Modern Prometheus*, ed. M. K. Joseph (1969), p. 9.

7 Cf. A. D. Harvey, "*Frankenstein* and *Caleb Williams*", *Keats-Shelley Journal*, 29 (1980), 21–7.

8 Charles Brockden Brown might be listed as a third "disciple", but in this case the influence was reciprocal. Cf. Chapter VI, above. Godwin's influence might have been important in one more career, had it not been cut short: his son William turned to writing just before he died, at the age of twenty-nine, in 1832. His only novel, *Transfusion*, was seen through the press by his father,

9 *The George Eliot Letters*, ed. Gordon S. Haight (1955). There is a reference to Mary Wollstonecraft in v, pp. 160–1.

10 *The Letters of Charles Dickens*, iii, ed. Madeline House, Graham Storey and Kathleen Tillotson (1974), p. 107. For Godwin's possible influence on the blacking factory scenes in *David Copperfield*, see Chapter V, above.

11 Jay Leyda, *The Melville Log: A Documentary Life of Herman Melville 1819–1891* (1951), p. 351.

Damon and Delia

1 Kegan Paul, i, pp. 20–1.

2 Burton R. Pollin, *Godwin Criticism: A Synoptic Bibliography* (1967) lists four reviews. The longest, discussed in some detail below, was in *The English Review. The Critical Review* and *The Westminster Magazine* both thought it "an amusing little tale" (Pollin, p. 49), while *The Monthly Review* dismissed it as "insipid" and "dull" (p. 127).

3 *Dictionary of National Biography*, ix, p. 68.

4 *DNB*, xvi, p. 287.

5 Joshua Toulmin, *The Life of Samuel Morton Savage, D. D.* (1796), p. 13.

6 Samuel Morton Savage, *National Reformation the Way to Prevent National Ruin. Considered in a Sermon . . . February 20, 1782* (1782), pp. 28–9.

7 See *DNB*, viii, p. 1253.

8 3 (1784), 135.

9 Ibid., p. 133.

Bibliography

I By William Godwin

The year of the first edition is given in brackets when a later edition has been used.

Antonio: A Tragedy in Five Acts. London, 1800.

Caleb Williams. [1794] Ed. David McCracken, London, 1970.

Cloudesley: A Tale. London, 1830.

Damon and Delia: A Tale. London, 1784.

Deloraine. London, 1833.

The Enquirer: Reflections on Education, Manners and Literature.[1797] New York, 1965.

Enquiry Concerning Political Justice and its Influence on Morals and Happiness. [1793] Vol. I–III. Ed. F. E. L. Priestley. Toronto, 1946.

Fleetwood: Or, The New Man of Feeling. [1805] London, 1832.

Four Early Pamphlets 1783–1784. Ed. Burton R. Pollin. Gainesville, Florida, 1966.

Godwin and Mary: Letters of William Godwin and Mary Wollstonecraft. Ed. Ralph M. Wardle. London, 1967.

Baldwin, Edward (i.e. William Godwin). *The History of England. For the Use of Schools and Young Persons*. [1806] London, 1807.

Baldwin, Edward (i.e. William Godwin), *History of Greece*. [1811] London, 1828.

Baldwin, Edward (i.e. William Godwin). *History of Rome*. [1806] London, 1811.

History of the Commonwealth of England. From Its Commencement, to the Restoration of Charles the Second. Vol. I–IV. London, 1824–28.

Imogen: A Pastoral Romance From the Ancient British.[1784] New York, 1963.

Italian Letters: Or, The History of Count de St. Julian. [1784] Ed. Burton R. Pollin. Lincoln, Nebraska, 1965.

Lives of the Necromancers. London, 1834.

Mandeville: A Tale of the Seventeenth Century in England. Edinburgh, 1817.

Memoirs of Mary Wollstonecraft. [1798] Ed. W. Clark Durant. London, 1927.

St. Leon: A Tale of the Sixteenth Century. [1799] London, 1831.

Sketches of History in Six Sermons. London, 1784.

Thoughts on Man: His Nature, Productions and Discoveries. [1831] New York, 1969.

Uncollected Writings 1785–1822. Ed. Jack W. Marken and Burton R. Pollin. Gainesville, Florida, 1968.

Manuscripts in Lord Abinger's Godwin Collection; photocopies deposited in the Bodleian Library.

II Secondary Sources

(a) *Books and articles on Godwin, and books containing chapters on Godwin (reviews of Godwin's works are not included).*

Allen, B. Sprague. "William Godwin as a Sentimentalist". *PMLA*, 33 (March, 1918), 1–29.

Allen, Walter. "Introduction" vii–xv, in Godwin, *Caleb Williams*. London, 1966.

Barker, Gerard. "Justice to Caleb Williams". *Studies in the Novel*, 6 (Winter, 1974), 377–88.

Beckett, Juliet. "Introduction", ix–xxix, in Godwin's *St Leon*. New York, 1972.

Boulton, James T. *The Language of Politics in the Age of Wilkes and Burke.* London, 1963.

Brown, Ford K. *The Life of William Godwin.* London, 1926.

Butler, Marilyn. *Jane Austen and the War of Ideas.* Oxford, 1975.

Clark, John P. *The Philosophical Anarchism of William Godwin.* Princeton, 1977.

Cruttwell, Patrick. "On *Caleb Williams*". *The Hudson Review*, 11 (Spring, 1958), 87–95.

Dowden, Edward. *The French Revolution and English Literature.* London, 1897.

Dumas, D. Gilbert. "Things As They Were: The Original Ending of *Caleb Williams*". *Studies in English Literature*, 6 (Summer, 1966), 575–97.

England, Martha Winburn. "Felix Culpa", 109–12, in Godwin, *Imogen*. New York, 1963.

Flanders, Wallace Austin. "Godwin and Gothicism: *St Leon*". *Texas Studies in Literature and Language*, 7 (Winter, 1967), 533–46.

Fleisher, David. *William Godwin: A Study in Liberalism*. London, 1951.

Furbank, P. N. "Godwin's Novels". *Essays in Criticism*, 5 (July, 1955), 214–28.

Gregory, Allene. *The French Revolution and the English Novel*. New York, 1915.

Grob, Alan. "Wordsworth and Godwin: A Reassessment". *Studies in Romanticism*, 6 (Winter, 1967), 98–119.

Grylls, Rosalie Glynn. *William Godwin and His World*. London, 1953.

Harvey, A. D. "*Frankenstein* and *Caleb Williams*". *Keats-Shelley Journal*, 29 (1980), pp. 21–27.

—. "The Nightmare of *Caleb Williams*". *Essays in Criticism*, 26 (July, 1976), 236–49.

Hazlitt, William. *The Spirit of the Age*. [1825] Ed. E. D. Mackerness. London, 1969.

Kelly, Gary. *The English Jacobin Novel 1780–1805*. Oxford, 1976.

Kiely, Robert. *The Romantic Novel in England*. Cambridge, Mass., 1972.

Kovačević, Ivanka. *Fact into Fiction: English Literature and The Industrial Scene 1750–1850*. Leicester, 1975.

Locke, Don. *A Fantasy of Reason: The Life and Thought of William Godwin*. London, 1980.

McCracken, David. "Godwin's Literary Theory: The Alliance between Fiction and Political Philosophy". *Philological Quarterly*, 49 (January, 1970), 113–33.

—. "Godwin's Reading in Burke". *English Language Notes*, 7 (June, 1970), 264–70.

—. "Introduction". vii–xxii, in Godwin, *Caleb Williams*. London, 1970.

Marken, Jack W. "Introduction". 9–18, in Godwin, *Imogen*. New York, 1963.

Meyer, Johannes. *William Godwins Romane: Ein Beitrag zur Geschichte des englischen Romans*. Weida, 1906.

Monro, D. H. *Godwin's Moral Philosophy: An Interpretation of William Godwin*. London, 1953.

Myers, Mitzi. "Godwin's Changing Conception of *Caleb Williams*". *Studies in English Literature 1500–1900*, 12 (Autumn, 1972) 591–628.

Bibliography

Ousby, Ian. "'My Servant Caleb': Godwin's *Caleb Williams* and the Political Trials of the 1790s". *University of Toronto Quarterly*, 44 (Fall, 1974), 47–55.

Paul, Charles Kegan. *William Godwin: His Friends and Contemporaries*. Vol. I–II. London, 1876.

Pollin, Burton R. *Godwin Criticism: A Synoptic Bibliography*. Toronto, 1967.

—. *Education and Enlightenment in the Works of William Godwin*. New York, 1962.

—. "Introduction", vii–xxxvi, in Godwin, *Italian Letters*. Lincoln, Nebraska, 1965.

—. "Primitivism in *Imogen*", 113–117, in Godwin, *Imogen*. New York, 1963.

—. "The Significance of Names in the Fiction of William Godwin". *Revue des Langues Vivantes*, 37 (1971), 388–99.

Priestley, F. E. L. "Introduction", 3–116, in Godwin, *Political Justice*. Vol. III. Toronto, 1946.

Primer, Irwin, "Some Implications of Irony", 118–21, in Godwin, *Imogen*. New York, 1963.

Prey, James A. *The Dean and the Anarchist*. Tallahassee, Florida, 1959.

Proby, W. C. [pseud.?] *Modern Philosophy and Barbarism: Or, A Comparison Between the Theory of Godwin, and the Practice of Lycurgus. An Attempt to Prove the Identity of the Two Systems, and the Injurious Consequences Which must Result to Mankind from the Principles of Modern Philosophy Carried Into Practice*. London, n.d. [1798?]

Rodway, Allan E. *Godwin and the Age of Transition*. London, 1952.

Rothstein, Eric. "Allusion and Analogy in the Romance of *Caleb Williams*". *University of Toronto Quarterly*, 37 (October, 1967), 18–30.

—. *Systems of Order and Inquiry in Later Eighteenth-Century Fiction*. Berkeley, 1975.

Sherburn, George. "Godwin's Later Novels". *Studies in Romanticism*, 1 (Winter, 1962), 65–82.

Smith, Elton Edward and Esther Greenwell Smith. *William Godwin*. New York, 1965.

Stallbaumer, Virgil R. "Holcroft's Influence on *Political Justice*". *Modern Language Quarterly*, 14 (March, 1953), 21–30.

Starr, G. A., 'Henry Brooke, William Godwin, and "Barnabas Tirrell/Tyrrel'", *Notes and Queries*, 25(1978), 67–8.

Stephen, Leslie. "William Godwin's Novels", 119–54, in *Studies of a Biographer*, Second Series, Vol. III. London, 1902.

Storch, Rudolf F. "Metaphors of Private Guilt and Social Rebellion in Godwin's *Caleb Williams*". *ELH*, 34 (June, 1967), 188–207.

Uphaus, Robert W. "*Caleb Williams*: Godwin's Epoch of Mind". *Studies in the Novel*, 9 (Fall, 1977), 279–96.

Walton, James. "'Mad Feary Father': *Caleb Williams* and the Novel Form". *Salzburg Studies in English Literature*, No. 47. Salzburg, 1975.

Wilson, Angus. "The Novels of William Godwin". *World Review*, New Series 28 (June, 1951), 37–40.

Woodcock, George. *William Godwin: A Biographical Study*. London, 1946.

(b) *Select list of other secondary sources*

Anon. [*i.e.* John Reynolds] *God's Revenge against Murder and Adultery; Remarkably displayed in a Variety of Tragical Histories, containing Examples, Historical and Moral*. London, 1771.

Anon. *The History of Mademoiselle De St. Phale. Giving an Account of the Miraculous Conversion of a Noble French LADY and her DAUGHTER to the Reformed Religion. With the Defeat of the Intrigues of a JESUIT, their Confessor*. The Ninth Edition. London, 1787.

—. *Mandeville; Or, The Last Words of a Maniac! A Tale of the Seventeenth Century in England. By Himself*. London, 1818.

—, *Memoirs of an Unfortunate Young Nobleman, Returned from a Thirteen Years Slavery in America where he had been sent by the Wicked Contrivance of his Cruel Uncle. A Story founded on Truth, and address'd equally to the Head and Heart*. London, 1743.

Bage, Robert. *Hermsprong or Man As He is Not*. [1796] Ed. Vaughan Wilkins. London, 1951.

—. *James Wallace*. [1788] London, 1824.

—. *Man as He is*. London, 1792.

Baillie, Joanna. *De Montfort; A Tragedy, in Five Acts*. London, 1807.

Battie, William. *A Treatise on Madness*. [1758] Ed. Richard Hunter and Ida Macalpine. London, 1962.

Beckford, William. *Vathek*. [1786] Ed. Roger Lonsdale. London, 1970.

Bentley, G. E. Jr. *Blake Records*. Oxford, 1969.

Berryman, John. "Introduction", 11–28, in M. G. Lewis, *The Monk*. New York, 1959.

Booth, Wayne C. *The Rhetoric of Fiction*. Chicago, 1961.

—. *A Rhetoric of Irony*. Chicago, 1974.

Brooks, Peter. "Virtue and Terror: *The Monk*". *ELH*, 40 (Summer, 1973), 249–63.

Burke, Edmund. *A Philosophical Enquiry into the Origin of our Ideas of the Sublime and Beautiful*. [1757] Ed. James T. Boulton. London, 1958.

Byrd, Max. *Visits to Bedlam: Madness and Literature in the Eighteenth Century*. Columbia, 1974.

Cobban, Alfred. *Edmund Burke and the Revolt Against the Eighteenth Century: A Study of the Political and Social Thinking of Burke, Wordsworth, Coleridge and Southey*. London, 1960.

Cowper, William. *The Poetical Works*. Ed. H. S. Milford. London, 1911.

Crane, R. S. "Suggestions Towards a Genealogy of the 'Man of Feeling'". *ELH*, 1 (December, 1934), 205–30.

Cranston, Maurice. *Locke*. London, 1961.

Davie, Donald. *A Gathered Church: The Literature of the English Dissenting Interest, 1700–1930*. London, 1978.

DePorte, Michael. *Nightmares and Hobbyhorses: Swift, Sterne and Augustan Ideas of Madness*. San Marino, 1974.

Edgeworth, Maria. *Castle Rackrent*. [1800] London, 1953.

—. *Life and Letters*. Ed. A. J. C. Hare. London, 1894.

Empson, William. *Seven Types of Ambiguity*. [1930]. London, 1953.

Forgus, Ronald H. *Perception: The Basic Process in Cognitive Development*. New York, 1966.

Foucault, Michel. *Madness and Civilization: A History of Insanity in the Age of Reason*. New York, 1965.

Godwin, Mary Wollstonecraft. *Letters Written during a Short Residence in Sweden, Norway and Denmark*. [1796] Ed. Sylva Norman. Fontwell, 1970.

—. *Maria: or, The Wrongs of Woman*. [1798] Ed. Moira Ferguson. New York, 1975.

—. *Original Stories from Real Life; with Conversations, Calculated to Regulate the Affections, and Form the Mind to Truth and Goodness*. London, 1791.

—. *A Vindication of the Rights of Woman*. [1792] Ed. Miriam Brody Kramnick. Penguin Books, 1975.

Gombrich, Ernst. *Art and Illusion*. Princeton, 1969.

Haslam, John. *Considerations on the Moral Management of Insane Persons.* London, 1817.

—. *Illustrations of Madness.* London, 1810.

—. *Observations on Insanity: With Practical Remarks on the Disease, and an Account of the Morbid Appearances on Dissection.* London, 1798.

Holcroft, Thomas. *The Adventures of Hugh Trevor.* Vol. I–VI. London, 1794–97.

—. *Anna St. Ives* [1792] Ed. Peter Faulkner. London, 1973.

—. *The Road to Ruin: A Comedy.* [1792] London, 1796.

Holmes, Richard. *Shelley: The Pursuit.* London, 1974.

Home, Henry Lord Kames. *Elements of Criticism.* [1762] Edinburgh, 1785.

Humphreys, A. R. " 'The Friend of Mankind' (1700–60) – An Aspect of Eighteenth Century Sensibility". *The Review of English Studies,* 24 (July, 1948), 203–18.

Inchbald, Elizabeth. *Nature and Art.* [1796] London, 1810.

—. *A Simple Story.* [1791] Ed. J. M. S. Tompkins. London, 1967.

—. *Such Things Are; A Play, in Five Acts.* London, 1788.

Josipovici, Gabriel. *The World and the Book.* London, 1971.

Littlewood, S. R. *Elizabeth Inchbald and her Circle: The Life Story of a Charming Woman (1753–1821).* London, 1921.

Lévy, Maurice. *Le Roman "gothique" anglais 1764–1824.* Toulouse, 1968.

Lewis, C. S. *The Allegory of Love: A Study in Medieval Tradition.* [1936] London, 1948.

Lewis, M. G. *The Monk.* [1796] New York, 1959.

Locke, John. *An Essay Concerning Human Understanding.* [1690] London, 1748.

Lukács, George. *The Historical Novel.* [1937] Penguin Books, 1969.

McKee, William. *Elizabeth Inchbald: Novelist.* Washington, D.C., 1935.

Mackenzie, Henry, *Julia de Roubigné* [1777] 397–514 in *Works,* London, 1816.

—. *The Man of Feeling.* [1771] Ed. Brian Vickers. London 1970.

Mandeville, Bernard. *The Fable of the Bees; or Private Vices, Publick Benefits.* Vol. I–II. [1714,1729] Oxford, 1924.

Marsh, Robert. "The Second Part of Hartley's System". *Journal of the History of Ideas,* 20 (April, 1959), 264–273.

Mayo, Robert D. *The English Novel in the Magazines 1740–1814.* London, 1962.

Nixon, Edna. *Mary Wollstonecraft: Her Life and Times*. London, 1971.

O'Connor, D. J. *John Locke*. Penguin Books, 1952.

Parreaux, André. *The Publication of* The Monk: *A Literary Event 1796–1798*. Paris, 1960.

Prickett, Stephen. *Romanticism and Religion: The Tradition of Coleridge and Wordsworth in the Victorian Church*. Cambridge, 1976.

Radcliffe, Ann. *The Italian, or The Confessional of the Black Penitents. A Romance*. [1797] Ed. Frederick Garber. London, 1968.

—. *The Mysteries of Udolpho*. [1794] Ed. Bonamy Dobrée. London, 1966.

Reeve, Clara. *The Progress of Romance Through Times, Countries, and Manners*. Colchester and London, 1785.

St Leon, Count Reginald De [pseud. for Edward Dubois]. *St Godwin: A Tale of the Sixteenth, Seventeenth, and Eighteenth Century*. London, 1800.

Smith, Charlotte. *Desmond. A Novel, in Three Volumes*. London 1792.

Tomalin, Claire. *The Life and Death of Mary Wollstonecraft*. London, 1975.

Tompkins, J.M. S. *The Popular Novel in England 1770–1800*. [1932] London, 1969.

Trench, Charles Chenevix. *The Royal Malady*. London, 1964.

Tuke, Samuel. *Description of the Retreat, An Institution near York, for Insane Persons of the Society of Friends*. [1813] London, 1964.

Vickers, Brian. "Introduction", vii–xxiv, in Henry Mackenzie, *The Man of Feeling*, London, 1970.

Watt, Ian. *The Rise of the Novel*. [1957] Penguin Books, 1963.

Woodward. E. L. *The Age of Reform 1815–1870*. Oxford, 1946.

Index